Time Sensitivity of Passengers and Market Structure in the Airline Industry

European University Studies
Europäische Hochschulschriften
Publications Universitaires Européennes

Series V
Economics and Management

Reihe V Série V
Volks- und Betriebswirtschaft
Sciences économiques

Vol./Band 2135

PETER LANG
Bern · Berlin · Frankfurt/M. · New York · Paris · Wien

Roland Fischer

Time Sensitivity of Passengers and Market Structure in the Airline Industry

A Model of International Air Transport

PETER LANG
Bern · Berlin · Frankfurt/M. · New York · Paris · Wien

Die Deutsche Bibliothek – CIP-Einheitsaufnahme

Fischer, Roland:
Time sensitivity of passengers and market structure in the airline industry : a model of international air transport / Roland Fischer. – Bern ; Berlin ; Frankfurt a. M. ; New York ; Paris ; Wien : Lang, 1997
(European university studies : Ser. 5, Economics and management ; Vol. 2135)
Zugl.: Fribourg, Univ., Diss., 1997
ISBN 3-906757-78-1

US-ISBN 0-8204-3418-3

Printed in Germany

To my parents

Preface

When studying Industrial Organization, the student learns about market structure, firm behavior, welfare, technology and many other things. But most importantly, he learns that the success of a firm always depends on the relationship with other firms. Similarly, the quality of research is enhanced by the support and advise of teachers, colleagues and friends. I am, therefore, grateful to all those who have contributed to the making of this book.

I especially thank Professor Gerhard Aschinger, who was the first examiner of my doctoral thesis. His courses in Industrial Organization originally inspired me to study air transport markets many years ago. I am grateful to him not only for the numerous encouraging discussions and profound comments on my work, but also for the good time I had working at the Economics Department of the University of Fribourg. I am also grateful to the second examiner, Professor Reiner Wolff, whose critical and detailed comments essentially contributed to the success of my dissertation.

With English not being my native language, finding the right words was not always easy. I therefore thank Anthony Clark and especially Ute Hellner for their time and advise. For the help and support I received for my empirical work, I am grateful to Peter Windlin and Björn Schmolck at the University of Fribourg and to Mr. Bisang from *Swissair*.

I further appreciate working together with Peter Windlin at the University, I enjoyed the discussions and good times in Fribourg. For many unforgettable hours during our studies and their friendship I thank Rafael Halm and Stefan Rapp. Finally, I especially thank Michèle Graber for her love, friendship and support.

Buchrain, Switzerland, Mai 1997 Roland Fischer

Contents

List of Figures

Chapter 1

Chapter 2

Chapter 3

Chapter 4

Chapter 5

List of Tables

Chapter 1

Chapter 2

Chapter 3

Chapter 4

Abbreviations

ADA	Airline Deregulation Act
ASK	Available Seat Kilometers
CAB	Civil Aeronautics Board
CRS	Computer Reservation System
DOT	US Department of Transportation
DPFI	Domestic Passenger Fare Investigation
EEA	European Economic Area
EU	European Union
FFP	Frequent Flyer Program
IATA	International Air Transport Association
OECD	Organization for Economic Cooperation and Development
OLS	Ordinary Least Squares Regression
RPK	Revenue Passenger Kilometer
RPM	Revenue Passenger Mile
SIFL	Standard Industry Fare Level
SUR	Seemingly Unrelated Regression Model
TACO	Travel Agent Commission Override Program
UK	United Kingdom
US	United States of America

Guide to Symbols

AC	average costs
AR	average revenue
b	market density for a unit time interval of preferred departure times
B	network density
BS	ratio of business class passengers to the sum of business and economy class passengers
c	passenger specific costs
C	total costs
d	market distance
D	number of connecting destinations at a hub airport
E	inverse load factor
f	flight specific costs
F	schedule density
g	capacity specific costs
G	environmental variables
h	hubbing costs
IAC	industry average costs
k	aircraft size in seats
K	total capacity
L	load factor
LI	Lerner Index
MC	marginal costs
MR	marginal revenue
n	number of firms
P	ticket price
q	demand for one time unit
Q	number of passengers, demand, perceived demand
r	discount rate
R	combination of supply variables
s	market share
S	demand shift parameter (market size)

t	time
T	total time units (per day)
v	time costs from frequency delay
V	consumer surplus
VS	social welfare (sum of consumer surplus and profits)
w	time costs from stochastic delay
W	number of regions
X	number of flights
y	expected trip time
Y	number of online connections
z	money value of one unit of time
Z	Lagrangian function
α	frequency elasticity of demand
β	capacity elasticity of demand
γ	network elasticity of demand
ε	price elasticity of demand
ζ	rate of return on investment
η	distance elasticity of cost (economies of scale with respect to distance)
θ	elasticity multiplier in competitive models
Θ	full price of air travel
λ	Lagrangian multiplier
ν	welfare change from local to global networks
Π	profit
ρ	probability
σ	homogeneity of competitors' services
τ	time lag
Φ	profit margin
Ψ	marginal output costs from variations in flights
ω	welfare ratio between local and global networks in the two area case
Ω	degree of deviation of a single firm from its pro-rata demand curve

Guide to Subscripts

0	departure of flight
c	passenger specific costs
d	cost shift parameter
D	per connecting destination
f	flight specific costs
g	capacity costs
G	at hub G
H	at hub H
i	firm *i*
j	firm *j*
k	market *k*
l	market *l*
L	local network - two area case
m	monopoly case
M	global network - two region case
min	minimum
N	local network - two region case
p	preferred by the passenger
Q	per passenger
R	regulatory case
RPK	per revenue passenger kilometer
U	global network - two area case
w	contestable case
W	two area case (‹world› case)
X	per flight

Introduction

Today, the airline industry is characterized by radical changes in market and firm structures. Starting in 1978 with the complete deregulation of the US airline industry, the regulatory environments for air transport in several countries are currently being revised. In the EU, for example, deregulation started in 1983 with the partial liberalization of local interstate connections and was completed in January 1997, when EU airlines were finally granted free choice in market entry, fares, capacities and frequencies for flights within the community. In addition, several European governments signed open-sky agreements with the US in the 90s. The new contracts provide more liberal frameworks for international air transport and have replaced the former restrictive bilateral agreements that favored cartel supply by a small number of specially designated national (flag) carriers. Although the majority of connections to South America, Asia, Africa and Australia are still characterized by restrictive bilateral agreements, it can be presumed that, together with the liberalization of international trade, many of these contracts will eventually be replaced, creating a large deregulated area where carriers are able to develop global networks.

However, with liberalization in the EU still in progress, deregulation in the US is the only major step towards free markets in air transport that has been completed so far in an economic area of significant size. It thus provides the only "natural experiment" available in order to analyze the effects of air transport liberalization and is often used as a model for other countries. In the US up to 1978, the regulatory authority *Civil Aeronautics Board* (CAB) controlled entry and set fares on the basis of long-run average costs reported by the airlines. The carriers were divided into trunk airlines, which were able to acquire transport rights all over the country, and local carriers only allowed to serve cities within a restricted area. Shortly after the *Airline Deregulation Act* (ADA) was passed by the US congress in 1978, legal entry barriers and fare regulations were abolished. As a result, numerous newly certified carriers started operation and challenged the well established traditional airlines with lower fares. The local airlines started to compete with the trunk carriers by expanding their networks into the formerly protected long-distance markets. The increase in competition was followed by lower fares in the majority of city-pair markets.[1] In addition, market structures changed considerably as carriers established nationwide hub-and-spoke networks that increased the number of online connections within the US.[2] However, although numerous empirical studies indicate that on average consumers have benefited from deregulation, the increase in the concentration of firms, which began in the mid 80s and eliminated most of the new entrants, raises worries about the long-term market structure of air transport and possible anti-competitive effects. Several economists are concerned about the concentration of firms at major hub airports, which may lead to higher fares and, therefore, distort the positive impacts on consumers that were achieved in the early days of deregulation. Moreover, competition only seems to prevail in long distance markets between major cities. The majority of short-distance connections to local destinations are still provided by monopolies.

As a result of numerous liberalized bilateral agreements, the increase in the concentration of firms first only observed in the US is continuing internationally. Because of restrictions with respect to foreign ownership of airlines in the US and the EU, US and European carriers have started to integrate their operations and networks by forming strategic alliances. Such agreements intend to establish multiple-hub networks covering North America and Europe in the context of the complete deregulation of air transport between the two economic areas. Since the respective hubs are usually located in different countries (EU) or states (US), and the networks can therefore be regarded as geographically differentiated products, the question of market dominance is an important issue for air transport over the Atlantic. The decrease in fares and the increase in the number of connections between Europe and North-America indicate that consumers have benefited from competition with global networks so far. But an increase in concentration may lead to the opposite effect. Thus, with international deregulation of air transport markets

1 A city-pair market is defined by the demand and supply of air traffic between two airports.

2 In a hub-and-spoke system, airlines offer indirect connections over a central (hub) airport instead of direct connections.

and the simultaneous restructuring of airlines and networks still in progress, the future design of market structures cannot easily be predicted and leaves open several questions: Will the industry be characterized by a high degree of competition or is there danger of collusive behavior? Do network externalities lead to natural monopoly situations? And what are the effects of an increase in competition on service quality and consumer welfare?

A common feature of transport services is the importance of time costs to passengers. Since time can be regarded as a scarce resource for the consumer, the ‹full price› of transport includes the ticket price as well as opportunity costs regarding the time needed to ‹consume› the service. One may basically distinguish three types of time cost. The first type is the actual trip time necessary using a particular mode of transport, e.g. the actual flight time between Zurich and London. A second type of cost arises from the time passengers need in order to have access to the chosen transport mode, e.g. the time needed to get to the airport. For individually owned equipment, like the car or the bike, access time and respective costs are virtually zero. But for public transport, the time necessary to get to the closest station or airport may even exceed actual transport time. The third type of time cost is related to the trade-off between the preferred departure or arrival time of consumers and the actual departure time given by the schedule of the carrier. For example, a passenger who prefers to fly at 2 p.m. cannot use his or her time as efficiently when there are no flights between 11 a.m. and 5 p.m. or when a flight scheduled at 2 p.m. is already fully booked by the time he or she would like to make a seat reservation. In both these cases, the passenger incurs time opportunity costs from waiting. The level of opportunity cost per time unit can be referred to as the time sensitivity of passengers. Therefore, consumers with high time opportunity costs are called time sensitive consumers, whereas consumers with low time opportunity costs may be regarded as time insensitive consumers. With respect to air transport, it is often suggested that business passengers are more time sensitive than tourists, because opportunity costs from a loss of work time are considered to be higher than those incurred from a loss of leisure time.

The three types of time cost introduced above are closely related to supply and demand in transport services. Taking time sensitivity of passengers into account, the actual ticket price is only one of many variables that influence demand for a particular transport service, as the following examples show for the airline industry. First, trip time may be higher when airlines offer indirect connections rather than direct connections between two cities, because the former involves at least one stopover at a third airport. Therefore, it can be assumed that consumers prefer direct flights to indirect flights. But when indirect flights cost less, the full price of air travel may be less for indirect flights than for direct flights, which then leads to the opposite order of choices. Second, time costs with respect to service access depend on the number of destinations in a given area. Suppose, for example, that air transport between the US and France is provided by a monopoly airline. If this carrier offers only flights to Paris, US citizens that would like to visit another French city may not take the trip, because access time from Paris is much too long. If, on the other hand, the airline offers connections to a variety of cities all over France, each preferred destination of US citizens may be located close to an airport that is served by the carrier. This leads to a higher demand compared to a network that only includes Paris. Third, an increase in the frequency of service lowers the average delay passengers incur from the trade-off between actual and preferred departure time, and a low average load factor reduces the probability that a flight is booked up. Therefore, an increase in quality in terms of destinations, frequency and capacity leads to an increase in demand, because time costs of passengers are reduced.

Empirical results indicate that airlines take time sensitivity of passengers into account when deciding on network structures, schedules and capacities. As a simple example, observe the numerous connections to small cities in the US, where carriers usually offer relatively dense schedules with small aircraft, while long-distance markets rather are served by relatively few flights with large aircraft. From a technical point of view, several flights with small aircraft may lead to higher costs per kilometer and, therefore, to higher fares than few flights with large aircraft. But since a high frequency of service reduces opportunity costs for time sensitive consumers, the full price of air travel may still be lower than for a low frequency, although the ticket price is higher. Moreover, because the quality of service influences costs, the time sensitivity of passengers determines the cost structure and, therefore, the profitability of firms operating in the market. This indicates that time sensitivity of passengers influences market structures.

In the economic literature on the airline industry, the basic contributions to the problem of time costs were provided by *DeVany (1974)* and *Douglas and Miller (1974)*. *DeVany (1974)* estimated the value of time to passengers in different market distance segments. He demonstrated that passengers in short-distance markets are more time sensitive than passengers in long-distance markets. *Douglas and Miller (1974)* introduced the concepts of *frequency* and *stochastic delay* in order to analyze optimal regulation of the US airline industry. Both concepts refer to costs associated with the trade-off between actual and preferred departure time. While frequency delay relates time costs to the number of flights offered, stochastic delay refers to time costs arising from the probability of a booked up flight and, therefore, depends on capacity. The theory was later used by several economists for the development of theoretical and empirical models that demonstrate the effects of entry and fare regulation in the US.[3] The results were in accordance with previously published empirical studies, which indicate that entry and fare regulation in the US led to competition on frequencies and capacities.[4] At the time the ADA was implemented, *Panzar (1979)* presented a model for a competitive environment based on frequency and stochastic delay costs and analyzed welfare effects of air transport deregulation.

In the early 80s, empirical studies mainly focused on the effects of deregulation on fares.[5] The concept of competition which underlaying most of these studies was the theory of contestable markets. The theory was especially appealing because of two technical features that are often attributed to airline city-pairs: economies of scale with respect to the number of passengers carried per flight (economies of aircraft size) and the absence of sunk costs. Whereas the first notion is generally accepted as an empirical fact, there are still doubts as to the existence of sunk costs. While the high market liquidity for equipment (airplanes) indicates the absence of sunk costs in city-pair markets, empirical studies reject the hypothesis of perfect contestability and have found only weak effects of potential competitors on fares. The reasons given by the authors of

3 See, for example, *De Vany (1975)* and *Schmalensee (1977)*.

4 See *Jordan (1970)* and *Keeler (1972)*.

5 See, for example, *Bailey and Panzar (1981)*, *Graham, Kaplan and Sibley (1983)*, *Caves, Christensen and Tretheway (1983)*, *Bailey, Graham and Kaplan (1985)*, *Moore (1986)*, and *Morrison and Winston (1987)*.

these studies are entry barriers like the scarcity of airport facilities and slots at large airports. However, a decline in fares after deregulation is a common result of the majority of empirical studies and this has led to the widespread opinion that deregulation is beneficial to consumers. With respect to time sensitivity of passengers *Graham, Kaplan and Sibley (1983)* conclude that market characteristics, such as distance and time sensitivity of passengers, explain most of the variation in fares across markets after deregulation.

In the mid 80s, when the industry was characterized by numerous mergers and acquisitions, several empirical studies analyzed the impacts of a growing industry concentration. Since many large US airports have become dominated by a single firm, some authors point to the problem of market power and sunk costs associated with hub-airports. They show that a dominant firm may be able to raise fares in markets which involve such hubs as one endpoint.[6] In addition, several theoretical models discuss network externalities and the cost efficiency of hub-and-spoke operations.[7] At the same time, the issue of quality in terms of network size, flight frequency and load factor was again raised in empirical investigations. *Morrison and Winston (1989)*, for example, estimated the welfare effects of six post deregulation mergers of US carriers, taking into account price and non-price variables. They found that the mergers led to a welfare loss from the increase in fares but to a welfare gain from the increase in cities served. Cumulatively, the results suggest that the mergers had a modest positive effect on consumer welfare. In a recent study, *Gaynor and Trapani III (1994)* calculated the difference in consumer surplus before and after deregulation for 70 US city-pair markets. They tested the hypothesis that the observed decrease in flight frequencies and increase in load factors after deregulation has reduced welfare. The finding of the empirical study is that welfare has increased after deregulation as a result of lower fares, but that this increase is lower if frequency and load factor variables are included in the analysis.

6 See, for example, *Borenstein (1989)*, *Borenstein (1990)* and *Evans and Kessides (1993)*.

7 See, for example, *Carlton, Landes and Posner (1980)*, *Brown (1991)*, *Brueckner and Spiller (1991)*, *Brueckner, Dyer and Spiller (1992)*, and *Hendricks, Piccione and Tan (1995)*.

However, although some of the literature cited above recognizes the importance of time sensitivity of passengers for market structures, and although the development of hub-and-spoke systems is one of the major features of industry studies today, there is no theoretical contribution known to the author that explores the influence of time sensitivity of passengers on the structure of hub-and-spoke systems. Specifically, it seems that the question of access time to an airlines' service and the respective effects on the extent and design of networks have been rather neglected in the past. The main purpose of this work, therefore, is to fill this gap by combining the two features time sensitivity of passengers and hub-and-spoke networks in a sequence of theoretical models, which may help to explain current and future developments of market structures in the international airline industry.

The theory developed in this work leads to the following principal findings: a basic model indicates that firms offer higher fares, lower load factors and higher frequencies in markets where passengers are more time sensitive than price sensitive. In addition, the ticket price increases but the ticket price per kilometer decreases with market distance due to economies of stage length.[8] However, the influence of distance on frequency and load factor is ambiguous. The results are supported by OLS regressions for *Swissair*'s European markets. In addition, the basic model demonstrates that the frequency of service, and therefore quality, increases with market size. A first extension of the model reveals that in a hub-and-spoke system, the size of the network in terms of connecting destinations increases with time sensitivity of passengers. Like frequency, the number of connecting destinations increases with market size. Using a model of monopolistic competition, it can be shown that an increase in the number of firms leads to a decrease in fares, schedule densities, and network densities, but to an increase in load factors.[9] Although this implies that competition leads to a decrease in quality, consumer surplus increases with the number of firms when price elasticity of demand is sufficiently large and time sensitivity of passengers is sufficiently small. In addition, the model

8 Stage length is a synonym for market distance often applied in the literature on the airline industry. Here both expressions are used interchangeably.

9 Schedule density and network density refer to the number of flights per passenger and firm and the number of connecting destinations at the hub per passenger and firm respectively.

demonstrates that air transport over a specific hub is likely to be a natural monopoly, especially when passengers are very time sensitive with respect to frequency. This result may aims at explaining the high concentration of firms at hub airports. Furthermore, it is shown that in providing air transport services between two regions, firms are tempted to develop multiple-hub networks in order to increase demand by reducing access time. This leads to an increase in the concentration of firms providing such services. However, because the development of multiple-hub networks leads to an increase in the number of destinations in a network, consumer welfare is likely to increase. The further development of the model predicts that the free-entry equilibrium number of firms in a given area increases with the size of this area, and that consumer welfare is more likely to increase from deregulation when the size of the deregulated area increases. Thus, as a main policy implication, it is suggested that international air transport deregulation should be introduced in and between as many countries as possible, so that firms are able to develop multiple-hub networks and that a concentration of firms can be avoided.

The present work is structured as follows. In Chapter 1, the international regulation of air transport and institutional arrangements between countries and firms are discussed, and the regulation and deregulation of the US airline industry is analyzed. Besides the implications for market structures, we focus especially on the development of hub-and-spoke systems and on the contestability hypothesis. Some recent attempts to relax regulatory constraints in the European Union and in international markets are also examined. Here, economic and institutional differences between the EU and the US are analyzed.

In Chapter 2 the basic model is developed. Specifically, after introducing a feasible cost function, the frequency and stochastic delay concepts and their applications in previous studies are discussed. Then, a demand function for a single city-pair market is specified, taking into account the fact that the frequency and capacity offered by a firm influence the decisions of consumers. Subsequently, the profit maximizing price, frequency and load factor of a monopoly airline are computed. In a further step, comparative statics results of this model are interpreted and tested in a case study on *Swissair*.

Chapter 3 first introduces a hub-and-spoke model for city-pair markets, where the number of connecting destinations at the hub is considered as an additional element of service quality. Moreover, it is assumed that airlines offering competitive services in a major city-pair market to a hub differentiate their products by offering connections to different local destinations from that hub. After calculating the respective equilibrium values for fares, load factors, schedule and network densities, the free-entry equilibrium number of firms is determined and the effects of competition on consumer welfare are discussed. This includes the calculation of a welfare maximum that may be achieved by a regulated monopoly. To complete the analysis of competition at hubs, we focus on the development of multiple-hub networks and their implications for the free-entry equilibrium number of firms and for consumer welfare.

In Chapter 4, the previously developed model is adjusted by the assumption that airlines differentiate products offering connections via hubs in different regions. Thus, we analyze competition *with hubs* instead of competition at hubs. After calculating the free-entry equilibrium number of firms and welfare effects for this model, a case study on the concentration of firms in the US airline industry after deregulation illustrates the theoretical findings.

Chapter 5 summarizes the model results and draws up respective propositions, which are then used to indicate the possible development of market structures following European and international deregulation. Subsequently, policy implications are derived. Here, we focus on competition policy, taking into account problems associated with the integration of firms and networks on the one hand and collusion on the other hand. We conclude with some final remarks and some hints for future research.

1. Regulatory Framework

1.1 Introduction

Despite the worldwide tendency towards the liberalization of air transport, airlines still face a variety of restrictions in international markets. In order to illuminate some institutional issues in international air transport regulation, bilateral agreements between governments as well as pool arrangements between airlines will be discussed in the opening section of this chapter. Besides the contents of multinational and bilateral agreements, this includes a brief description of some attempts at regulatory reform in the EU and the UK. Today, the US and the EU constitute the only large geographic areas with liberalized airline industries. The subsequent section, therefore, deals with the deregulation and the change of market structures in the US. First, the history of US airline regulation and some empirical results will be presented. Then, the impact of deregulation and the development of hub-and-spoke systems is analyzed. In addition, the theory of contestable markets is introduced, which is one of the most important tools in analyzing the effects of deregulation. However, although airline city-pair markets were considered as contestable in the years following the *Airline Deregulation Act*, later studies found that fares are positively correlated with the number of firms in the market, which rather supports traditional oligopoly models. Thus, the reasons for this result are discussed. The fourth section deals with the liberalization of air transport in the EU and in intercontinental markets. Among other things, we consider whether the results from US deregulation may equally apply to European markets. The concluding section sets out some of the requirements for a new theoretical model that may improve the understanding of recent developments in the airline industry as discussed in this chapter.

1.2 Institutional Arrangements for International Air Transport

The basic multilateral agreements regulating international civil aviation services were signed at the *Chicago Convention of 1944*. While the convention established multilateral agreements for issues like safety standards, communication and the exchange of technology, commercial rights were left to be negotiated between single countries. At least, according to a report of the *OECD*, the member states of the future *International Civil Aviation Organization* agreed on the principle that «every state has complete and exclusive sovereignty over the airspace above its territory»[1].

For international air transport this principle means that commercial flights require the permission of the respective governments concerned. The failure to achieve a multinational agreement was due to the different interests of the European governments and the US. While the European governments favored regulatory constraints in order to protect their war-damaged airline industry from competition, the US tried to establish a multinational agreement, according to which every country would have to guarantee five different ‹freedoms›-rights defined by the convention. The five ‹freedoms› to be granted to airlines flying scheduled services are as follows:[2]

1st freedom:	the right to overfly a foreign country without a stop-over in that country;
2nd freedom:	the right to land and take off in the foreign country for technical purposes (e.g. to refuel, change crew etc.) without taking passengers and cargo from that country;
3rd freedom:	the right to take passengers and cargo from the home country to a foreign country;
4th freedom:	the right to take passengers and cargo from a foreign country to the home country;
5th freedom:	the right to transport passengers and cargo between two foreign countries, if the flight begins or ends in the home country.

1 *OECD (1988)*, p. 26.

2 An illustration of the freedom rights is presented in the Appendix.

Although a multinational agreement ensuring the five freedoms would have restricted the sovereignty of the countries, it would still have protected national markets from international competition, because the five freedoms only cover international transport rights for flights involving the home country of an airline. Therefore, analysts often refer to additional (never officially defined) freedom rights:

6th freedom: the right to take passengers and cargo from a foreign country to another foreign country, if the flight includes a stop-over in the home country;
7th freedom: the right to take passengers and cargo from a foreign country to another foreign country directly;
8th freedom: the right to take passengers and cargo from a destination in a foreign country to another destination in the same country (cabotage).

The establishment of all the eight freedom rights would have led to free entry into every international and national city-pair market. However, at the *Chicago Convention* in 1944, only an agreement granting the first and second freedom rights, the *International Transit Agreement*, was signed by a majority of the participating governments.

The lack of multinational rules led to a large number of restrictive bilateral agreements, which still form the basic regulatory framework for international air transport services. Today, every country usually governs more than 70 bilateral agreements. Only between member states of the EU has commercial air service been regulated in a broader multinational. For a large number of bilateral agreements, the 1946 contract between the UK and the US – the *Bermuda I* agreement – served as the model. Although there is wide variation in the content of subsequent agreements between other countries, they all include more or less the following rules first set up by the Bermuda I agreement [see *OECD (1988)*, p. 27)]:

- scheduled air service between two countries is provided by one or more airlines designated by each country to provide that service;

- an airline designated by a country must be substantially owned and effectively controlled by the country designating it or by nationals of that country;
- ticket prices should be agreed on by the designated airlines, approved by the *International Air Transport Association* (IATA) and approved by both governments;
- each country's designated airline should have fair and equal opportunity to operate on the routes between the countries;
- the city-pair markets to be operated are specified in the agreement or in schedules attached to the agreement.

Some agreements established 5th freedom rights, which, of course, had to be negotiated with the respective third country. The contents of *Bermuda I*-type contracts show that bilateral agreements basically regulate market entry and total capacity provided on the routes between the two countries, while fares are negotiated between the designated airlines directly. The rate fixing agreements between airlines are governed through the *International Air Transport Association* (IATA), which is composed of most international airlines providing scheduled services. Since the national governments usually approve the proposed tariffs automatically, the IATA may be considered as a cartel for setting monopoly tariffs. In addition to rate fixing, airlines usually form pooling arrangements, which extend the provisions of the bilateral agreements to daily operations.[3] The formal commercial agreements between airlines are often supplemented by ‹confidential understandings› and ‹side agreements›, which may differ from the published pooling arrangements. *Figure 1.1* illustrates the basic regulatory framework of international air transport. In detail, the pooling agreements usually contain the following elements:[4]

3 In this work, the term ‹pooling agreement› is used in its broader sense, covering all elements of commercial agreements between airlines. In its narrower sense, the term is also used for revenue sharing agreements between airlines for a specific market. Here, revenue sharing is only one element of pooling arrangements besides others discussed below.

4 See *OECD (1988)*, p. 69ff.

Figure 1.1: Regulation of international air transport with bilateral agreements

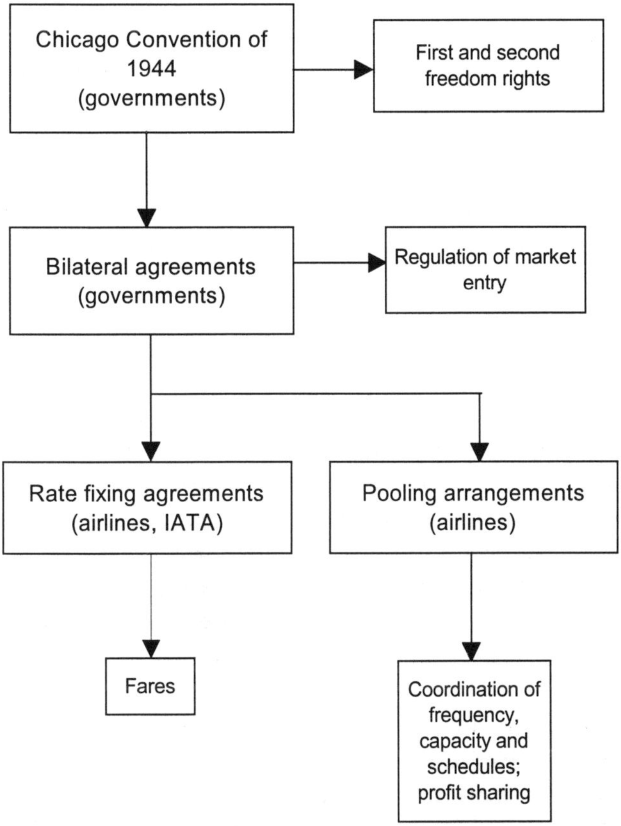

– *Capacity and frequency agreements*
The control of capacity and frequency serves as an instrument for securing monopoly rents of the designated airlines. Control is established by either fixing the total available seat kilometers (ASK) the airlines will be flying in a market, the frequency of flights, or the type of aircraft used. In practice, capacity may be divided for individual routes or for the whole country-pair. Because of their strong anti-competitive effects, capacity and

frequency arrangements are illegal in markets within the United States just as price fixing agreements are.

- *Joint scheduling agreements*
  Joint scheduling agreements are closely related to capacity and frequency arrangements. The cooperating airlines integrate each others flights into their own schedules and coordinate the flights. They set up a schedule as if they were one single airline. On the one hand, scheduling agreements may be beneficial because they save costs or avoid congestion at major airports at peak times. On the other hand, they limit competition between the airlines.

- *Revenue pools*
  A revenue pool basically involves the transfer of part of the revenues of the colluding firms operating in a market, so that each airline receives an equal share of total market revenue. Airlines and governments justify revenue sharing agreements on the grounds that they compensate for the lower income of the carrier with less convenient departure times. Actually, revenue sharing agreements lead to very strong anti-competitive effects arising from the calculation of the revenue shares. The mechanism for transfer is usually based on a ‹notional revenue› instead of the actual revenue of the participating airlines. The notional revenue is defined as the previous year's income per passenger multiplied by the number of passengers transported in the present year. This discourages airlines from increasing the number of passengers by offering lower fares, because they may would have to transfer revenue they did not earn. Besides single revenue pools, there also exist revenue-cost pools that involve the sharing of costs as well. Revenue sharing is also used by airlines cooperating with code sharing agreements. However, in this case, the anti-competitive effects may be offset by the increase in utility passengers incur from an increase in online connections.[5]

5 Code sharing agreements are discussed below. Online connections refer to indirect flights, where passengers have to change planes at a large airport, but where they are

- *Joint operation*
  In a joint operation agreement only one airline operates in the market instead of the designated carriers. The operating airline can be one of the designated airlines or a third airline. Joint operation usually involves a joint cost and/or revenue sharing agreement in mutual interest.

- *Royalty agreements*
  In a royalty agreement, one airline pays a royalty, e.g. a substantial amount of cash, to the other airline for the privilege of serving a joint market as a monopoly. Thus royalty agreements are similar to joint operation, since only one airline offers flights in a market where both airlines have transport rights.

- *Code sharing*
  A code sharing agreement involves the appearance of the two cooperating airlines' flights under the two letter identification code of each airline. Originally, code sharing agreements were signed between major carriers and commuter airlines that provide connecting services from local airports to hubs. The flights of the feeder airline are indicated with the code of the larger carrier on computer reservation systems (CRS), thus appearing as one single airline offering online flights. Today, there is a growing number of code sharing agreements between US and European carriers in the Trans-Atlantic market. Online flights are usually more beneficial to consumers than interline flights.[6] Especially in the US, where each airline has its own terminal, an online connection requires less time to change the aircraft, is based on an adjusted schedule, and reduces the probability of baggage arriving late or being lost.

transported by the same carrier. In contrast to this, a change of airplane involving different carriers is called an interline flight.

6 See, for example, *Carlton, Landes and Posner (1980),* who estimated passenger valuation of online flights relative to interline flights in view of the merger of *North-Central Airlines* and *Southern Airways* as *Republic Airlines* in 1979.

- *Interlining*
  In an interline agreement, cooperating airlines accept each others tickets for their city-pair markets. This means that a passenger who purchases a ticket from one carrier can use this ticket to fly with another airline offering flights to the same destination. The tickets sold by each participating airline are cleared with the number of passengers actually transported at the IATA-Clearing House. The Interline system offers several advantages to passengers and carriers. Passengers benefit from greater flexibility in changing flights spontaneously or in case they miss a flight. For carriers, interline agreements facilitate cooperation. Actually, interlining may only be feasible for cooperating airlines, because airlines should charge the same or at least similar ticket prices for the same markets.[7]

A quick look at European markets before deregulation by the EU shows how intensively airlines made use of pooling agreements in order to exploit monopoly rents. According to the *Report on Competition in Intra-European Air Services* (COMPAS-Report) of 1982, 75-85% of the ton-kilometers offered on intra-European scheduled flights were carried out under pooling agreements. The dominance of national carriers may be underlined by the fact that none of the agreements involved more than two carriers. Among the European pooling agreements in 1982, all involved revenue sharing, 10-15% agreed on cost sharing, 15-20% limited the capacity of each partner, and a large number limited total capacity provided by the pool. About two thirds agreed on frequencies and one third involved forward planning of capacity, load factors and frequency more than 12 months ahead.[8] However, in the 1980s, several more liberal bilateral agreements were signed, especially between the UK and other European countries.[9] These contracts were less restrictive on market entry, capacity and tariff-fixing, but still did not abolish the anti-competitive

7 According to *Göpfert (1994),* p. 460, about 280 airlines were integrated in the Interline system in 1994.

8 Cf. Report on Competition in Intra-European Air Services, European Civil Aviation Conference, Doc. No. 25, Paris 1985; cited from *OECD (1988).*

9 See *Button and Swann (1989).*

pooling arrangements. Moreover, until recently, agreements on capacity, schedules and, to a certain extent, tariffs were still tolerated by the EU despite the deregulation process.

The bilateral agreements for international air transport prevent competition in airline markets. Because of entry restrictions, airlines do not develop efficient networks according to passenger demand. On the contrary, due to the pooling agreements, consumers face cartel supply in almost every international market. Although airlines should be highly profitable in this environment, many national carriers incur losses, especially those controlled by their governments. Therefore, the absence of competitive markets may trigger X-inefficiencies.[10] In addition, since a majority of carriers still is controlled by governments, further inefficiencies are created. Whereas private firms set fares, offer schedules and develop networks in order to maximize profits, destinations and schedules of publicly owned carriers are often influenced by governments for political reasons. European countries, for example, may maintain unprofitable services to former colonies, or large countries may want to guarantee a certain level of domestic services to small cities.

In contrast to scheduled services, charter airlines are less regulated, especially with respect to capacities, fares and market entry. Usually, only technical requirements must be met in order to obtain transport rights. However, charter services are restricted to group travel and firms are not allowed to sell tickets to passengers directly. In general, travel agencies buy a fixed number of seats and allocate them to holiday packages. Due to the absence of bilateral restrictions, pool arrangements are virtually absent in the charter industry, which indicates that there is tougher competition between charter airlines than between airlines offering scheduled services.

Although air transport is still highly regulated today, there are large economic areas with liberalized markets. In the US, the ADA abolished restrictions on entry, fares, capacities and frequencies on domestic operations. In the EU, all the eight freedom rights have been granted for services within the community since April 1997. Every EU based carrier is allowed to offer flights between any destinations within the EU without restrictions. Therefore, the ‹common market› has replaced the former bilateral agreements between

10 For X-efficiency theory, see *Leibenstein (1981)*.

member states. In addition, rate fixing and pooling agreements are now illegal under the competition law provisions of the *Treaty of Rome*, and governments are encouraged to privatize their flag carriers. However, it is important to note that several bilateral agreements have already led to a partial deregulation of air transport between European countries before the member states agreed on a common European policy. The UK especially has always been a proponent of a liberal policy for the airline industry in the past and, consequently, partially deregulated domestic traffic in the early 80s. Moreover, the former flag carrier *British Airways* was privatized in 1986. Today, the deregulation of scheduled air transport markets within the framework of bilateral agreements seems to be continuing on the intercontinental level, especially between EU member states and the US.

1.3 The Deregulation of the US Airline Industry

1.3.1 The History of Airline Regulation and Deregulation in the US

The regulation of air transport in the US basically involved entry and price regulation by the *Civil Aeoronautic Board* (CAB). The CAB's authority was initially established by the *Civil Aeoronautics Act* of 1938. In accordance with the provisions of the act, the CAB controlled entry into and exit from the industry, regulated fares, awarded direct subsidies (mainly for service to small communities), controlled mergers and agreements between firms and investigated unfair methods of competition.[11] The CAB set fares in order to achieve an average rate of return for the industry based on actual industry operating costs. With respect to market entry, not all carriers were able to obtain permission to operate in any market within the United States. The CAB subdivided the airlines into different categories according to their size and their primary area of operation. Only the ‹trunk carriers› were permitted to develop nationwide networks. The ‹local carriers› were restricted to city-pair markets

11 See *Bailey, Graham and Kaplan (1985).*

within areas that covered a small number of states, but were not allowed to offer services across the US. In order to guarantee air transport to small communities, these services were subsidized by the CAB. A third group, the ‹commuter carriers›, operated on short distance and low density routes. Commuters' entry and fares were exempted from CAB regulation, but they were only allowed to operate aircraft with less than 30 revenue seats. A small group of airlines, the ‹intra-state carriers›, were not regulated by the CAB since they were only offering connections within one single state. However, because of the relatively small size of most states, only California and Texas enjoyed networks of intra-state carriers.

Stigler (1971) suggests that any industry regulation satisfies the regulated firms' goals rather than public interests. Indeed, after two decades of CAB control of the US airline industry, observers discovered a number of inefficiencies associated with regulation in the late 60s and 70s. *Stigler*'s theory implies that CAB regulation may be regarded as a government supported cartel with an attempt to capture monopoly rents. As will be discussed below, this would explain the extraordinarily high fares on most city-pair markets during the decades of regulation. *Jordan (1970)* and *Keeler (1972)* compared the non-regulated intra-state carriers operating in California with the regulated airlines and demonstrated the inefficiency of CAB regulation compared to free markets. *Jordan (1970)* discovered that the intra-state carriers offered lower fares but still incurred higher profits than the regulated local and trunk carriers. *Keeler (1972)* found that the monopoly rents were competed away by schedule rivalry. Since the number of daily flights on a particular route was not regulated by the CAB, carriers replaced price competition by competition with flight frequency and capacity. Although this probably increased welfare, several economists demonstrated that this welfare gain was more than offset by the negative impacts of higher fares.[12] Furthermore, the CAB determined fares according to an average of industry costs reported by the airlines. As airlines increasingly competed with flight frequency and capacity, fares rose almost automatically.

The analysis of *Keeler (1972)* on frequency and capacity competition is of further interest with respect to the present work. Therefore, it is analyzed in more detail. *Keeler (1972)* proceeds in several steps. For the comparison of the

12 See, for example, *Douglas and Miller (1974)*.

efficiency of firms in the two different regulatory regimes, one would first have to know how the regulated airlines would price in an unregulated environment. To calculate the hypothetical fares of interstate carriers in free markets, *Keeler (1972)* therefore estimates a cost function using data from the regulated interstate carriers, and then adjusts it for ‹efficient› operation variables of the non-regulated California carriers such as load factors and seating densities. Second, he estimates passenger trip costs for 30 routes, taking into account stage length as well as costs incurred from airport and traffic congestion. The resulting trip costs are then used as estimates of competitive, unregulated ticket prices. As a test, *Keeler (1972)* predicted the fares on two unregulated California routes. For both routes the simulated fares were extremely close to actual fares (within a range of 3% on both routes). The estimation of competitive unregulated fares for the interstate markets and the comparison with actual fares revealed that there are large markups on almost all the markets investigated. In addition, *Keeler (1972)* found that the markup tends to rise with stage length. Nevertheless, although the large markups would suggest excessively high profits for the interstate carriers, they earned only ‹normal› profits. One reason for this result may be cross subsidies from long-haul to short-haul markets. However, since load factors on interstate routes were generally lower than on California routes, *Keeler (1972)* concludes that with fares at high ‹cartel› levels, airlines have competed away profits through excess capacity.[13]

Completing the above results, *Bailey, Graham and Kaplan (1985)* show that service and frequency competition mainly occurred in high density and long haul markets, whereas short distance markets to small communities were characterized by relatively low service and inconvenient departure times. They found that although the CAB price-regulation formula took into account economies of scale with respect to stage length, long distance fares were usually set too high and short distance fares too low. Therefore, airlines were tempted to put more resources for frequency and capacity competition into long-haul markets than into short distance flights. This conclusion is in accordance with the higher markups *Keeler (1972)* estimated for long-haul compared to short-

13 In Chapter 2, two articles are presented, *DeVany (1975)* and *Schmalensee (1977)*, that model frequency competition under fare and entry regulation.

haul markets. Higher markups between the regulated and the ‹efficient› competitive fares allow for a higher degree of frequency and capacity competition.

In 1977 the economist *Alfred Kahn*, having become the new head of the CAB, initiated the first steps towards the deregulation of airline markets. Several new entry applications were accepted and the airlines enjoyed greater pricing flexibility as the CAB started to set fare intervals and discount fares instead of fixed rates. But the major step towards complete deregulation was made by the US Congress which passed the *Airline Deregulation Act* (ADA) in 1978. With the ADA, US carriers gained complete freedom to enter any city-pair market in the United States and, gradually, in setting fares. The ADA reduced the regulatory power of the CAB until its liquidation in 1983. The remaining regulatory responsibilities, mainly concerned with security standards and slot allocation, were transferred to the *US Department of Transportation* (DOT).

The ADA led to an increase in competition as several newly certified carriers entered the industry. Since they had some cost advantages due to the lower degree of unionization of their employees, they started to challenge the established local and trunk carriers by setting considerably lower fares in long distance markets. The local carriers expanded their (local) networks by offering long distance flights to other regions in the US. The commuter carriers took over several short haul markets to local destinations that were abandoned by the local carriers after deregulation. With their fleets that were composed of small propeller aircraft, the commuters started to offer high frequency services from small airports to the hubs of the former local and trunk carriers. Today, this service mainly suits local business passengers traveling to large cities.

As a result of the growing extent of competition, carriers improved efficiency by adjusting fares, frequency and capacity to the needs of different passenger segments. Whereas fares decreased considerably in long haul markets, they increased in short-haul markets.[14] In addition, carriers started to develop ‹peak load pricing› strategies.[15] For flights at peak times, when

14 See, for example, *Moore (1986)*.

15 *Steiner (1957)* provides an introduction into the economics of peak load pricing strategies.

demand is relatively high, firms charge higher fares than at off-peak times, when demand is smaller. In order to reduce costs, airlines started to develop hub-and-spoke systems, which allow firms to economize on the number of flights and capacity.[16] Although lower fares, improved schedules, and the large number of newly certified carriers point to the benefits of deregulated air transport markets for consumers, several changes in market structures have led to concern about the welfare effects of deregulation. More than a decade after the US congress passed the ADA, the majority of city-pair markets remain dominated by one single firm. In addition, the industry became more concentrated on the national level in the late 80s as several mergers, acquisitions and bankruptcies reduced the number of carriers considerably.[17] By the end of this concentration process, the majority of the local and commuter carriers and almost all of the newly certified carriers were not able to survive as independent firms. The growing importance of hub-and-spoke systems also led to a concentration of firms at major airports. Market concentration, the increasing dominance of single carriers at major airports, and higher fares in some markets weakened the long believed hypothesis that city-pair markets are contestable. In the following section, therefore, the nature of hub-and-spoke systems and the theory of contestable markets are presented together with some empirical studies on market power and the contestability of airline markets.

1.3.2 Hub-and-Spoke Networks and Market Power

The main reason for the development of hub-and-spoke systems is cost saving. The following simplified example illustrates this property of airline markets. Consider an airline that provides services between several destinations in two different areas, as depicted in *Figure 1.2*. For simplicity it is assumed that there is only demand between the destinations of different areas (foreign destinations) but that there is no demand between destinations in the same area (local destinations). In panel (a) a network is depicted where the services are carried

16 See *Figure 1.2 (b)* and the respective comments in the section below.

17 Market concentration in the US after deregulation is discussed more detailed in the case study in section 4.4.3.

out by direct flights. In order to guarantee connections between every pair of foreign destinations, the airline has to offer nine return flights or a total number of 18 flights. Denoting the costs for operating one flight by f and the cost for transporting one passenger by c, total costs of providing the service for the constant total demand Q are

$$C = 18f + Qc.$$

By using this rather simple cost function, we additionally assume that Q is equally distributed over all flights and that the airline uses only one type of aircraft, so that c is the same for all flights.

In panel (b), the network is completed by a hub-airport in the center between the two areas. Instead of offering direct flights between any foreign destination, the airline offers only 6 return flights between the destinations and the hub. In a network like this, passengers are transported from the originating destinations to the hub, where they change aircraft and continue their trips to their final destination. Of course, the hub-and-spoke network requires that the flight schedules to and from the destinations are adjusted, such that passengers do not have long waiting times on the hub and that there is enough time to reload baggage. In a hub-and-spoke system as depicted in panel (b), all the connections between foreign destinations can be offered by only 12 flights to and from the hub. Assuming that flight cost, passenger cost and total demand are the same as for direct flights, total costs are lower for a hub-and-spoke system compared to a network with only direct flights,

$$C = 12f + Qc.$$

For a given number of passengers, the lower total costs imply lower average costs (costs per passenger), which leads to lower fares and, therefore, induces higher demand. Of course, the airline has to take into account that there might be a reduction in demand because of the increased trip time. It can be reasonably assumed that passengers only prefer indirect flights to direct flights if the cost saving exceeds the money value of increased trip time.

Figure 1.2: Network with direct flights vs. hub-and-spoke system

(a) Direct flights

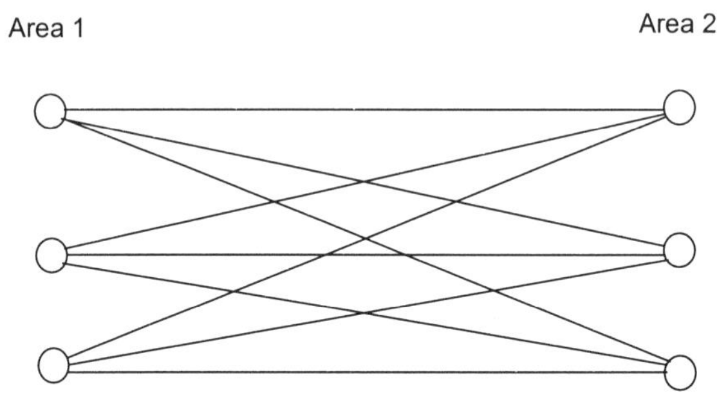

(b) Hub-and-spoke system

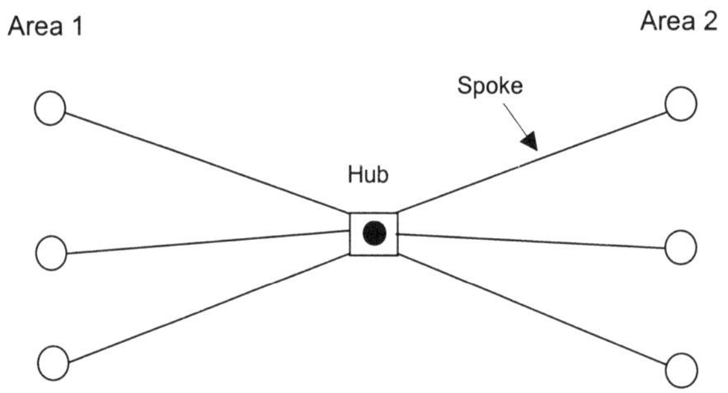

The extent of hub-and-spoke operations today suggests that indirect flights are efficient in this respect for a majority of city-pair markets. However, direct flights were not completely abandoned. Especially between large cities, where numerous newly certified carriers started offering direct flights at discount prices, carriers were very reluctant in replacing direct flights. The most significant improvements from the development of hub-and-spoke systems were achieved in services to local destinations. The concentration process among the former local carriers in the mid 80's and the integration of commuter carriers into the networks of large airlines led to several nationwide and even international networks, which are composed of flights between large cities as well as small towns.

Although hub-and-spoke systems may have improved consumer welfare due to an increased number of online connections, there is growing concern about the implications of the increased market power of hub dominating firms. Due to capacity limitations, only a few airports are sufficiently large to serve as a hub for more than one carrier. Therefore, several large and medium sized airports are dominated by one airline that uses this airport as its major hub. This dominant firm may obtain market power on the spokes, because the large share of destinations it offers in the region enables it to implement frequent flyer programs (FFPs) and travel agent commission override programs (TACOs) more effectively than competitors.[18] In addition, airport dominance may also result in a greater influence on the distribution of gates and slots, which are one of the critical inputs at large airports.[19] Gates and slots are usually distributed by the airport operator on the basis of long term leases. Because of the high revenues it creates, the dominant firm may influence decisions with respect to the distribution of gates and slots and with respect to the expansion of airport facilities to accommodate new entrants. When slots are traded on markets, the dominant firm presumably has a large market share and, therefore, dominates the slot market as well. In order to prevent profitable entry, it may even accumulate slots it does not need.

Airport dominance and its effects on market power in the US airline industry was investigated by *Borenstein (1989)*. He found that a single airline's traffic share on the route and at the endpoints of the route enables it to raise fares on that route relative to the fares of competitors on the same route. *Evans and Kessides (1993)* also demonstrate that fares are correlated with airport

18 Frequent flyer programs (FFPs) give passengers a gift, usually free travel, after he or she has used a certain amount of flights with that airline. Travel agent commission override programs (TACOs) pay bonuses to travel agents who generate a specified level of revenue for that airline. See *Borenstein (1989)*, pp. 345ff.

19 Gates are physical assets at airports like buildings and jetways. A slot is the right to land or take off at an airport during a certain time period.

market shares. But in their analysis, fares are independent of route market shares. To the authors, this result is not surprising. They note that the primary impediments to entry and sources of product differentiation between firms for a specific city-pair market are gates, slots, FFPs and TACOs. All these factors are clearly related to airport market shares rather than to route market shares. Once they are controlled for by airline fixed effects and airport dominance variables, firms offer rather homogeneous products and fares on markets with no entry barriers.

However, since *Borenstein (1989)* and *Evans and Kessides (1993)* both stress the importance of airport market shares, the question arises as to how exactly airport dominance is transformed into pricing power. *Evans and Kessides (1993)* identify scarce airport facilities and computer reservations systems as the main features. The two variables are therefore integrated into the econometric analysis. The authors then find that scarce airport facilities and computer reservation systems both *augment* a firms local pricing power, but do not eliminate the statistically significant airport dominance effect. Thus, they are not considered as the root cause of market power. *Evans and Kessides (1993)* therefore suggest three alternative sources of local market power at airports. First, the high prices may reflect high sunk costs at the airport level, which creates an additional entry barrier. Second, the largest firm at the airport may be offering a different product, which may be characterized by more convenient service, more attractive terminals, or more convenient locations for terminals than competitors. Third, the dominant airline may ‹cream skim› by attracting the high-paying traveler. *Evans and Kessides (1993)* therefore conclude that the higher prices may not reflect anticompetitive effects, but are due to the price premium passengers are willing to pay for higher quality services. This suggests that hub airports are characterized by a certain degree of product differentiation.

Brueckner, Dyer and Spiller (1992) discuss the problem of hub-and-spoke systems from a different viewpoint in that they specifically analyze network effects on fares. *Brueckner et. al.* argue that average costs per passenger fall when the airline develops a hub-and-spoke system, because it is able to use larger aircraft. In a hub-and-spoke system, each flight can be considered as a multiple product service, because it transports passengers with different origins or destinations, which increases the number of passengers per flight. Economies of scale with respect to the number of passengers are usually called *economies of aircraft size* or *economies of density*. The exploitation of economies of density by increasing the network size therefore should lead to lower fares, especially for connecting flights. *Brueckner et. al.* investigate 4-segment city-pair markets, which are defined as markets requiring a connection at a hub. The empirical results prove the theoretical predictions. For an increase in the number of 4-segment city-pairs of 100 (for a large network this is easily obtained by adding a relatively small number of additional destinations), fares decrease by 0.5%. The results have interesting implications for the analysis of airline mergers, especially in cases where both parties already had large airport shares at a specific airport prior to the merger. Whereas the increase in the merged airline's market share at the (common) hub airport leads to higher fares on direct markets to that airport (see *Borenstein 1989* and *Evans and Kessides 1993*), the increase in the number of online connections leads to a decrease in fares for these connections. However, although the results of *Brueckner et. al.* are very impressive, they do not answer the question of net welfare effects of hub-and-spoke networks.

1.3.3 The Theory of Contestable Markets

The theory of contestable markets is one of the most important tools for the analysis of deregulation in the US airline industry. In the following, the contributions of contestability theory to the analysis of airline markets is discussed, taking into account merits and deficiencies. The theory was developed in the early 80s and presented a new way of looking at competition and industry structures.[20] The main proposition of the theory is that marginal cost pricing may occur even in monopolistic and oligopolistic industries due to the existence of potential competition. As a starting point, consider an industry where the production of a good or service is characterized by economies of

20 See *Baumol, Panzar and Willig (1982)*. A short introduction into the main features of the theory is presented by *Aschinger (1984)* for the one product case, and *Aschinger (1986)* for the multiproduct case. Contestable equilibria for multiproduct firms are simulated in *Aschinger (1991)*.

scale for a certain interval of output. This implies that for a given demand function, a small number of firms or even a monopoly can produce the whole industry output at lowest cost. As a result, firms may incur market power, which can lead to deviations from marginal cost pricing and reduce consumer welfare. Therefore, it was long believed that industries with large economies of scale should be regulated in order to prevent monopoly rents. The theory of contestable markets states that if firms charge prices above average costs and, therefore, incur supranormal profits, potential competitors would enter the market, offer a lower price, still make a positive profit and satisfy the whole market demand. To deter this kind of entry, incumbent firms set prices equal to average costs, which leads to zero profits and thereby eliminates entry incentives. Thus, contestable markets can be interpreted as a market entry game.

As a necessary condition, contestable markets require free and costless entry and exit of firms. Otherwise, incumbent firms are able to charge prices above their average cost without the risk of entry of a potential competitor, because the latter incurs sunk costs from market entry. It further is assumed that the Bertrand-Nash condition holds, according to which the price change lag of incumbent firms exceeds the entry lag of entrants. In addition, contestable markets require *feasible* and *sustainable* industry configurations. The feasibility condition requires market clearing and no negative profits for incumbent firms. The sustainability condition requires that the industry configuration is feasible and that no profitable entry is possible. Under the assumption that all firms face the same cost function, this implies a cost minimizing industry structure. If an alternative industry structure had lower costs, at least one firm could enter the market profitably by offering a slightly lower price. Because of the absence of monopoly rents and production at minimum costs, contestable markets are efficient. If the number of firms exceeds one, it can be shown that a sustainable industry configuration leads to prices equal to average and marginal costs. In the case of a natural monopoly, as it is shown in *Figure 1.3*, sustainability usually leads to a second best solution, where the price equals average cost but exceeds marginal cost. Thus, a sustainable monopoly still is efficient with respect to production, but is inefficient with respect to the structure of consumption. In fact, the sustainable price-quantity pair satisfies the *Ramsey solution*, where consumer surplus is maximized subject to the break-even constraint of the firm.[21]

Figure 1.3: Contestable equilibrium in a natural monopoly situation

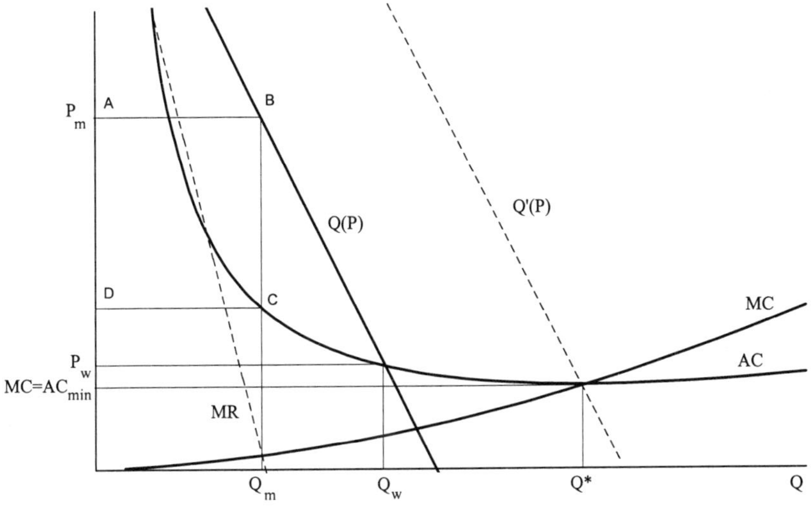

The theory of contestable markets for the natural monopoly is illustrated for a single product in *Figure 1.3* using U-shaped average costs. For the market demand function $Q(P)$, point B represents the supply of a monopoly without potential competition. The firm maximizes profits when marginal costs MC equal marginal revenue MR, which leads to the Cournot monopoly price P_m and to the monopoly profit given by the surface $ABCD$. In a contestable market, the industry is only in equilibrium if markets clear and if incumbent firms incur zero profits. In the case of a natural monopoly, these conditions are only satisfied if the firm produces Q_w at the price P_w. It can be seen that $P_w < P_m$ and $Q_w > Q_m$, which indicates that consumer surplus is higher if a

21 See for example *Baumol and Bradford (1970)*.

market with economies of scale is contestable. In addition, *Figure 1.3* shows that P_w is only a second best solution because it exceeds marginal costs. A first best solution is obtained if the demand function intersects the average cost curve AC at its minimum ($AC = MC$), as is the case for market demand $Q'(P)$.

Figure 1.4: Contestable equilibria for oligopolies

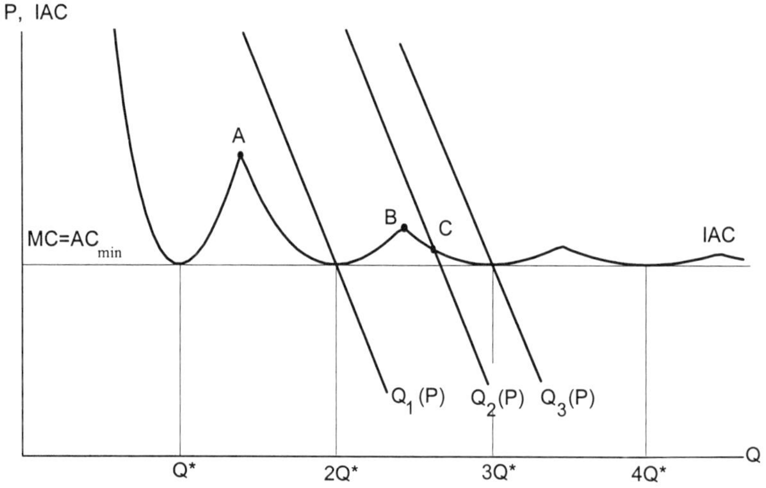

Figure 1.4 shows contestable equilibria with more than one firm operating profitably. In this case, the average cost curve is replaced by the industry average cost curve IAC, which represents the lowest average cost at which a given output can be produced. The industry average cost curve together with the market demand curve determines the optimal industry structure straightforwardly. For example, up to the output at point A, any output is produced at lowest costs by only one firm. Between point A and B, any output is produced at lowest average cost by two firms, and so on. However, only points where $P = AC = MC$ are sustainable and, therefore, represent contestable equilibria. This condition is satisfied if the demand curve intersects at a local

minimum of the industry average cost curve. This indicates that contestable equilibrium outputs in the oligopoly case are multiples of the Pareto-optimal monopoly output . As can be seen in *Figure 1.4*, $P = AC = MC$ is satisfied for the demand functions $Q_1(P)$ and $Q_3(P)$, but not for $Q_2(P)$. Actually, point C is an unsustainable point. Any of the three firms producing the product has incentives to sell the product at a slightly lower price and increase its output, which would lead to a loss and, therefore, exit for at least one firm. However, the resulting industry structure, which would imply profits for the remaining firms, induces entry of another firm again. The situation may be improved if we allow the average cost curve to have a flat-bottom. Depending on the length of the flat bottom, the number of possible contestable equilibria increases.[22]

1.3.4 The Contestability of City-Pair Markets

Airline city-pair markets are characterized by decreasing average costs with respect to stage length and aircraft size. *Table 1.1* shows that average costs for a given load factor are highest for short distance markets and small aircraft and are lowest for long distance markets and large aircraft. *Bailey and Panzar (1981)* show that short distance city-pair markets in particular were served by only one firm in 1980, which indicates natural monopoly situations. Therefore, airline city-pair markets seem to be a good example of contestable markets. This proposition may be underlined by the assumption that entry does not involve substantial sunk costs, because in today's airline industry, there is a large market for used aircraft. Thus, if airline city-pair markets are contestable, a deregulated airline industry is beneficial to consumers despite the high concentration of firms. However, although early studies support this view, the contestability of city-pair markets was later questioned by a number of authors.
Bailey and Panzar (1981) analyzed the pricing behavior of commuter, local and trunk carriers during the process of deregulation. They found that medium and long distance routes served by local carriers were nearly perfect contestable in late 1979 and early 1980 due to potential competition by trunk carriers, whereas trunk carriers were rather constrained by actual competition. As noted earlier,

22 This case is illustrated in *Aschinger (1984)*.

the CAB lifted fare regulation only gradually. In the first years of deregulation, the CAB set upper and lower bounds around the *Standard Industry Fare Level* (SIFL), which was based on a formula established along with the *Domestic Passenger Fare Investigation* (DPFI) in 1975. The DPFI formula sets equal fares for flights of equal distance based on industry average costs, average load factors, and a mileage formula that takes into account economies of scale with respect to market distance. The computation of the SIFL was periodically adjusted according to operating costs per available seat-mile. The CAB set different fare ceilings for trunk and local airlines because the DPFI formula has been known for many years to underprice short distance services. Therefore, according to the CAB policy set out in August 1978, the trunk airlines were allowed to put fares up to 10% above the SIFL in markets with four or more carriers and up to 5% in markets with fewer carriers, whereas locals could set fares up to 30% above the SIFL. The commuter carriers enjoyed complete pricing flexibility, as was already the case before deregulation.

Bailey and Panzar (1981) demonstrate that in markets in which commuter carriers are providing the only nonstop service, firms do not charge fares above the level permitted to local carriers, despite complete pricing flexibility. Moreover, fares are widely dispersed around the SIFL. According to *Bailey and Panzar (1981)* this result suggests that commuter fares are constrained by potential competition from local carriers. For the monopoly markets of locals the results are ambiguous. Whereas in short distance markets locals predominantly price between the SIFL and the upper bound permitted, fares are closer to the SIFL in long distance markets. In fact, in longer markets the local airlines seemed to set fares around the ceiling permitted to trunks. Therefore, *Bailey and Panzar (1981)* conclude that potential competition did constrain the locals in their pricing flexibility in long distance markets. On the other hand, fares in shorter markets indicate a lack of contestability. This may be due to the fact that short distance markets were not very attractive for trunk carriers to enter, because their fleets were composed of aircraft too large for local markets and they were not yet operating at the respective local endpoints. Moreover, there was a shortage in aircraft following deregulation, which prevented carriers from their fleets in the short run. For similar reasons, commuter carriers also did not provide a sufficient threat to the high fares of locals in the short distance segment. Firms operating aircraft with less than thirty seats were exempted from regulation, which mainly applied to commuter carriers. Thus, the fleets of the commuters probably were composed of aircraft too small to enter the locals' markets. The trunk carriers predominantly priced at the permitted ceiling. The high number of entries in markets served by trunk airlines indicates that fares in these markets may have been constrained by actual competition.

*Table 1.1: Average costs in ¢ per Revenue Passenger Mile (RPM)**

Aircraft type:	DC-9-30	DC-737-200	B-727-100	B-727-200	DC-10-10	B-747
Seats:	115	121	125	164	371	500
Milage						
200	12.0	*11.7*	14	12.1	12.5	15.4
400	8.3	8.1	9.5	8.1	*7.8*	9.0
600	7.1	6.9	8.0	6.8	*6.2*	6.9
800	6.5	6.3	7.2	6.2	*5.5*	5.9
1,000	6.1	6	6.8	5.8	*5.0*	5.2
1,250	-	-	6.4	5.5	*4.6*	4.7
1,500	-	-	6.2	5.2	*4.4*	4.4
1,750	-	-	-	-	4.2	*4.1*
2,000	-	-	-	-	4.0	*4.0*
2,250	-	-	-	-	3.9	*3.8*
2,500	-	-	-	-	3.9	*3.7*

* Direct aircraft-operating costs for domestic trunk airlines, June 1980 - June 1981.

Source: Bailey, Graham and Kaplan (1985), Table 3.4, p.51.

However, subsequent empirical investigations did not support the contestability hypothesis for airline city-pair markets. *Graham, Kaplan and Sibley (1983)* tested the contestability hypothesis by determining a fare equation for city-pair markets that includes the Herfindahl index, the presence of newly certified carriers, market density, market distance, passengers' value of time, and the presence of a slot constrained airport as exogenous variables.[23] If airline city-pair markets are contestable, fares should be independent of market concentration but should be closely related to costs. This implies that in the fare equation the coefficient for the Herfindahl index should be insignificant. The results of *Graham, Kaplan and Sibley (1983)* show the opposite. Fares significantly increase with the Herfindahl index and decrease with the presence of newly certified carriers in the market, which indicates that fares are constrained more by actual than by potential competition. The other exogenous variables, reflecting cost and time sensitivity of passengers, all have significant coefficients, except for market density. Although these results reject the contestability hypothesis, one has to take into account the fact that the data stem from the fourth quarter of 1980 and the second quarter of 1981. Because the data were collected shortly after deregulation, market structures still reflected the situation prior to deregulation at least partially, where local airlines' operations were restricted to their home regions. Therefore, potential competitors may not have been able to establish themselves at a great number of local airports in this short time period.

Later, *Bailey, Graham and Kaplan (1985)* and *Moore (1986)* also found that fares depend on market concentration. However, *Morrison and Winston (1987)* criticize the methodology of previous studies because they do not specifically integrate the number of potential competitors into the empirical model. They argue that «although it is inconsistent with the hypothesis that a given market is perfectly contestable, a finding that market concentration influences efficiency does not preclude the presence of potential competition also having an effect».[24]

23 The Herfindahl-Index *H* is defined as follows:

$$H = \sum_{i=1}^{n} (s_i)^2 ,$$

where s_i is the market share of firm *i*, *n* is the number of firms in the market, and $\sum_{i=1}^{n} s_i = 1$. See, for example, *Tirole (1988)*, pp. 221-223.

24 *Morrison and Winston (1987)*, p. 56.

Morrison and Winston (1987) point to the distinction between the concepts of perfect contestability developed by *Baumol, Panzar and Willig (1982),* and imperfect contestability, which corresponds to the ideas of potential competition of *Bain (1959)*. To test perfect contestability, *Morrison and Winston (1987)* analyze whether markets with potential competitors have achieved welfare maximizing performance or not. To test imperfect contestability, they determine the amount by which additional potential competitors influence market welfare. The difference of passenger welfare between the deregulated environment and the optimal welfare was measured by compensating variation, which then was used as the dependent variable in the empirical analysis. Perfect contestability implies that this welfare measure should be zero for those markets with at least one potential competitor. In the case of imperfect contestability, the welfare measure should depend on the number of actual and potential competitors in the market. The results of the empirical analysis lead to the rejection of the perfect contestability hypothesis, but statistically significant coefficients were found for the number of actual and the number of potential competitors in a regression analysis. *Morrison and Winston (1987)* therefore conclude that airline city-pair markets are only imperfect contestable.

From a theoretical point of view, the imperfect contestability of city-pair markets may be explained by the notion that scheduled air transport does not fully meet the assumptions underlying the theory of perfect contestability:

(1) As an implicit assumption of contestable markets, quantities should change faster than prices, which corresponds to the Bertrand-Nash condition that the price change lag exceeds the entry or exit lag. Otherwise, incumbent firms can charge monopoly or oligopoly prices until they face actual entry. For scheduled services, the latter is more likely to apply, since today fares are altered quickly at low menu costs due to computer reservation systems, while entry takes time and can be observed by competitors in advance, so that they can react. In relation to this problem *Baumol and Willig (1986)* state that

> *... transportation by trucks, barges or even buses may be more highly contestable than passenger air transportation. Barges and trucks have business firms rather than individual consumers as their primary customers,*

and that facilitates the provision of service via contracts on which potential entrants can effectively bid against incumbents. (p. 24)

In the case of contracts and in absence of entry costs, an incumbent firm will not charge a price higher than average costs even if it has monopoly power. Any bid by the monopoly can be undercut by a slightly lower bid by a potential competitor. The bidding process then goes on until one firm offers the service at the price that equals average cost. Therefore, any potential entrant faces an industry where no profitable entry is possible, which reflects the sustainability concept of the theory of contestable markets. In this regard, it is important to note that charter airlines have business firms rather than individual consumers as customers. Thus, charter services may be more contestable than scheduled services.

(2) The assumption that there are no or only small entry costs for city-pair markets turned out to be wrong. Especially at large airports, ground facilities and slots are scarce, which leads to severe problems with respect to their distribution. The acquisition of ground facilities causes sunk costs for new entrants when there are long-term leasing contracts between the airport authorities and incumbent firms. In this case, the entrant can only sublease gate space from competitors who are able to seek monopoly rents if they control a large proportion of gates at one airport. The limited number of slots at congested airports may cause an additional barrier to entry, especially if there is no competitive allocation process that eliminates discrimination against new entrants. Like gates, slots are also often distributed through long-term leases. In addition, some large airports face environmental constraints that prevent airport authorities from complete utilization of capacity. This may also lead to discriminatory restrictions for new entrants or new services. The importance of the availability of ground facilities and slots to entrants is demonstrated in *Bailey and Panzar (1981)*. Of the 449 new nonstop services established between July 1 1978 and July 1 1979 in the US, 270 were supplied between destinations where carriers already owned ground facilities at both airports, 170 were provided between destinations where carriers already owned ground facilities at one airport and only nine were opened

between destinations where carriers had to acquire ground facilities at both airports.

(3) The development of hub-and-spoke systems after deregulation led to additional entry costs. In a hub-and-spoke network, airlines group passengers with different destinations on the same flights and transport them to a hub, from where they continue their trip to their final destinations. Thus, the transportation of passengers with different final destinations on the same flights can be regarded as the joint production of different services. As the theory of contestable markets predicts, there may be natural monopolies with respect to hub-and-spoke networks due to economies of scale and scope. But networks are even more resistant to the influence of potential competition. In the case of a hub-and-spoke system, a potential competitor should be able to quickly match the whole network of the incumbent, which is hardly possible if the entrant does not already own the ground facilities and aircraft needed. For example, the lack of a consistent network may be a reason for the failure of most newly certified carriers after deregulation in the US.

(4) If passengers in a city-pair market have distinct preferences with respect to final destinations, there is a wide scope for product differentiation for scheduled air transport. In this case, airlines may be tempted to gain local monopoly power by offering distinct products, e.g. distinct networks. This does not mean that airlines do not compete on particular city-pair markets at all. But the development of hubs at different airports and the concentration of activities in different regions after deregulation in the US indicate product differentiation on the network level. Again, scheduled services differ from charter services in this respect. Airlines with scheduled services are bound to schedules and networks they have made public in advance and on which customers rely. Carriers therefore have to restrict themselves to a finite number of destinations, at least in the short run. In contrast to this, charter airlines may fly to any destination at short notice. Therefore, they offer rather homogenous services relative to scheduled air transport, which facilitates entry and potential competition.

The above comments show that only city-pair markets for charter services are likely to be contestable, and only in the absence of sunk costs at airports. In addition, *Caves, Christensen and Tretheway (1984)* found that there is no evidence of economies of scale with respect to firm size, where firm size is defined as the number of markets served. Thus, large airlines do not have cost advantages compared to small carriers. This implies that if the analysis of air transport is extended from the single city-pair market to the level of networks, the theory of contestable markets also provides only limited insight.

1.4 Deregulation in the EU and International Liberalization

The deregulation of air transport in Europe started with more liberal bilateral agreements initiated by the UK. In the mid 80s, Great Britain revised the agreements with the Netherlands, West Germany, Belgium, Ireland and Switzerland. The treaty between the UK and the Netherlands signed in 1984 later served as the model for contracts with other countries.[25] It guarantees the freedom of market entry for any British or Dutch airline designated by their governments, abolishes capacity and frequency restrictions and introduces the ‹double disapproval rule› for fares. The ‹double disapproval rule› implies the freedom to offer any fare unless it is explicitly disapproved by both governments.

In 1987, the EU implemented a first package of deregulation measures for all its members. However, the rules were still based on the concept of bilateral agreements. The guidelines define minimum liberalization standards for air transport between EU member states, such as the possibility of multiple designation in high density markets, free entry for EU carriers in international markets between hub and local airports, restrictions on capacity sharing agreements and limited freedom to compete with fares. The guidelines include a definition of high density markets and of hub and local airports. Multiple designation means that bilateral contracts must allow each participating

25 See *Marín (1995)*, p. 143.

government to designate more than one carrier. Some of the earlier bilateral agreements required that the two designated airlines divide up total capacity offered in a city-pair market into shares of 50% each. The 1987 guidelines required that an increase of a single firm's capacity up to 60% be tolerated in bilateral agreements. Limited competition with fares was bound to restrictions on tickets, such as early booking or a minimum length of stay for return flights. This indicates that the fare provision was basically designed to allow discount fares for tourists. In addition, the 1987 guidelines guarantee 5th-freedom rights if the indirect service involves at least one local airport and only uses 30% of the total capacity offered on the respective spokes. This rule was probably implemented in order to facilitate hub-and-spoke operations, which may not be carried out on the international level unless 5th freedom rights are granted. However, the EU commission exempted air transport from the competition law provisions set down in the *Treaty of Rome*. Thus, anti-competitive measures of airlines such as revenue sharing and rate fixing agreements were still tolerated and, therefore, widely used.

In 1990, the EU took further measures to gradually increase competition. The new guidelines guaranteed the freedom to offer any fare within certain bounds and implemented the double disapproval rule for air transport within the community. Furthermore, 3rd, 4th and 6th freedom rights were established for all carriers based in the EU, and 5th freedom rights were granted with a 50% capacity share restriction for respective services on the spokes involved. In 1993, a third package was implemented, which established free entry for cross-border services for EU based airlines. Thus, only 8th freedom rights were missing compared to completely liberalized markets. Capacity and frequency restrictions were abolished and the freedom to offer any fare was granted, unless it was ‹regarded as either too high and, therefore, harmful to the consumers, or so low that it produces losses for all the companies involved.›[26] In addition, the EU started to apply its competition law provisions to air transport and abolished exemptions. In this respect, subsidies to carriers as well as agreements of firms that fix capacities, frequencies and fares are illegal now. In April 1997, the EU granted the freedom of entry in any market and the freedom to offer any fare to EU carriers for services within the European

26 *Marín (1995)*, Table 1, p. 143.

Economic Area (EEA). However, unlike in the US, where airlines are owned privately, the majority of EU airlines is still owned or, at least partially, controlled by the respective governments. Unfortunately, the EU commission has been very reluctant to fully apply the competition law and has approved several subsidy packages of national governments for their carriers.

Marín (1995) measured the effects of the introduction of liberal bilateral agreements and of the first package of EU guidelines on European routes. He subdivided European markets into routes serving pairs of countries that have signed liberal bilateral agreements, and routes serving pairs of countries in which only the 1987 guidelines apply. The first group was further subdivided into markets with a relatively high traffic volume and markets with a relatively low traffic volume. In general, *Marín (1995)* found that while the 1987 guidelines had no observable effects, the liberal bilateral agreements were followed by entry and competition. Especially in markets with a relatively high traffic volume, the growth rate of leisure fares was negative, whereas it was positive in all other markets. In markets with a lower traffic volume, entry of additional carriers after the introduction of liberal bilateral agreements led to considerably higher growth rates of frequencies and capacities compared to the other markets.

Although these results demonstrate some possible changes in market structures following liberalization in Europe, they may not clearly indicate the effects of complete deregulation in the EU and the effects of liberal bilateral agreements between single EU countries and the US. The lessons learned from the deregulation of the US airline industry may be of additional interest in this respect. Probably the most important conclusion is given by the empirical results that demonstrating that city-pair markets for scheduled services and networks are not contestable. Thus, oligopoly pricing will probably persist and anti-trust authorities are urged to pay attention to possible collusive behavior. But it is important to note that a number of economic differences between the US and Europe on the one hand, and Europe and the rest of the world on the other hand do not allow clear forecasts from US results. As *Goods, Röller and Sickles (1993)* note, different characteristics with respect to the demand for air transport, fare and network policies prior to deregulation may influence overall results.

While Europe is larger than the US in terms of population, it is geographically much smaller. The difference in geographical size means that average stage lengths are smaller in Europe than in the US. As a result, European carriers are more likely to face competition from other modes of transportation, especially from Europe's highly subsidized railroads. Another distinct feature is the low percentage of inter-European traffic of European carriers (21.7%) compared to inter-US traffic of US airlines (72%).[27] This implies that despite the deregulation within Europe, the largest proportion of European carriers' routes will still be affected by bilateral agreements. However, this may change when airlines become more competitive within Europe and if the high subsidies for the railroads are abolished.

Because charter travel is more common in Europe than in the US, European city-pair markets may be more contestable. The charter sector always has been exempted from bilateral agreements and pooling arrangements, which favored competitive behavior. Indeed, taking into account the relatively low price offerings of tour operators for holiday packages within Europe, we may presume that the charter business is already very competitive.

Since European air transport has been organized by bilateral agreements for a long period of time, European carriers had already built hub-and-spoke systems prior to liberalization, although they were not used as efficiently as in the US today. Since bilateral agreements usually restrict scheduled air transport to third and fourth freedom rights, airlines were only allowed to offer point to point connections out of the home country into a foreign country. Due to the relatively small geographical size of European countries, each national carrier concentrated its operations at one airport. Regulation, therefore, led to the development of one major hub for each national carrier, where international flights started or terminated. However, many European carriers that are not based in a country in the center of Europe probably face the new deregulated environment with a hub in the wrong place. Furthermore, the small geographical size of Europe limits the applicability of hub-and-spoke networks for intra European air transport. Unlike the US, Europe's major centers of economic activity are located relatively close together, which favors direct flights.

27 The data stem from IATA and AEA, see *Good, Röller and Sickles (1993)*.

The results of the partial liberalization of the North-Atlantic market may be used as an example of the implications of future worldwide airline deregulation. Today, the liberalization process between Europe and the US is still based on reformed bilateral agreements between some EU member states and the US, since an open-sky agreement between the US and the EU has not been signed yet. Nevertheless, European airlines have started to establish interlining and code-sharing agreements with US carriers in order to develop international multiple-hub networks. In this kind of a network, European passengers with US destinations are grouped at a hub airport in Europe, transported to a large US hub, from where they reach connecting destinations all over the US. For example, a passenger flying from Kansas City to Vienna can choose between the connections of *Delta Airlines, Swissair, Sabena* and *Austrian Airlines* via the hubs in Atlanta and Zurich, *Northwest Airlines* and *KLM* via Minneapolis St. Paul and Amsterdam, *United Airlines* and *Lufthansa* via Chicago and Frankfurt, and soon *American Airlines* and *British Airways* via Chicago and London. Furthermore, EU and US airlines increasingly integrate across the Atlantic by mutually holding minor stock shares. Thus, the deregulation of most of the North-Atlantic market has led to competition between different groups of airlines, each composed of at least one European and one US firm. As more international markets become deregulated in the future, multiple-hub networks may be extended accordingly, providing online services between a large number of destinations all over the world.

1.5 Summary and Conclusions

In this opening chapter we have shown that international air transport is characterized by a variety of regulatory frameworks. Although the recently deregulated industries in the US and the EU point to the increased dominance of free markets, intercontinental connections, even in the North-Atlantic market between the US and the EU, are still governed by bilateral agreements between single countries. These contracts usually restrict entry, capacity and fares in order to assure market power for the national carriers involved. However, many countries have revised restrictive bilateral agreements recently in order to provide more competition and lower fares to consumers. Taking into account that many of these markets may be completely liberalized in the future, the question arises as to what international air transport will look like in a deregulated environment.

The deregulation of the US airline industry has shown that the increase in competition led to a decrease in fares on average but also to an increase in market concentration. Today, the majority of direct city-pair connections in the US is still provided by monopolies. In this respect it was shown that scheduled air transport in the US is not perfect contestable. While authors demonstrate that local city-pair markets were contestable shortly after the implementation of the ADA, later studies indicate that fares are positively correlated with market concentration. However, since it was also found that the number of actual and potential competitors both influence fares, airline city-pair markets may be considered as imperfectly contestable. It is important to note that the assumptions for perfect contestable markets do not apply to scheduled air transport. First, scarce slots and gates at large airports can be considered as entry barriers and may cause large sunk costs to competitors. Second, the Bertrand-Nash condition of quasi fixed prices in the short run does not apply to today's scheduled air transport, because CRS allow for a quick adjustment of fares, while entry takes time and can be observed by incumbent firms in advance. Moreover, airport dominance in connection with the development of large hub-and-spoke networks led to market power in city-pair markets to the respective hubs and with respect to the distribution of slots and gates at the dominated airports. On the other hand, hub-and-spoke networks are beneficial to consumers because they lead to an increase in online connections, lower costs and, therefore, lower fares per mile. Thus, the analysis of the long run welfare implications of air transport deregulation should include features of hub-and-spoke systems.

Taking these empirical results from US deregulation and recent developments in international markets into account, a theory of air transport should basically be able to explain the following features: (1) despite deregulation and free market entry, many city-pair markets are still characterized by monopolies; (2) fares per mile differ widely among different markets and market segments; (3) large airports are often dominated by one firm that uses this airport as its hub; (4) in the long run, deregulation has increased industry concentration; (5) international air transport in a deregulated environment is characterized by multiple-hub networks. The following chapters will show that a model using time sensitivity of passengers as well as elements of product differentiation theory can help to explain these features.

Appendix

The eight freedom rights for international air transport

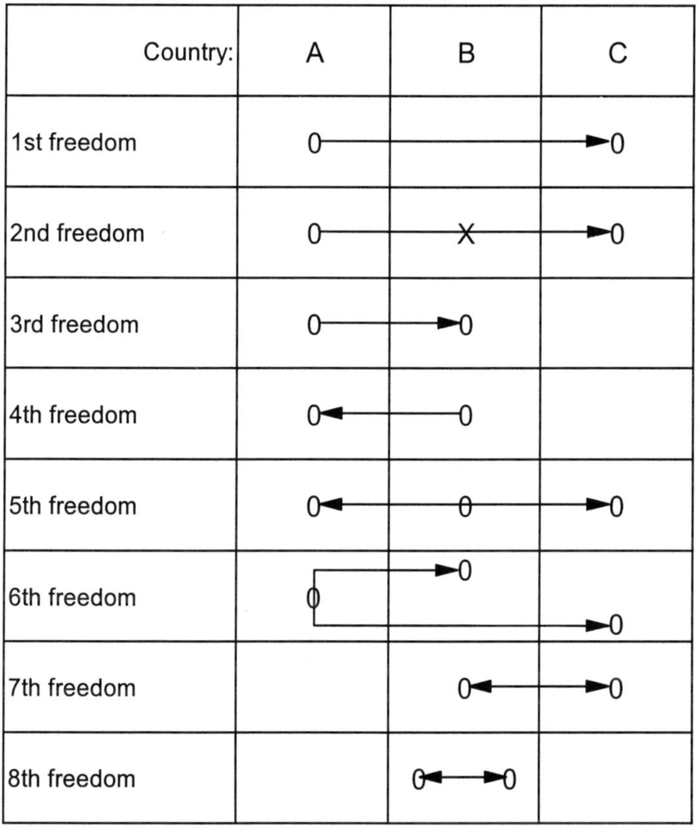

Country A is the home country

0—— Origin of flight

—►0 Destination of flight

—✕— Stopover without picking up or dropping off passengers

—θ— Stopover picking up or dropping off passengers

2. The Monopoly Airline

2.1 Introduction

In the transport industry, time components essentially determine the structure of demand. Not only the selling price but also the time the service is offered and the time needed to consume the service are of great importance. Thus, the ‹actual price› consists of the selling price and time costs. As it is shown in *Table 2.1* from a survey by *Doganis (1985)*, various elements of supply in air transport markets are ranked differently by passengers depending on the segment they belong to. The most clearly observable distinctions are found in the valuation of price on the one hand and other supply variables on the other hand. Whereas business passengers tend to put more emphasis on time and quality attributes, tourists prefer a low ticket price.

We can presume that airlines take the different needs of passengers into account when they set fares, purchase suitable types of aircraft and develop schedules. As *Bailey, Graham and Kaplan (1985)* show in *Table 2.2*, airlines offer different ticket prices, flight frequencies and load factors in different markets. For example, load factor and frequency increase, whereas fares per mile decrease with increasing market distance and market size. In addition tourist markets are characterized by lower fares, higher load factors and lower frequencies than non-tourist markets. Moreover, OLS estimates by *Graham, Kaplan and Sibley (1983)* show that most of the variation in fares across markets can be explained by market characteristics such as market distance and time sensitivity of passengers.

Table 2.1: Customer ranking of different supply variables (very essential = 5, not essential = 1)

passenger segment supply variables	emergency business	routine business	weekend holiday	two-week holiday
Low fare	1	2	4	5
Seat available on demand	5	3	3	1
high frequency of service	5	4	3	2
ability to cancel or change reservations	5	4	3	1
stop-over en route	3	5	2	1
in-flight standards and comfort	5	4	3	1
quick check-in and check out	5	4	2	1

Source: *Doganis (1985)*.

In this chapter a theoretical model is developed that aims at exploring profit maximizing behavior of airlines in city-pair markets, taking into account three supply variables indicating the different preferences of passengers: *ticket price*, *frequency of service* and *seats available on demand*. In this respect the *load factor*, which is defined as the ratio of the number of passengers actually flown to the number of seats offered, is used to denote the relative number of seats available on demand. Following a brief description of a feasible cost function, demand for airline services is modeled, using theoretical concepts and empirical observations from *Douglas and Miller (1974)*, who analyzed airline regulation in the US. Additional features of the analysis are based on the models by

DeVany (1975), *Schmalensee (1977)* and *Panzar (1979)*. *DeVany (1975)* and *Schmalensee (1977)* explore scheduling rivalry of airlines under price and entry regulation, while *Panzar (1979)* develops a model of price competition in unregulated markets. After computing the optimal ticket price, flight frequency and load factor of a monopoly airline, some comparative statics features of city-pair markets under different cost and demand parameters are presented. Finally, the model results are illustrated by a case study on supply variables of the Swiss national carrier *Swissair*.

Table 2.2: Load factor, flight frequency and fares in the US after deregulation

	Market size (201-500)			Market size (501 +)		
Market distance (miles)	Load factor	Flights*	Fare**	Load factor	Flights*	Fare**
501-1500	62%	1.5 - 3.8	80	54%	3+	76
	60%	1.6 - 3.9	92	60%	3.4+	95
1500+	68%	0.9 - 2.1	64	69%	1.7+	56
	64%	1.2 - 3.1	79	61%	2+	70

* Flights per day, determined by the ratio of market size to average equipment size

** Fares as a percent of the *DPFI*-value. The *DPFI* formula was used for the calculation of the fare to be charged by airlines in a specific market during the period of regulation on the basis of market distance and long run industry costs.

Source: *Bailey, Graham and Kaplan (1985)*, Table 3.7, pp. 55.

2.2 Cost Function for a City-Pair Market

For a first part of the analysis, a *city-pair market* is defined by the demand and supply of direct air traffic between two airports. It is assumed that total costs for an airline operating in one city-pair market vary with the *number of passengers* transported, the *distance* between the two airports, the *number of flights* offered and the *size of the aircraft* used. For this reason, three different types of costs are distinguished. *Passenger related costs* include costs for reservations, sales, food, fuel and ground service to passengers such as baggage handling and collecting tickets at the gate. *Flight specific costs* vary with the number of flights and include landing fees, expenses for ground service to aircraft and the flight deck crew. *Capacity costs* consist of aircraft ownership costs, such as interest and depreciation, and the costs of operating capacity, mainly fuel costs but also expenses for the cabin crew. Note that fuel costs are subdivided into *passenger related* and *capacity related costs.* This is at variance with many statistics, where fuel costs are subsumed under *flight specific costs*. But fuel costs for one flight vary with the weight of the aircraft, thus they increase with its size and the load. Therefore, it seems reasonable to treat fuel expenses as part of costs for operating capacity and transporting passengers. In the model capacity refers to the number of seats flown.

It is assumed that all three types of costs only partially increase with market distance, which implies economies of scale with respect to trip length. While passenger related costs for sales, reservations and ground service to passengers do not vary with market distance, costs for fuel and food certainly increase with trip time. For flight specific costs, expenses for ground service and landing fees do not vary with the distance flown, while the salaries for the cabin and flight crews increase with trip time and, therefore, with market distance. Similarly, while capacity ownership costs are constant with respect to market distance, operating costs for one seat increase with the length of the flight. In order to illustrate economies of scale with respect to market distance, which are called *economies of stage length*, the three types of costs may be denoted as follows:

$$c = c_d \cdot d^{\eta_c},\ f = f_d \cdot d^{\eta_f} \text{ and } g = g_d \cdot d^{\eta_g}, \tag{2.1}$$

$$\text{with } 0 < \eta_c, \eta_f, \eta_g < 1.$$

The variables *c, f,* and *g* denote the cost per passenger, per flight and per seat respectively. Thus, they are called *passenger specific*, *flight specific* and *capacity unit costs* respectively. The variable *d* stands for market distance in kilometers, and c_d, f_d, and g_d are cost shift parameters, which can be interpreted as the cost level. According to the above definitions, total costs of an airline operating in one market for one day are a linear function of the number of passengers *Q*, the number of flights *X*, and the size of the aircraft, denoted by the respective number of seats *k*.

$$C = cQ + fX + gK \ .$$

Denoting the total number of seats, that is total capacity, by $K = kX$, total costs are

$$C = cQ + fX + gK. \tag{2.2}$$

For a given market distance, marginal costs with respect to output, the number of flights and capacity are constant. Thus, *c*, *f* and *g* also denote marginal passenger costs, marginal flight costs and marginal capacity costs for a given stage length respectively. Besides the economies of stage length, the cost function indicates economies of scale with respect to the number of passengers carried, as the subsequent average cost function (AC_Q) indicates for a given flight frequency, capacity and market distance:

$$AC = \frac{cQ + fX + gK}{Q} = c + \frac{fX + gK}{Q}.$$

Economies of scale with respect to the number of passengers are called *economies of density*. Dividing average costs AC_Q by market distance *d* then leads to the cost per *revenue passenger kilometer* (RPK), which denotes the cost incurred by transporting one passenger one kilometer:

$$AC_{RPK} = AC_Q / d = c_d d^{\eta_c - 1} + (X/Q) f_d d^{\eta_f - 1} + (K/Q) g_d d^{\eta_g - 1}.$$

The above equation shows that costs per RPK decrease with market distance and increase with flight frequency and capacity. Therefore, it indicates that for variable flight frequency and capacity, costs per RPK are lowest if the airline offers the lowest possible capacity and number of flights. Thus, assuming the size of the airplane not to be limited by technology, a cost minimizing airline would always offer only one flight per day at a load factor of 100%. In reality this is usually not the case. By contrast we can observe, even in monopoly markets, that flight frequency often exceeds one flight per day and load factors are generally lower than 100%. One explanation for this phenomenon may be the existence of technological limitations of aircraft capacity. However, given the number of passengers, the airline would use the largest aircraft available on the market. Only when demand exceeds the capacity of the largest airplane would more than one flight be offered. Nevertheless, this cannot explain the fact that airlines often offer several flights with small aircraft, although only one flight with a big aircraft would cause lower average costs for an equal number of passengers. The reason for this behavior is to be found in the nature of the demand function for air transport services, which is determined by price and time sensitivity of passengers.

2.3 Demand in a City-Pair Market

2.3.1 Stochastic Delay

In the following it is assumed that in a city-pair market airlines do not simply offer a ticket price for air transport between the two cities, but provide a ‹supply package› containing a ticket price, a daily frequency of service and a certain amount of free seats available on demand for each flight. Whereas passengers can observe price and frequency directly, they have to rely on the reputation of the carrier with respect to the availability of seats. This means that passengers know at any time the probability of still getting a seat on the preferred flight of a specific carrier. In order to model the valuation of frequency and seats available on demand, two concepts are now introduced that describe the influence of these supply variables on passengers' demand: *stochastic delay* and *frequency delay*, which are subsumed under the notion *schedule delay*.

We focus on capacity first. *Table 2.1* shows that passengers' valuation of a carrier's supply depends on the availability of seats. Suppose a flight is booked up at the time a passenger prefers to fly. This passenger either has to accept another flight at a less convenient departure time, or to take a flight of another airline, or to use different means of transportation. Referring to *Douglas and Miller (1974)* the time the passenger loses thereby is called *stochastic delay*. In a situation like this, the passenger incurs time costs because of the non-availability of seats at his preferred departure time. Therefore, taking into account that the true price a consumer faces contains the selling price (ticket price) and time costs, demand for air transport services in a city-pair market increases with the availability of seats.

Time costs from stochastic delay are not the same for all passenger segments. Because time sensitive passengers (e.g. business passengers) incur high opportunity costs from the use of time compared to less time sensitive passengers (tourists), the former put more emphasis on the availability of seats at the preferred departure time. Tourists, on the other hand, are rather price sensitive and the availability of seats for a specific flight is not as important to them. Thus tourists incur lower time costs from stochastic delay than business passengers. In addition, passengers that are more price but less time sensitive usually book in advance, while passengers that are less price but more time sensitive book closer to departure time. Therefore, there is much more uncertainty about effective demand in city-pair markets where the demand consists of mainly business passengers. This implies that airlines always have to set aside a sufficiently high number of seats in order to meet short term demand of business passengers, which leads to lower average load factors compared to tourist markets.

Douglas and Miller (1974) estimated expected stochastic delay with a queuing model. In the present work, like the model of *Panzar (1979)*, the effect of stochastic delay on demand is simplified by taking the average load factor as a measure for the availability of seats.[1] The average load factor is defined as the total number of passengers transported relative to the total number of seats offered within a defined period of time. Denoting the total number of seats, that is total capacity, by $K \equiv kX$, the load factor is $L \equiv Q/K$, where it is assumed that $K \geq Q$. This condition reflects the notion that the airline cannot transport more passengers on a flight than there are seats provided. Taking into account capacity costs, airlines therefore have incentives to provide exactly the amount of seats necessary to satisfy daily demand. But daily demand is very difficult to forecast because passengers sometimes cancel reservations or book flights at the last minute. Therefore, when demand exceeds the number of seats offered, some consumers have to be rejected and incur time costs. Moreover, even when reliable forecasts are available, the daily variation in demand would call for a very flexible use of aircraft of different sizes in order to provide exactly the number of seats needed. Of course, the operation of such a diversity of aircraft would be too costly. Therefore, carriers offer capacity according to *expected demand*, taking into account that they may have to reject some consumers or may fly with some empty seats.

1 The basic method and the results of *Panzar (1979)* are discussed in section 2.3.3 below.

Figure 2.1: Cumulative normal distribution of passengers per day given capacity

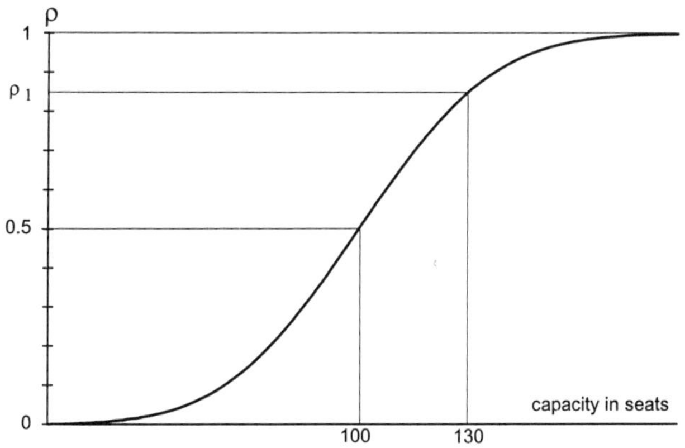

Assume that daily demand for a flight within a well-defined period of time, for example one year, is normally distributed with a mean of 100 passengers. In *Figure 2.1* the respective cumulative normal distribution is depicted. When the airline uses an aircraft of exactly 100 seats, the average load factor is 100%. For convenience, we may use the inverse of the load factor as a measure of the availability of seats, which is denoted by $E \equiv 1/L = K/Q$ and equals 1 in this particular case. *Figure 2.1* indicates that for a normal distribution of daily demand, the probability that demand exceeds capacity is one half. This means that on half the days in the year, the airline has to reject consumers because there are not a sufficiently high number of seats available. If the airline increases daily capacity to 130 seats, the average load factor decreases to 77% ($E = 1.3$), and the probability that demand exceeds capacity decreases to $1 - \rho$. This implies that less passengers have to be rejected on average, which increases the availability of seats. Therefore, the availability of seats can be expressed by ρ. Since expected demand increases with the availability of seats, average demand is an increasing function of ρ and, therefore, also an increasing function of the inverse load factor *E*. Taking into account that demand is additionally influenced by the ticket price, we may specify the following demand function for a given time period:

$$Q = U\left(\underset{-}{P}, \underset{+}{E}\right), \tag{2.3}$$

where Q is average demand over the time period, for example the number of passengers per day. Note that equation (2.3) establishes an implicit relationship with respect to the number of passengers, since $E = K/Q$. It therefore is assumed that the firm is able to obtain any desired inverse load factor by choosing the appropriate number of seats K, taking into account the respective implicit effects.

If the demand for one flight is normally distributed, it follows that demand increases with a growing inverse load factor at a decreasing rate. This can be seen in *Figure 2.1*. The additional reduction of the probability that demand exceeds capacity is smaller for a high inverse load factor relative to a low inverse load factor. Thus the improvement of the availability of seats is smaller for a high E than for a low E.

2.3.2 Frequency Delay

Among other quality elements of supply, *Table 2.1* points to the sensitivity of passengers with respect to the frequency of flights, which indicates that flight frequency influences demand in a city-pair market. If there is only one flight per day at a particular departure time, this flight would - although it might suit a few passengers very well - be inconvenient for all the passengers who prefer flying at another time. Considering the value of time, a passenger's total travel cost increases with growing deviation of the actual from his preferred departure time. *Douglas and Miller (1974)* called this time differential ‹frequency delay›. As in the case of stochastic delay, time costs from frequency delay increase with the time sensitivity of passengers. As more flights are added, actual and preferred departure times fit better, which lowers the margin between actual ticket prices and total costs for the passenger. Therefore, given the ticket price and load factor, the demand for air transport increases with additional flights. Thus, airlines have incentives to offer more flights with, *ceteris paribus*, smaller aircraft.[2] Of course it is not rational for an airline to match its flights to the preferred departure times of all consumers, since this would lead to a large number of flights with very few passengers and would reduce economies of scale. *DeVany (1975)* showed that demand increases less than proportionately with the number of flights. Thus, with a growing number of flights, additional flights become less efficient. For that reason, the airline maximizes the profit not only by choosing optimal ticket prices and load factors but also by choosing an optimal number of flights.

The concept of *frequency delay* may be illustrated by a simple geometric model, like for example *Panzar (1979)* used in his model of airline competition. Consider a market, where consumers are located on and uniformly distributed over a circle representing 24 hours.[3] The specific location of a passenger indicates his preferred departure time, which is denoted by t_p. The uniform distribution of passengers implies that for each time unit the number of passengers is the same. If a monopoly airline, for example, offers a flight at $t_0 = 8$pm., total travel cost will increase for passengers as their preferred departure time differs from the actual departure time of the flight at t_0.

Let $t = |t_p - t_0|$, which is the number of time units on the time circle between the preferred departure time of a consumer and the actual departure

2 See *Bailey, Graham and Kaplan (1985)*, p. 52.

3 The concept of the circular market is frequently used to model product diversity, as for example in the model of *Salop (1979)* for monopolistic competition. The location of the firm on the circle represents the location in the product space. *Panzar (1979)* assumes product differentiation with respect to departure times of flights, with each firm operating one flight at a different time on the circle. The model of *Brown (1991)* for competition in hub-and-spoke systems is also based on this concept.
In this section, the circular model of departure times is used to show the allocation of flights of *one firm* rather than to model product differentiation. In Chapter 3, however, the circular market will be used again to illustrate product diversity with respect to networks.

time of the flight. Assuming a constant time sensitivity for all passengers in the market, time costs $a(t)$ are an increasing function of *t*. It further is assumed that $a(t)$ is linear and integrable in *t*, and that time costs of a passenger with preferred departure time t_0 is zero, $a(0)=0$. The time costs include time opportunity cost the passenger faces because he is not able to fly at his preferred departure time. For frequency delay, the reduction of demand for a specific time t_p is denoted by $-ba(t)$, where *b* is a parameter that increases with market density, that is the number of passengers at a unit time interval around t_p. Since passengers are uniformly distributed over the time circle, *b* is constant for every t_p.

Let *T* be the total number of time units on a circle representing one day. If there were no time costs from frequency delay, total demand for one day, depending on the ticket price and the inverse load factor, would be $Q=U(P,E)$ and $q=U(P,E)/T$ for one time unit. With costs from frequency delay, demand for air transport at a unit time interval around t_p is

$$q=\frac{U(P,E)}{T}-ba(t). \tag{2.4}$$

In order to guarantee a nonnegative demand at any location on the time circle, we assume that $U(P,E)/T>ba(t)$ for all t_p. If the airline offers one flight at departure time t_0, total demand is computed by adding the demands for all preferred departure times t_p ‹on both sides of t_0› on the time circle. This corresponds to the area under the function $U(P,E)/T-ba(t)$ on both sides of t_0. In this case, total demand for one flight is denoted by q_1. Note that for one flight at t_0, no passenger is ‹located› further away from t_0 than *T*/2 time units. Thus $\max t = T/2$. Taking into account that $t=0$ for a passenger with preferred departure time t_0, total demand for a market with one flight is given by the area

$$Q=q_1=2\int_0^{T/2}\left(\frac{U(P,E)}{T}-ba(t)\right)dt=2\left[\frac{U(P,E)}{T}t-bA(t)\right]_0^{T/2}, \tag{2.5}$$

$$\text{with } \frac{dA(t)}{dt} = a(t),$$

$$\text{and } A(0) = 0.$$

The concept just described is illustrated by *Figure 2.2*, where demand equals the gray area.

Figure 2.2: Time costs from frequency delay and demand for one flight

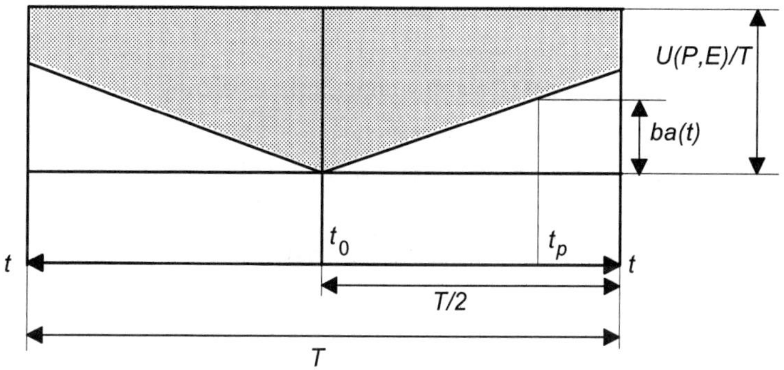

If the airline adds another flight at $t_0 + T/2$, total demand is now shared by two flights and the number of time units on one side for one flight equals *T*/4, which indicates that no passenger is ‹located› further away from the next flight than *T*/4 time units. When the airline provides three flights a day, demand for one flight is one third of the total demand and the maximum *t* reduces to *T*/6. Therefore, the maximum delay *t* for one flight is *T*/(2*X*), *X* being the number of flights, with departure times uniformly distributed on the circle.[4] Thus demand for a single flight, denoted by q_X, depends on the number of flights per day:

4 Note that *frequency delay* of a passenger decreases with the number of flights in the market at a decreasing rate. This property of the frequency delay function corresponds

$$q_X = 2\left[\frac{U(P,E)}{T}t - bA(t)\right]_0^{\frac{T}{2X}}. \tag{2.6}$$

Total demand for one day is equal to the demand for one flight multiplied by the number of flights per day:

$$Q(P,E,X) = q_X X = 2X\left[\frac{U(P,E)}{T}t - bA(t)\right]_0^{\frac{T}{2X}}$$

$$= U(P,E) - 2XbA\left(\frac{T}{2X}\right). \tag{2.7}$$

In *Figure 2.3*, total demand for a monopoly airline offering *two* flights per day with departure times t_0^I and t_0^{II} corresponds to the sum of the gray areas 1 and 2. *Figure 2.4* shows daily demand for a market with three flights. In this case, departure times are t_0^I, t_0^{III} and t_0^{IV}. When an airline with two flights adds another flight, the net increase of demand is shown by the total of areas 1 minus area 2, which is a positive number. The airline gains some additional passengers around the new departure times, but loses some passengers around the former departure time t_0^{II}. However, the difference between areas 1 and 2 decreases as more flights are added. Thus an airline is able to expand its output by additional flights, but only at a decreasing rate.[5]

to empirical results from *Douglas and Miller (1974)*. They estimated the average difference between a passenger's preferred departure time and the closest scheduled departure time by simulation. After measuring the pattern of demand for the specific market, they determined, for any number of daily flights, a schedule of departures which equalizes the number of passengers per flight. For a hypothetical market, they found that expected per-passenger frequency delay is a decreasing function of the number of flights.

5 A proof is given in Appendix A.

Figure 2.3: Time costs from frequency delay and demand for two flights

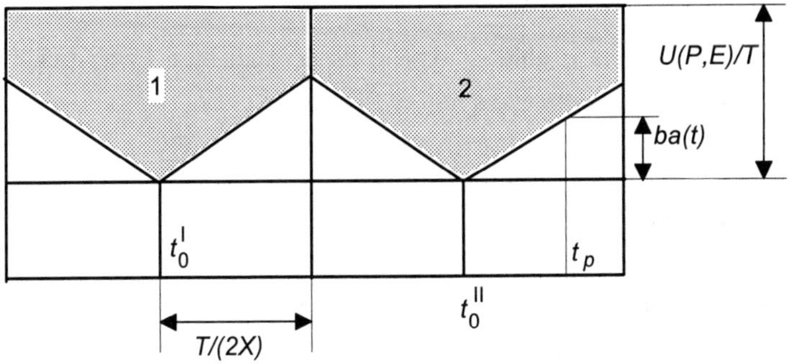

Figure 2.4: Demand increase due to an increase in flights

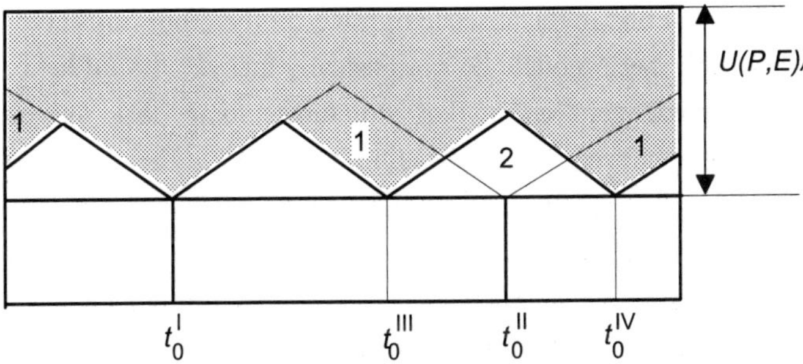

Summarizing the influence of stochastic delay and frequency delay on demand, total demand for one airline in a given time period is

$$Q = Q(P, E, X), \tag{2.8}$$

which is assumed to be at least twice differentiable in P, E and X. We then have

$$\frac{\partial Q}{\partial E} > 0, \ \frac{\partial Q}{\partial X} > 0 \text{ and } \frac{\partial Q}{\partial P} < 0, \text{ and } \frac{\partial^2 Q}{\partial E^2} < 0, \ \frac{\partial^2 Q}{\partial X^2} < 0.$$

Therefore the airline is able to expand its demand by a lower ticket price, a higher inverse load factor and a higher flight frequency.

2.3.3 Frequency and Stochastic Delay in Other Models of Air Transport

The concepts of stochastic and frequency delay introduced by *Douglas and Miller (1974)* were first applied in the models of *De Vany (1975)* and *Schmalensee (1977)*. Both models investigate schedule rivalry under price and entry regulation, as it was conducted by the CAB before deregulation. The models basically include comparative statics properties of schedule densities, load factors, profits and costs with respect to fare changes and entry restrictions, taking into account that in the absence of price competition, firms compete with quality. Although these models do not basically analyze the influence of time sensitivity of passengers on market structures, some basic issues can be extracted for the subsequent analysis in this work. The model of airline competition in unregulated markets developed by *Panzar (1979)* includes frequency and stochastic delay. However, competition only involves price changes, which implies that frequency and capacity are not treated as choice variables of the carrier and, therefore, determined indirectly by the price and costs. In the following, the three models mentioned above are introduced by discussing the respective demand, cost and profit functions and by looking at the main results. A tabular comparison of the models with the subsequent approach in this work is provided in Appendix D.

DeVany (1975)

In *De Vany (1975)*, flight frequency influences demand via the full price of air travel. The full price of air travel Θ is defined as the fare P and the value passengers place on their expected trip time y. Expected trip time includes flight time, airport access, and schedule delay. Taking into account that schedule delay decreases with the number of flights, total expected trip time is defined as a function of the number of flights per time unit X and other environmental variables G, which are not further specified in the model:

$$y = y(X, G); \quad \frac{\partial y}{\partial X} < 0.$$

The full price of air travel then is

$$\Theta = P + zy(X, G),$$

where z is the value passengers place on one unit of their time. The demand function is given as follows:

$$Q = Q[\Theta(P, X)] \equiv J(P, X)$$

with

$$\frac{\partial J}{\partial P} = \frac{\partial Q}{\partial \Theta}\frac{\partial \Theta}{\partial P} = \frac{\partial Q}{\partial \Theta} < 0,$$

$$\frac{\partial J}{\partial X} = \frac{\partial Q}{\partial \Theta}\frac{\partial \Theta}{\partial X} = \frac{\partial Q}{\partial \Theta} z \frac{\partial y}{\partial X} > 0$$

In order to use a more compact notation of the above market demand function for the subsequent analysis, *De Vany (1975)* writes:

$$Q = Q(P, X).$$

De Vany (1975) first analyzes a monopoly situation. The airline's cost function is based on a production function for flights and a production function for the output in terms of passengers conditional to the level of flights. The resulting cost function is

$$C = C(Q, X).$$

The monopoly profit then is given by

$$\Pi = PQ(P, X) - C(Q, X),$$

which is concave in X whenever $Q(P, X)$ is concave, which would require that there are eventually diminishing returns to flight frequency. Therefore, $\partial^2 Q / \partial X^2 < 0$ for some X. Since the ticket price is regulated, the monopoly airline maximizes profits by choice of the number of flights subject to the constant ticket price. The first order condition for a profit maximum is

$$\left(P - \frac{\partial C}{\partial Q}\right)\frac{\partial Q}{\partial X} - \frac{\partial C}{\partial X} = 0.$$

The above equation can be changed to

$$P\frac{\partial Q}{\partial X} = \frac{\partial C}{\partial Q}\frac{\partial Q}{\partial X} + \frac{\partial C}{\partial X},$$

which shows that the monopoly produces at the point where marginal revenue equals marginal output costs from variations in flights.

De Vany (1975) does not explicitly calculate the monopoly flight frequency, but determines the solution graphically. In *Figure 2.5*, the monopoly airline offers the number of flights X^*, where marginal revenue MR_X equals the sum of marginal passenger costs from variation in flights and marginal flight costs, $MC_Q + MC_X$, which corresponds to the above first order condition.[6] Assuming

6 In detail,

$$MR_X = P\frac{\partial Q}{\partial X}, \ MC_Q = \frac{\partial C}{\partial Q}\frac{\partial Q}{\partial X}, \text{ and } MC_X = \frac{\partial C}{\partial X}.$$

a constant (regulated) ticket price P and constant marginal costs with respect to the number of passengers and to the number of flights, the MC_X curve is a horizontal line, whereas the other curves are concave.[7] This is due to the assumption that first there are increasing and then diminishing returns to flight frequency.

Figure 2.5: Total number of flights in the monopoly and competitive equilibrium under fare regulation

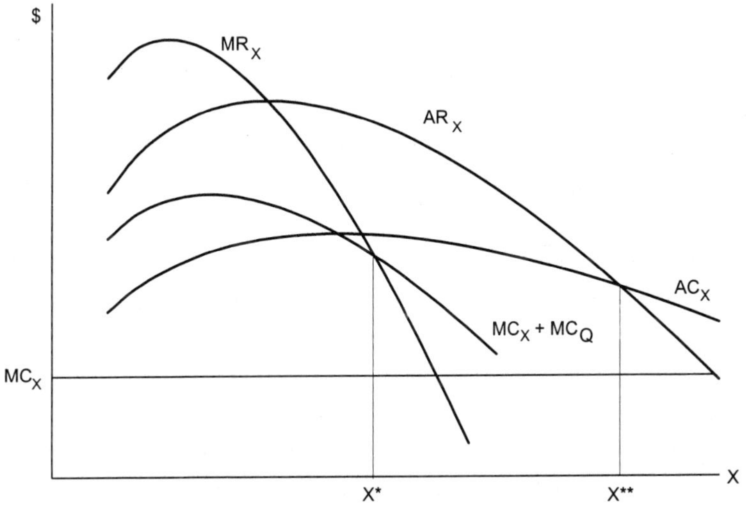

Source: *De Vany (1975)*, Figures 1 and 3, p. 330.

Since *De Vany (1975)* assumes a fixed aircraft size, the load factor is proportional to the ratio between the output and flight frequency and can be

7 A cost function like this may take the form $C = fX + cQ(P, X)$, where f are flight specific costs and c are passenger specific costs.

determined endogenously. *De Vany (1975)* concludes that because the profit maximizing output exceeds the output that leads to minimum average cost, the airline produces with excess capacity.

Second, a competitive solution is developed, assuming that the firms are symmetrical with respect to their size and costs. Thus, every firm offers the same number of flights and transports the same number of passengers per time period. Since fares are regulated, the firms are price takers and compete on frequency. Entry then leads to an increase in the total number of firms and flights until profits are eliminated. In analogy to the conventional price taker model, it is assumed that each firm feels that revenue per flight is a constant over which its actions have no influence. *De Vany (1975)* shows that for each profit maximizing firm marginal revenue from variations in flights equals average revenue and marginal costs from variations in flights equal average costs in the competitive zero-profit equilibrium. Assuming that the competitive industry faces the same market demand function as faced by the monopolist and, again, constant marginal costs with respect to the number of passengers and to the number of flights, the competitive industry has the same revenue and cost curves as the monopolist. Thus, in *Figure 2.5* the solution for frequency competition is determined by the intersection of average revenue per flight, AR_X, and average costs per flight, AC_X. As indicated in by X^{**}, competition leads to an increase in the total number of flights of the industry compared to the monopoly solution. The increase in the total number of flights corresponds to an increase in output. Because of decreasing returns to flight frequency, the increase in the total number of flights also leads to an increase in average costs and in excess capacity, which are followed by a decrease in load factors.

De Vany (1975) additionally investigates the effect of a change in the regulated fare. He shows that if demand is inelastic, the total number of flights increases as a result of an increase in the fare. On the other hand, if demand is sufficiently elastic, an increase in the fare leads to a decrease in the total number of flights.

Schmalensee (1977)

Schmalensee (1977) investigates the effects of entry and price regulation on rates of return, load factors, flight frequencies, and profit. Unlike *DeVany (1975)*, *Schmalensee (1977)* directly develops a competitive model, where the (symmetric) demand functions for the single firms are assumed to depend directly on the flight frequencies of all firms in the market and the regulated ticket price:

$$Q_i = \frac{X_i}{X} Q(X,P) S,$$

where Q_i and X_i are the output and the number of flights of the single firms respectively and S is a demand shift parameter. $Q(X,P)$ is the market demand function, which is increasing and concave in the total number of flights X and decreasing in the ticket price P. The above equation supports the assumption that the single firm's market share is proportional to its share in the number of flights. Assuming further a fixed seating configuration k, the capital stock a firm employs is proportional to the number of flights offered per firm:

$$K_i = kX_i .$$

The linear cost function for each firm includes passenger specific costs and flight specific costs, the latter being composed of capital costs of capacity and operating costs of flights:

$$C_i = cQ_i + (gk + f)X_i .$$

In difference to the cost function (2.2) introduced in Section 2.2, g represents the cost of capital funds and f include the costs of operating capacity in the model of *Schmalensee (1977)*. The profit per firm then is

$$\Pi_i = (P - c)Q_i - (gk + f)X_i .$$

In addition, *Schmalensee (1977)* is interested in the accounting rate of return on investment, which is defined as follows:

$$\zeta = \frac{(P-c)Q_i - fX_i}{K_i}.$$

It is assumed that each firm chooses its capital stock (or, equivalently, the number of flights) to maximize its profit at the regulated price, treating the capital stocks of the other firms in the market as fixed. Like the model of *De Vany (1975)*, load factors are determined endogenously and are based on the exogenous aircraft size. Profits are nonnegative if exit is free and costless.

Schmalensee (1977) finds that an increase in the regulated fare lowers the load factor but does not affect the accounting rate of return on investment. For the influence of fare changes on flight frequencies and profits no unique results can be obtained. In order to show the properties derived by *Schmalensee (1977)*, the following index is defined:

$$I \equiv \frac{(P-c)}{P}|\varepsilon|,$$

where $\varepsilon = (\partial Q/\partial P)(P/Q) < 0$ is the price elasticity of total demand. If $I < 1$ ($I > 1$), the flight frequency of the single firm increases (decreases) as a result of an increase in fares. If firms have positive profits, profits increase (decrease) with an increase in the regulated fare if $I < 1$ ($I > 1$). With respect to entry policies, *Schmalensee (1977)* finds that entry leads to an increase in the total number of flights in the market, but leads to a reduction in total profits, profits per firm, rates of return, and load factors.

Panzar (1979)

Panzar (1979) develops a model of price competition in unregulated markets, taking time costs from frequency and stochastic delay into account. The purpose of the model is to compare welfare effects of deregulation. In the model firms differentiate products by choosing different flight departure times on a time circle of duration *T*. For simplicity, it is assumed that each firm offers only one flight. Therefore, the distribution of flights over the time circle is equivalent to the distribution of firms. Passengers' desired departure times are assumed to be uniformly distributed over *T*. As in *De Vany (1975)*, demand for one firm is modeled as a function of the full price of air travel, but with expected trip time being a function of both flight frequency and the load factor. The full price of air travel then is

$$\Theta = P + v(t) + w(n, L),$$

with $$\frac{dv}{dt} \geq 0, \; \frac{\partial w}{\partial n} \leq 0, \; \frac{\partial w}{\partial L} > 0, \; \frac{\partial^2 w}{\partial L^2} > 0.$$

In the above equation, t is the number of minutes between the desired departure time of a representative passenger and the departure time of the most convenient flight, $v(t)$ represents time costs from frequency delay, n is the number of firms (or flights), L is the load factor, and $w(n, L)$ is time costs from stochastic delay. Note that in this model, the length of the wait until the next flight is an additional component of stochastic delay costs. As in the frequency delay model introduced in Section 2.3.2., the number of passengers carried by each flight or firm on the time circle is

$$Q_i(P, n, L) = 2\int_0^{T/(2n)} q(\Theta) dt,$$

where $q(\Theta)$ denotes the demand density at any point in the circle. Each firm i incurs passenger specific costs c and a cost $f(k)$ of flying a plane with k seats:

$$C_i = c + f(k).$$

This leads to the following profit function for the single firm:

$$\Pi_i = 2(P - c)\int_0^{T/(2n)} q(\Theta) dt \; - f$$

It is important to note that, as in *De Vany (1974)* and *Schmalensee (1977)*, the load factor is implicitly determined by the demand function, because aircraft size is assumed to be fixed. We therefore face the identity $L \equiv Q_i / k$.

Since flights are distributed over the time circle, products are differentiated with respect to departure times, which suggests a monopolistically competitive model of airline markets. In a first step, *Panzer (1979)* analyzes regulation by maximizing social welfare with respect to the price and the number of firms. Social welfare, denoted by *VS*, is defined as the sum over all firms of the consumers' surplus areas under the full price demand functions and the profits.

$$VS = 2n \int_0^{T/(2n)} \int_{\Theta}^{\infty} q(\Theta) d\Theta dt + n\Pi_i$$

Panzar (1979) shows that the welfare optimal choices of *P* and *n* result in non-positive profits for the single firm. Contrary to the models of *De Vany (1975)* and *Schmalensee (1977)*, the model of *Panzar (1979)* does not explain the competition with frequency and capacity that was observed in the regulated US airline industry, although it realistically assumes fare and entry regulation. Since it is assumed that each firm offers exactly one flight and that the aircraft size is fixed, flight frequency and the load factor are directly determined by the (regulated) number of firms.

Subsequently, the unregulated free entry equilibrium is calculated, where it is assumed that firms maximize profits by changing the ticket price and taking the rivals' prices as constant. This leads to a non-cooperative Nash-equilibrium in prices, where excess profits are zero due to free entry. The result reveals that, compared to the welfare maximum, competition leads to higher fares, lower load factors, and more firms (flights).

The models of *DeVany (1975)* and *Schmalensee (1977)* show that for regulated fares price competition is replaced by quality competition. The model of *Panzar (1979)* indicates that price competition leads to welfare losses in unregulated markets. Although all three models recognize time sensitivity of passengers by considering the influence of flight frequencies and load factors in the demand function, they do not account for the notion that variations in load factors may be chosen by the firm according to preferences of passengers rather than being endogenously determined. In all models, load factor variations arise from variations in the number of flights given the aircraft size. But the assumption that seating configurations are fixed may be too restrictive, especially if markets with different time and price sensitivities of passengers and with different stage lengths are explored. As *Table 2.2* indicates, flight frequencies, load factors and aircraft sizes vary with passenger segments, market size and stage length. In order to account for these distinctive features of market structures in theory, the models would have to extended. In addition, the assumptions of *Panzar (1979)* may be questioned, according to which each firm offers only one flight and differentiates its product by offering the flight at different departure times. As the example in Section 3.2. shows, firms often have similar departure times but differentiate products with respect to routes to connecting destinations. The similarity of departure times may be due to the fact that in the airline industry there are demand peaks in the morning, at noon, and in the evening.[8] In order to be where the demand is, airlines are tempted to adjust schedules to peak times, which tends to lead to similar departure times rather than to differentiated products.

In the following, a demand function is specified, where the *fare*, the *flight frequency* and the *inverse load factor* are assumed to be choice variables of the airline. In addition, markets with different stage lengths are considered, which is what primarily influences the cost function. In the monopoly model, the endogenous determination of aircraft size is one of the results. In addition, the competitive models developed in Chapters 3 and 4 assume equal departure times for all firms, but product differentiation with respect to the network.

8 See, for example, *Bailey, Graham and Kaplan (1985)*, Figure 3.1, p. 57.

2.3.4 Specification of a Demand Function

Using the notation introduced in the previous sections, a Marshallian market demand function may takes the following form:

$$Q = SP^{\varepsilon} X^{\alpha} E^{\beta}, \tag{2.9}$$

where $\varepsilon = (\partial Q/\partial P)(P/Q) < 0$ is the *price elasticity of demand*, $\beta = (\partial Q/\partial E)(E/Q) > 0.$ denotes *capacity elasticity of demand* and $\alpha = (\partial Q/\partial X)(X/Q) > 0$ denotes *frequency elasticity of demand.* It is assumed that these elasticities are constant for a given market. S is a shift parameter indicating market size, for example as a function of the population at the endpoints of the city-pair market, which may be interpreted as the potential number of passengers. By using a demand function with constant elasticities, it is implicitly assumed that the elasticity of substitution between any two of the arguments equals one. This assumption is very restrictive and may not be supported by empirical tests. However, it will become clear later in this work that the constant elasticity demand function simplifies the technical analysis of firm behavior in several ways, especially when taking into account the fact that the firm has at least three choice variables.

The parameter β increases with the time sensitivity of passengers with respect to stochastic delay, because in markets with a high time sensitivity of passengers each additional seat will result in greater additional demand than in markets with a low time sensitivity of passengers. This is due to the fact that the value of time is higher for passengers with a high time sensitivity than for those with a low time sensitivity. Therefore time sensitive passengers incur a larger reduction of stochastic delay costs from an additional seat, which leads to a larger increase in demand. Frequency elasticity increases with time sensitivity of passengers for similar reasons as capacity elasticity. Time sensitive passengers incur a larger reduction of frequency delay costs from an additional flight than other passengers, which leads to a larger increase in demand. Constant elasticities and the assumption that demand increases with flight frequency and the inverse load factor less than proportionately require the conditions $0 < \beta < 1$ and $0 < \alpha < 1$.

Besides the effects from passenger segmentation time sensitivity of passengers in specific markets may also be influenced by market distance. *De Vany (1974)* estimated time sensitivity of passengers at various trip distances with a full price demand model. He assumed that the full price of a good, for example air transport, is composed of the selling price and the consumption time multiplied by the wage. The price or time elasticity then is the product of the elasticity with respect to the full price and the elasticity of the full price with respect to the money price or time. *De Vany* found that the absolute value of time elasticity decreases, whereas the absolute value of price elasticity increases with market distance. Thus, passengers in long-distance markets are less time sensitive compared to passengers in short-distance markets. However, the relationship between distance and time sensitivity of passengers may be biased. For short-distance trips it can be presumed that price sensitive passengers, like tourists, prefer other modes of transportation to flights, whereas time sensitive passengers prefer faster, but also more expensive, air transport. For long-distance trips, this difference between the two passenger segments vanishes, because ground transportation is either not possible or at least becomes more inconvenient relative to air transport as distance increases. Therefore, short-distance flights mainly transport time sensitive passengers whereas on long-distance flights the composition of time and price sensitive passengers is more balanced, which may explain *De Vany*'s results. For this reason, and in order to keep the model as simple as possible, it is assumed that elasticities are constant with respect to variations in market distance.

2.4 Monopoly Solution

In the following, the behavior of a monopoly airline in a city-pair market is analyzed, using the demand function introduced above and the linear cost function elaborated in Section 2.2. The analysis of firm behavior differs from the models discussed in Section 2.3.3. in that the airline maximizes profit with respect to the three supply variables price, frequency, and inverse load factor. Using the cost function (2.2) and the demand function (2.9), the profit of a monopoly airline is given by

$$\Pi = PQ(P,X,E) - \left[cQ(P,E,X) + fX + gK\right]. \tag{2.10}$$

Since the inverse load factor is given by $E = K/Q$, total capacity K can be replaced by QE. The profit function then takes the following form:

$$\Pi = PQ - (c + gE)Q - fX. \tag{2.11}$$

For a profit maximum, the first partial derivatives must vanish,

$$\frac{\partial \Pi}{\partial P} = Q + P\frac{\partial Q}{\partial P} - (c + gE)\frac{\partial Q}{\partial P} = 0, \tag{2.12}$$

$$\frac{\partial \Pi}{\partial X} = P\frac{\partial Q}{\partial X} - (c + gE)\frac{\partial Q}{\partial X} - f = 0, \text{ and} \tag{2.13}$$

$$\frac{\partial \Pi}{\partial E} = P\frac{\partial Q}{\partial E} - (c + gE)\frac{\partial Q}{\partial E} - gQ = 0. \tag{2.14}$$

At this point the profit function is concave in *P*, *X*, and *E* for $0 < \alpha < 1$, $0 < \beta < 1$, and $\varepsilon < -1$, such that equations (2.12)-(2.14) represent a maximum.[9]

9 See Appendix B.

Taking into account the fact that the demand function is monotonic in *P*, equation (2.12) can be written as follows:

$$\frac{\partial P}{\partial Q}Q + P = c + gE, \qquad (2.15)$$

which indicates that in the monopoly equilibrium, marginal revenue of output equals the sum of marginal passenger cost c and marginal capacity cost from variations in passengers gE.

From (2.13), net marginal revenue of the number of flights equals marginal flight costs:

$$\frac{\partial Q}{\partial X}\left(P - c - gE\right) = f. \qquad (2.16)$$

This condition indicates that the airline increases the number of flights as long as the additional net revenue from this increase exceeds additional costs. Further transformation of (2.16) shows that in the monopoly equilibrium, price equals marginal output costs from variations in flights Ψ_Q:[10]

$$P = \left(c + gE\right) + \frac{f}{\frac{\partial Q}{\partial X}} \equiv \Psi_Q. \qquad (2.17)$$

Marginal output costs from variations in flights represent the additional costs the airline faces due to an additional passenger as a result of an increase in the number of flights. These costs include marginal passenger costs and marginal capacity costs for a constant inverse load factor. The term $f/\left(\partial Q/\partial X\right)$ denotes the additional flight specific costs per additional passenger. Thus equation

10 This feature of the model has been adapted from *De Vany (1975)*. Total output costs are implicitly a function of the number of flights: $\Psi(Q) = (c + gE)Q + fX(Q)$, where $X(Q)$ is the inverse function of market demand given *P* and *E*. Marginal output costs Ψ_Q from variations in flights are calculated by taking the first order derivative $\Psi_Q = (c + gE) + f\left(\partial X/\partial Q\right)$, that corresponds to equation (2.17).

(2.17) shows again that the airline increases the number of flights as long as the additional expenses are covered by revenue. As $\partial Q/\partial X$ is positive but decreasing with the number of flights, marginal output costs increase with the number of flights.[11] Additionally, marginal output costs tend to infinity with $\partial Q/\partial X$ decreasing asymptotically to zero.

Rewriting (2.14) shows that in the equilibrium net marginal revenue per passenger from an increase of the inverse load factor equals marginal capacity costs,

$$\frac{\partial Q}{\partial E}\frac{(P-c-gE)}{Q}=g\,. \tag{2.18}$$

The airline increases capacity relative to demand as long as additional net revenue per passenger from the additional capacity exceeds additional capacity costs. Like optimal flight frequency, price equals marginal output costs from variations in the inverse load factor in the equilibrium:

$$P=(c+gE)+\frac{gQ}{\dfrac{\partial Q}{\partial E}}\,. \tag{2.19}$$

Marginal output costs from variations in the inverse load factor stand for the costs for an additional passenger due to an increase in the inverse load factor. They include marginal passenger and marginal capacity costs due to the increase of passengers as well as the additional capacity costs incurred because the inverse load factor has increased for the entire demand, which is denoted by

11 The first derivative of Ψ_Q with respect to X,

$$\frac{\partial \Psi_Q}{\partial X}=\left(-f\,\frac{\partial^2 Q}{\partial X^2}\right)\Bigg/\left(\frac{\partial Q}{\partial X}\right)^2>0\,,$$

shows that Ψ_Q is an increasing function of X for all X, because $\partial^2 Q/\partial X^2$ is negative.

the term $gQ(\partial E/\partial Q)$. This term indicates again that the airline increases capacity as long as the additional costs from this increase are covered by the ticket price.

In order to determine the equilibrium values of the ticket price, the inverse load factor and the flight frequency, the three conditions for a profit maximum have to be analyzed. The first condition, denoted by equation (2.15), determines the monopoly price. This price is given by the *Lerner Index*, indicating that the ratio between the profit margin and the monopoly price is the inverse of the price elasticity of demand:[12]

$$\frac{P-c-gE}{P}=-\frac{1}{\varepsilon}. \tag{2.20}$$

Therefore, the monopoly price is

$$P_m=\frac{c+gE}{1+\frac{1}{\varepsilon}}. \tag{2.21}$$

The optimal ticket price can now be inserted into the second and third condition for a profit maximum (2.16) and (2.18). In order to characterize the *inverse load factor*, both sides of (2.18) are multiplied by *E*. Thus, taking into account that $(\partial Q/\partial E)(E/Q)=\beta$, the *inverse load factor* is

$$E=\frac{\beta(P-c-gE)}{g}. \tag{2.22}$$

12 See for example *Tirole (1988)*, p. 66. The *Lerner Index* can be derived from equation (2.16):

$$\frac{\partial P}{\partial Q}\frac{Q}{P}P+P=c+g,$$

where $(\partial P/\partial Q)/(Q/P)=1/\varepsilon$.

Similarly, in order to determine the *flight frequency*, the second condition for profit maximization is used. Since $(\partial Q/\partial X)(X/Q) = \alpha$, multiplying (2.16) by X/Q leads to

$$X = \frac{\alpha Q(P - c - gE)}{f} \tag{2.23}$$

By solving (2.21), (2.22) and (2.23) for *P*, *E* and *X* we obtain the monopoly ticket price, inverse load factor and flight frequency,[13]

$$P_m = \frac{c}{\left(1 + \frac{1+\beta}{\varepsilon}\right)}, \tag{2.24}$$

$$E_m = -\frac{c}{g}\frac{1}{\left(1 + \frac{1+\varepsilon}{\beta}\right)}, \text{ and} \tag{2.25}$$

$$X_m = -\frac{\alpha c Q_m}{f(\varepsilon + 1 + \beta)}\ ^{14}. \tag{2.26}$$

In order to get a feasible solution of the model, it is necessary that $\varepsilon < -(1+\beta)$. It is assumed that this condition is always satisfied throughout the analysis in this work.

Note that the ticket price and the inverse load factor can be calculated without using the profit maximum condition for flight frequency given by equation (2.23). The model, therefore, has a block-recursive structure, which is due to the notion that flight specific costs are independent of the number of passengers and of total seating capacity. In fact, in the profit function, the total of

13 See Appendix C for the detailed derivation of these results.

14 In reality the equilibrium number of flights of course has to be an integer. For reasons of simplicity, this is ignored in the model. However, it is theoretically possible to see an optimal number of flights, let's say, of 0.5 flights per day as one flight every second day.

flight specific costs can be regarded as fixed costs related to a specific level of quality (e.g. frequency in this case). Thus, in the profit maximum of the monopoly, only the output level but not the values of the ticket price and the inverse load factor are influenced by flight frequency. Moreover, since in the profit function the inverse load factor and the number of passengers implicitly depend on each other, they can only be determined jointly.

While the optimal ticket price and the inverse load factor are determined by the elasticity and cost parameters, the optimal number of flights additionally depends on the monopoly output $Q_m = Q(P_m, X_m, E_m)$ and, therefore, on market size. Since Q_m increases with *S*, flight frequency also increases with market size. Therefore, with equal fares and inverse load factors, passengers traveling in high density markets enjoy a higher quality of service in terms of frequency than passengers traveling in low density markets. Although the relation between the optimal number of flights and market size is a quite realistic result of the model, it restricts comparison of different flight frequencies to markets of equal density. It, therefore, is useful to define a more general term that defines flight frequency relative to output. We may use the number of flights per passenger or, in other words, *schedule density F*, instead. From (2.26), schedule density of the monopoly airline is

$$F_m \equiv \frac{X_m}{Q_m} = -\frac{\alpha c}{f(\varepsilon + 1 + \beta)} . \tag{2.27}$$

With the aid of the above equilibrium supply variables, the monopoly output can be calculated. Replacing the number of flights with schedule density according to equation (2.27), the number of passengers transported is

$$Q_m = S P_m{}^{\varepsilon} (F_m Q_m)^{\alpha} E_m{}^{\beta},$$

which is equal to

$$Q_m = S^{\left(\frac{1}{1-\alpha}\right)} P_m^{\left(\frac{\varepsilon}{1-\alpha}\right)} F_m^{\left(\frac{\alpha}{1-\alpha}\right)} E_m^{\left(\frac{\beta}{1-\alpha}\right)} . \tag{2.28}$$

Finally, the profit maximizing aircraft size of the monopoly airline is determined. Average aircraft size may be defined as the number of seats offered per flight, and therefore is equal to the ratio of total capacity offered and the total number of flights,

$$k_m \equiv \frac{K_m}{X_m} = \frac{E_m Q_m}{F_m Q_m}.$$

Since demand can be eliminated in the numerator and the denominator, aircraft size is the ratio of the inverse load factor to schedule density, and therefore is determined by cost and time sensitivity parameters,

$$k_m = \frac{f\beta}{g\alpha}.$$

The interpretation of this result is straightforward. If passengers have relatively high preferences of seat availability compared to a high frequency, the airline is tempted to offer high capacity but not necessarily a large number of flights. The airline therefore offers few flights with large aircraft. On the other hand, if passengers are rather sensitive with respect to a high flight frequency, the airline offers many flights with small aircraft. Similar influences can be traced with respect to costs. If flight specific costs increase relative to capacity specific costs, the airline uses larger aircraft. If capacity costs rise relative to flight specific costs, the airline uses smaller aircraft. However, clear comparative static results for aircraft size with respect to time sensitivity of passengers and market distance cannot be determined on the theoretical level, since time sensitivity and market distance influence the inverse load factor and schedule density in the same direction. Because of the limited power of this result and because it is determined by two other supply variables, aircraft size will not be used in subsequent discussions and extensions of the model.

2.5 Comparative Statics

In this section, a brief qualitative comparative statics analysis is first presented in order to determine the influence of different price elasticity, time sensitivity and cost parameters on the monopoly solution. In a second step, the influence of market distance on supply variables is analyzed. As the optimal ticket price, inverse load factor and schedule density depend on the demand and cost structures in the city-pair market, tourist and non-tourist markets as well as long-distance and short-distance markets are differentiated. The surveys by *Doganis (1985)* and *Bailey, Graham and Kaplan (1985)* suggest that tourists are more price sensitive but less time sensitive than business passengers (non-tourists). Furthermore, the cost function indicates a positive influence of market distance on all the cost parameters. The main comparative statics results are presented in *Table 2.3*, where the respective relations of the parameters to tourist, non-tourist, short-distance and long-distance markets are also indicated. Note that the effects of single parameters on supply variables are indicated taking the other parameters as constant.

Throughout this work, we call price elasticity of demand as high if its absolute value is high. Accordingly, an increasing price elasticity means an increase in its absolute value. While the influences of price elasticity and marginal passenger costs on ticket price is well known from monopoly theory, the influence of time sensitivity on the inverse load factor and flight frequency is of further interest. As equations (2.24) to (2.27) indicate, the inverse load factor is high (low) for a high (low) capacity elasticity of demand. When passengers value the availability of seats very highly, the airline offers a high number of seats relative to average demand in order to reduce the probability of non-availability of seats. However this tactic is restricted by marginal capacity costs, whose influence on the inverse load factor is negative. Because marginal capacity costs are comparably high in long-distance markets, the provision of a high number of empty seats relative to average demand costs more in these markets than in short-distance markets. Therefore the inverse load factor is higher in long-distance than in short-distance markets. The influence of frequency elasticity of demand on schedule density is explained as follows: a high valuation of frequency by passengers means high time costs. Therefore, everything else being equal, time costs are reduced and the number of passengers increased with additional flights. Like the inverse load factor, schedule density decreases with increasing marginal flight specific costs. Thus, schedule density is lower in long-distance markets than in short-distance markets.

Table 2.3: Comparative statics for price, inverse load factor and schedule density.

	passenger or distance segment		P_m	E_m	F_m
$\|\varepsilon\|$	tourist:	high	low	low	low
	business:	low	high	high	high
α	tourist:	low	-	-	low
	business:	high	-	-	high
β	tourist:	low	low	low	low
	business:	high	high	high	high
c	short-distance:	low	low	low	low
	long-distance:	high	high	high	high
f	short-distance:	low	-	-	high
	long-distance:	high	-	-	low
g	short-distance:	low	-	high	-
	long-distance:	high	-	low	-

The influence of price elasticity on the inverse load factor and schedule density is the opposite compared to the time sensitivity parameters. This is due to the fact that a high price elasticity, for example, leads to a low ticket price, which augments the financial restrictions for the provision of additional capacity and flights. Similarly, the price increases with increased capacity elasticity of demand, indicating that passengers pay more attention to the availability of seats than to the ticket price. Finally, price, schedule density and the inverse load factor increase with increasing passenger specific costs.

Table 2.4: Equilibrium variables for tourist versus business and short-distance versus long-distance markets.

	P_m	P_m/d	E_m	F_m
Tourist markets	low	low	low	low
Business markets	high	high	high	high
Short-distance markets (low *d)*	low	high	?	?
Long-distance markets (high *d)*	high	low	?	?

Whereas *Table 2.3* shows the influence of single time sensitivity and cost parameters on equilibrium supply variables for constant values of the other parameters, *Table 2.4* indicates the net influence of tourist, business, short-distance and long-distance markets. In addition, fares per kilometer are indicated in order to compare fares across markets with different stage lengths. The results in *Table 2.4* are obtained by further analyzing equations (2.24) to (2.27). Using (2.1) and (2.24), the monopoly fare is

$$P_m = \frac{c_d \cdot d^{\eta_c}}{\left(1 + \frac{1+\beta}{\varepsilon}\right)}, \tag{2.29}$$

and the fare per kilometer thus is

$$\frac{P_m}{d} = \frac{c_d \cdot d^{(\eta_c - 1)}}{\left(1 + \frac{1+\beta}{\varepsilon}\right)}. \tag{2.30}$$

Since $0 < \eta_c < 1$ and, therefore, $\eta_c - 1 < 0$, the monopoly fare increases but the fare per kilometer decreases with market distance. This effect is due to economies of scale with respect to market distance. Unlike the effects on the fare, the influence of market distance cannot be determined for schedule density and the inverse load factor. As the following equations show, the direction of the influence of market distance on the two depends crucially on the extent of scale economies involved with passenger, flight and capacity specific costs.

$$E_m = -\frac{1}{\left(1 + \frac{1+\varepsilon}{\beta}\right)} \frac{c_d}{g_d} d^{(\eta_c - \eta_g)} \tag{2.31}$$

$$F_m = -\frac{\alpha}{(1 + \beta + \varepsilon)} \frac{c_d}{f_d} d^{(\eta_c - \eta_f)} \tag{2.32}$$

On the one hand, because an increasing trip time increases marginal flight and capacity costs, schedule density and the inverse load factor ought to decrease with market distance. On the other hand, because an increase in market distance leads to an increase in marginal passenger specific costs, schedule density and the inverse load factor should rather increase with distance. Thus, when economies of scale are smaller for flight and capacity specific costs than for passenger specific costs ($\eta_f, \eta_g > \eta_c$), schedule density and the inverse load factor decrease with market distance. Otherwise, when economies of scale are larger for flight and capacity specific costs than for passenger specific costs ($\eta_f, \eta_g < \eta_c$), schedule density and the inverse load factor increase with market distance. Therefore, empirical work is required to extend the model to accommodate this.

2.6 Case Study: The Supply Variables of *Swissair*

In what follows, the theoretical model introduced above is tested with a regression analysis using *Swissair* data. The relations to be examined are the dependencies of supply variables on market distance and passenger segments, as formalized in equations (2.29) - (2.32). It is important to note that there are difficulties with respect to the determination of passenger segments. For *Swissair*'s services, single city-pair markets cannot easily be assigned to specific passenger segments, because passengers of different segments often use the same flights. Flights from Zurich to London, for example, are offered to tourists and to business passengers as well. Moreover, the most important tourist destinations for Swiss people like Paris or London are probably among the most important business centers as well. Therefore, in order to determine the appropriate segment for a specific market, the ratio between tourist and business passengers should be known. In this regard, one may think of aircraft subdivision into first class, business class and economy class seats. But this classification does not basically reflect time sensitivity of passengers. Taking into account that business class passengers usually get better in-flight service and larger seats, for which they pay higher fares, the distinction is also based on the willingness of passengers to pay for higher quality. Moreover, business passengers do not always fly business class for cost reasons and not all tourists are satisfied with economy class seats. Nevertheless, assuming that passengers flying business class are predominantly composed of business passengers, and that passengers flying economy class are mostly tourists, the subdivision of consumers into business class and economy class passengers provides a good proxy variable for measuring the time sensitivity of passengers in a given market. A relatively *large share of business class passengers*, therefore, should correspond to *high fares*, *high schedule densities* and *high inverse load factors*, and vice versa.

The data reflect 60 European international city-pair markets from Zurich and Geneva in 1993. The data for the computation of supply variables and time sensitivity were collected from *Swissair* route profit and loss accounts for 1993, and market distance was determined on a map of Europe. Therefore, market distance is approximated by the direct distance between the observed cities. Schedule density F_k is the ratio of the total number of flights in this year to the total number of passengers in this year for market *k*. The inverse load factor E_k is the inverse of the average passenger load factor, the ratio of the total passenger revenue to the total number of passengers is used as the ticket price P_k, and market distance d_k is the direct distance between the two cities in kilometers. The variable BS_k is the ratio of business class passengers to the sum of business class and tourist class passengers, which is also reported in the *Swissair* profit and loss accounts.[15] The ratio implies that $0 \leq BS_k \leq 1$. Assuming that business class passengers have a high time sensitivity and a low price elasticity, whereas economy class passengers have a low time sensitivity and a high price elasticity, BS_k is a measure of the time sensitivity of passengers on a scale from 0 to 1. Therefore, a relatively low value of BS_k indicates that the *k*th market is dominated by price sensitive passengers, whereas a relatively high value of BS_k indicates that this market is dominated by time sensitive passengers. *Table 2.5* presents an overview of the data.

In order to simplify the analysis, all markets are considered as monopoly markets. This assumption is justified by the fact that Switzerland is not a member of the EU or the European Economic Area EEA, which implies that air transport is still regulated through bilateral agreements and pool arrangements. Passengers, therefore, face monopoly (that is cartel) supply in most international city-pair markets of *Swissair* (see Section 1.2).[16]

15 First class passengers are not included in this statistic, because in many European markets, only business and economy class seats are offered.

16 Unless the partner airlines in the markets concerned offer the same supply variables and have equal market shares, the analysis may be distorted due to this assumption. However, since a lot of bilateral agreements explicitly fix supply variables and market shares, we assume that this condition holds.

Table 2.5: Description of data (60 European markets)

	mean	standard deviation
P_k (ticket price in SFr.)	327	77.808
F_k (schedule density)	0.017	0.005
E_k (inverse load factor)	1.94	0.32
d_k (market distance in *km*)	916.75	490.809
BS_k (time sensitivity)	0.299	0.12

With respect to the specification of the empirical model, the theoretical solutions for the equilibrium supply variables suggest the use of logarithmic functions. According to (2.29), (2.31) and (2.32), we have

$$\ln P = \ln c_d + \eta_c \ln d + \ln\left(\frac{\varepsilon}{\varepsilon+\beta+1}\right), \tag{2.33}$$

$$\ln E = \ln\left(\frac{c_d}{g_d}\right) + \left(\eta_c - \eta_g\right)\ln d + \ln\left(\frac{-\beta}{\varepsilon+\beta+1}\right), \text{ and} \tag{2.34}$$

$$\ln F = \ln\left(\frac{c_d}{f_d}\right) + \left(\eta_c - \eta_f\right)\ln d + \ln\left(\frac{-\alpha}{\varepsilon+\beta+1}\right). \tag{2.35}$$

Note that all three equations have a constant term consisting of cost shift parameters, a second term relating costs to market distance, and a third term that is composed of the elasticities and, therefore, reflects the passenger segment. Due to the assumption stated earlier that $\varepsilon < -(1+\beta)$, the third terms are positive in all equations. Although depending on different combinations of parameters, the third term increases with time sensitivity (parameters α and β) and decreases with price elasticity ε in all three equations. In the empirical model, the third terms therefore are replaced by the proxy variable for time sensitivity *BS*.

Since least squares provide the best linear unbiased estimators (BLUE) of parameters (Gauss-Markov Theorem), equations (2.33)-(2.35) are estimated with OLS regressions for markets $k = \{1 \ldots 60\}$:

(I) $$\ln P_k = x_0 + x_1 \ln d_k + x_2 BS_k + \mu_k,$$

(II) $$\ln E_k = y_0 + y_1 \ln d_k + y_2 BS_k + \lambda_k, \text{ and}$$

(III) $$\ln F_k = z_0 + z_1 \ln d_k + z_2 BS_k + \chi_k,$$

where μ_k, λ_k and χ_k are the residuals. By using the Linear Regression Model we imply the following basic set of assumptions:[17]

1. Linear relationship between dependent and independent variables
2. *Zero mean of the disturbances:* $E[\mu_k] = E[\lambda_k] = E[\chi_k] = 0$ for all *k*.
3. *Homoscedasticity:* $Var[\mu_k], Var[\lambda_k], Var[\chi_k]$ constant for all *k*.
4. *Nonautocorrelation:* $Cov[\mu_k, \mu_l] = Cov[\lambda_k, \lambda_l] = Cov[\chi_k, \chi_l] = 0$ if $k \neq l$
5. *Uncorrelatedness of regressors and disturbances:*

   $Cov[\mathbf{X}, \mu], Cov[\mathbf{X}, \lambda], Cov[\mathbf{X}, \chi] = 0$, where $\mathbf{X}$ is the $k \times 2$ data matrix of the two variables $\ln d_k$ and BS_k, and μ, λ, and χ are the error vectors.
6. *No exact linear relationship among variables:* $\mathbf{X}$ is nonstochastic with full column rank.
7. *Normality*: $\mu_k \sim N[0, \sigma_1^2]$, $\lambda_k \sim N[0, \sigma_2^2]$, and $\chi_k \sim N[0, \sigma_3^2]$.

17 See, for example, *Greene (1993)*, pp. 170ff. The assumptions on the data are supported by respective tests, except for the normality of residuals in equation (I). However, we assume that this violation does not distort our results considerably.

Assumption 7 is necessary for the application of *t*-tests. Note that the analysis consists of a system of regression equations, which basically implies that the errors in each equation are not independent from each other. More specifically, since we test reduced form equations, we face a Seemingly Unrelated Regression Model (SUR). However, the equations have identical explanatory variables. Therefore, it is possible to estimate each equation individually by OLS.[18]

With respect to the coefficients it is important to note that the effects of market distance on the different cost parameters in the schedule density and inverse load factor equations may neutralize each other, as equations (2.31) and (2.32) and the comparative static properties in *Table 2.4* show. Whereas we can expect a clearly positive influence of market distance on fares, the net effect on schedule density and the inverse load factor may be very small or even zero.

The results reveal that the supply variables of *Swissair*'s European services are in accordance with these theoretical considerations, as *Table 2.6* shows. In the price equation (I) all the coefficients are significant at the 0.01% level. This clear result is not surprising. First, it is very plausible that marginal passenger costs increase with distance. As the theoretical model predicts, the coefficient for distance in the fare equation, representing η_c and therefore reflecting economies of scale, is positive and smaller than 1. Second, since business class passengers usually pay higher fares than tourist class passengers, a higher *BS* leads to an increase in *P*.

18 See for example *Greene (1993)*, p. 488. A mathematical proof of the property is found in *Dwivedi and Srivastava (1978)*.

Table 2.6: OLS regressions on distance and passenger segment (t-values in parenthesis)

	Dependent variable	Constant	ln*d*	*BS*	$\bar{R}^2$	Durbin-Watson
I	ln*P*	1.8471	0.5286	1.2895	0.716	1.6773
		(5.2878)	(11.7693)	(5.9355)		
II	ln*E*	0.0732	0.0474	0.8684	0.2556	1.78
		(0.2084)	(1.05)	(3.9758)		
III	ln*F*	-4.5292	0.0061	1.2522	0.2033	1.7741
		(-6.6303)	(0.0699)	(2.9470)		

The coefficients for *BS* in equations (II) and (III) are significant at the 0.01% level, which indicates that inverse load factors and schedule densities are influenced by the time sensitivity of passengers relative to their price elasticity. But, unlike the fare equation, the hypothesis that the distance coefficients for inverse load factors and schedule densities are zero cannot be rejected. This result supports the above notion that the various effects of market distance on cost parameters may neutralize each other in the frequency and capacity equations. However, as *Figure 2.6* shows, this result is biased because in the sample *BS* decreases with market distance.[19] As already mentioned above (cf. section 2.3.4.), this correlation may be due to the fact that in short-distance markets, price sensitive tourists prefer other modes of transportation like the car or the railway for cost reasons, whereas time sensitive passengers prefer the

19 From a linear regression of *BS* on *d* we find that $R^2 = 0.5$.

faster, but also more expensive, air transport. For long-distance trips, this difference between the passenger segments vanishes, because ground transportation is not possible or becomes inconvenient even for passengers with a very low time sensitivity. Therefore, the respective coefficients only capture the net effects of market distance on the supply variables. This leads to the following interpretation of the results: Whereas we cannot conclude that load factors and schedule densities are independent of stage length, we may still find that the net effect of stage length is zero because increasing effects of stage length on marginal passenger costs and marginal capacity and flight costs may neutralize each other.

Figure 2.6: Correlation between passenger segment and market distance

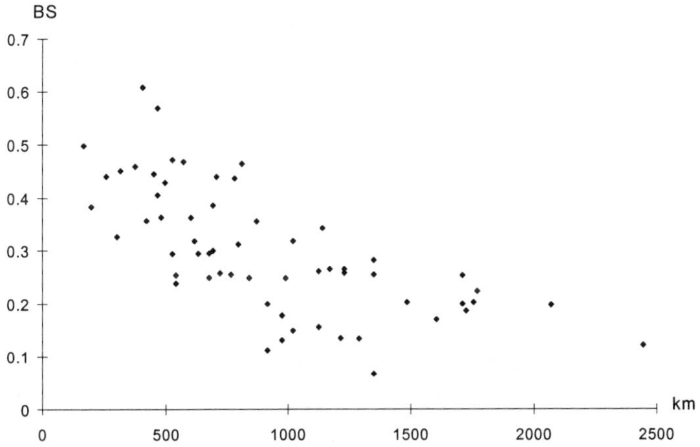

The high $\overline{R}^2$ in equation (I) indicates that market distance and the passenger segment, as defined above, explain most of the variation in fares. Although this result is in favor of the predicted influences of time sensitivity and distance on fares, it has to be interpreted very carefully. Because business class passengers usually get better service, for example larger seats, they cause higher passenger specific and capacity costs. Therefore, markets with a large share of business passengers may also incur higher average revenues because the level of marginal passenger costs c_d, and therefore fares, is higher independently of market distance. This means that the total effect of *BS* may be divided into a cost component and an elasticity component. The same is true for the other two supply variables, especially for inverse load factors, where a higher value of *BS* may also lead to higher capacity costs.

Unlike the fare equation, the empirical model only explains a small proportion of the variations in inverse load factors and schedule densities, as the respective $\overline{R}^2$ show. This result may be due to a lack of flexibility in the provision of capacity. Recall that in the model it was assumed that the airline is able to choose the number of seats that would lead to the desired average inverse load factor for a given expected demand exactly. In reality, an airline may not be able to meet this requirement. Aircraft have a fixed number of seats, where only the ratio between business class and economy class seats can be varied at most. Since an airline can economize on aircraft maintenance costs when it uses a large number of aircraft of the same type, the number of seats offered is an integer. The flights in the data set for example are mainly carried out by only four different types of aircraft. Thus, the observed capacity offered in one market is only an approximation to the optimal number of seats. Similarly, flight frequency was assumed to be a real number rather than an integer, which also neglects technical and organizational restrictions. For this reason, the daily schedule may also is not optimal. Therefore, unlike fares, a large part of the variation in inverse load factors and schedule densities is due to variables and parameters not included in the simple model analyzed. Despite these objections, we may conclude that *Swissair*'s supply variables for its European markets support the theoretical model.

2.7 Summary and Conclusions

The monopoly solution of the basic model presented in this chapter shows that price, load factor and flight frequency in a city-pair market are determined by the time sensitivity relative to the price sensitivity of passengers and by cost parameters. In markets for business passengers a monopoly airline will offer relatively high prices, low load factors and high schedule densities, whereas tourist markets are characterized by relatively low prices, high load factors and low schedule densities. In addition, the model demonstrates that flight frequency increases with market size. Whereas an increase in market distance leads to an increase in fares, the net effect of stage length on schedule density and the inverse load factor cannot be determined in the model. This is due to the fact that besides marginal passenger related costs, stage length also influences capacity and flight specific costs. Therefore, the net effect of stage length on those supply variables may be zero. This feature and problems with respect to the collection of feasible data restrict the testing of the model. Nevertheless, if we assume that business class passengers are more time than price sensitive, and that economy class passengers are more price than time sensitive, the coefficients from OLS regressions do not contradict the model with respect to the predicted effects of time sensitivity of passengers and market distance on supply variables.

The influence of demand and cost conditions on airlines' load factors has to be emphasized, because load factors are often used to measure the productivity of firms. At the market level, load factors are only a valuable measure of productivity if markets with equal demand and cost conditions are compared. At the firm level, the respective demand and cost conditions in the city-pair markets have to be analyzed and aggregated if the average load factor is used to assess the productivity of an airline. Thus, comparing firms by their load factors can cause difficulties and there is a high probability of misjudgment. For example, a comparison of the load factors of competitors in the North-Atlantic market may be feasible, because we can expect similar demand and cost conditions. But the comparison of overall load factors of the respective firms is not advisable, because airlines provide distinct networks, where the different city-pair markets served are characterized by different demand and cost conditions. Furthermore, especially in markets with time sensitive passengers, a low load factor may be more efficient than a high load factor. Although an increasing load factor and a decreasing schedule density may increase factor productivity of a firm, it may reduce revenue because of large frequency and stochastic delays.

Appendix A

In the following it is shown that demand increases with an increasing number of flights at a decreasing rate. According to equation (2.7),

$$\frac{\partial Q}{\partial X} = -2bA\left(\frac{T}{2X}\right) + b\frac{dA}{dt}\left(\frac{T}{2X}\right)\frac{T}{X}.$$

If $a(t)$ is linear, then $a(t) = \bar{a}t$ and

$$A = \int \bar{a}t = \tfrac{1}{2}\bar{a}t^2 + y,$$

where $\bar{a} > 0$ and constant, and y is the constant of integration, which we assume to be zero. Thus

$$\frac{\partial Q}{\partial X} = -b\bar{a}\frac{T^2}{4X^2} + b\bar{a}\frac{T}{2X}\frac{T}{X}$$

$$= b\bar{a}\frac{T^2}{4X^2} > 0.$$

Additionally,

$$\frac{\partial^2 Q}{\partial X^2} = -b\bar{a}\frac{T^2}{2X^3} < 0. \qquad \text{q.e.d.}$$

In order to demonstrate the concavity of the profit function at the extreme, we proceed in two steps. First we show that Π is globally concave in X and in E respectively. Then we find that Π is concave in P at the extremum.

For simplicity, the variables held constant in each particular step of the following analysis are replaced by single constants. The profit function (2.11) therefore can be rewritten as follows:

$$\Pi = \Gamma_1 X^{\alpha} - fX,$$

where $\Gamma_1 = (P - c - gE)SP^{\varepsilon} E^{\beta}$, which is constant for variations in X. For positive profits we have $(P - c - gE) > 0$ and, therefore, $\Gamma_1 > 0$. Since the second partial derivative for the profit function with respect to X is negative for $0 < \alpha < 1$, Π is concave in X:

$$\frac{\partial^2 \Pi}{\partial X^2} = \alpha(\alpha - 1)\Gamma_1 X^{\alpha - 2} < 0$$

Similarly, the profit may be denoted by

$$\Pi = \Gamma_2 E^{\beta} - \Gamma_3 E^{\beta + 1} - fX,$$

with $\Gamma_2 = (P - c)SP^{\varepsilon} X^{\alpha}$ and $\Gamma_3 = gSP^{\varepsilon} X^{\alpha}$. For positive profits $\Gamma_2 > 0$. The second order partial derivative with respect to E is

$$\frac{\partial^2 \Pi}{\partial E^2} = \beta(\beta - 1)\Gamma_2 E^{\beta - 2} - (\beta + 1)\beta\Gamma_3 E^{\beta - 1}.$$

This function is negative for $0 < \beta < 1$ and, therefore, Π is concave in E.

With respect to the ticket price the profit function is only concave in a certain range of values of P. Again, the constant variables in the profit function can be replaced by constants for simplicity. We therefore have

$$\Pi = \Gamma_4 P^{\varepsilon+1} - \Gamma_5 P^{\varepsilon} - fX,$$

where $\Gamma_4 = SX^{\alpha} E^{\beta}$ and $\Gamma_5 = (c + gE)SX^{\alpha} E^{\beta}$. The first order partial derivative with respect to *P*, which is later used to calculate the profit maximum, is

$$\frac{\partial \Pi}{\partial P} = (\varepsilon + 1)\Gamma_4 P^{\varepsilon} - \varepsilon \Gamma_5 P^{\varepsilon-1}.$$

Concavity requires that

$$\frac{\partial^2 \Pi}{\partial P^2} = (\varepsilon + 1)\varepsilon \Gamma_4 P^{\varepsilon-1} - \varepsilon(\varepsilon - 1)\Gamma_5 P^{\varepsilon-2} < 0,$$

that is equal to

$$(\varepsilon + 1)\Gamma_4 - (\varepsilon - 1)\Gamma_5 P^{-1} < 0.$$

Solving for *P* reveals that the profit function is only concave in *P* for

$$P < \frac{(\varepsilon - 1)\Gamma_5}{(\varepsilon + 1)\Gamma_4}. \tag{B.1}$$

It can be shown that the value of *P* in the extremum always belongs to this range. A maximum or a minimum requires that

$$\frac{\partial \Pi}{\partial P} = (\varepsilon + 1)\Gamma_4 P^{\varepsilon} - \varepsilon \Gamma_5 P^{\varepsilon-1} = 0,$$

which can be simplified to

$$(\varepsilon + 1)\Gamma_4 - \varepsilon \Gamma_5 P^{-1} = 0.$$

Solving for the ticket price leads to

$$P = \frac{\varepsilon \Gamma_5}{(\varepsilon + 1)\Gamma_4}.$$

For $\varepsilon < -1$, this price satisfies condition (B.1) and, therefore, maximizes the profit for constant inverse load factor and flight frequency. Note that $\varepsilon < -1$ is also a necessary condition for the existence of the Cournot solution to the monopoly problem. We therefore conclude that the profit function, as defined in equation (2.11) and using the constant elasticity demand function (2.9), is concave for the relevant range of prices.

Appendix C

In this appendix the supply variables for the monopoly airline in their reduced form are developed. First, we calculate the ticket price. Equation (2.22) can be written as follows:

$$\beta(P-c) - \beta gE = gE .$$

From this we obtain

$$gE = \frac{\beta(P-c)}{(1+\beta)}, \tag{C.1}$$

which now can be inserted into equation (2.21). We therefore have

$$P = \frac{c + \dfrac{\beta(P-c)}{(1+\beta)}}{1+\dfrac{1}{\varepsilon}}.$$

Solving for *P* leads to the monopoly ticket price,

$$P_m = \frac{c}{\left(1+\dfrac{1+\beta}{\varepsilon}\right)}. \tag{C.2}$$

By inserting the monopoly price (C.2) into (C.1) we obtain

$$gE = \frac{\beta}{(1+\beta)}\left(\frac{\varepsilon c}{\varepsilon+1+\beta} - c\right).$$

This expression can be simplified, which leads to the inverse load factor of the monopoly airline,

$$E_m = -\frac{c}{g}\frac{1}{\left(1+\frac{1+\varepsilon}{\beta}\right)}. \tag{C.3}$$

Finally, the monopoly flight frequency is calculated by using equations (2.23), (C.2) and (C.3). This first leads to

$$X = \frac{\alpha Q}{f}\left(\frac{\varepsilon c}{\varepsilon+1+\beta} - c + \frac{\beta c}{\varepsilon+1+\beta}\right),$$

which is reduced to

$$X_m = -\frac{c}{f}\frac{\alpha Q_m}{(1+\beta+\varepsilon)}.$$

Appendix D

	De Vany (1975)	*Schmalensee (1977)*	*Panzar (1979)*	*Basic model in Chapter 2*
Object:	- profit maximization under price regulation	- profit maximization under price regulation	- welfare effects of deregulation	- determination of monopoly supply
Main assumptions:	- fixed (regulated) ticket price - constant aircraft size	- fixed (regulated) ticket price - constant aircraft size	- regulated price and number of firms in a basic model - free entry and price competition in the extension	- constant demand elasticities - market distance influences costs
Application of frequency and stochastic delay:	- flight frequency influences full price of air travel - endogenous determination of load factors	- flight frequency influences demand directly - endogenous determination of load factors	- flight frequency and load factor influence full price of air travel - endogenous determination of load factors	- flight frequency and inverse load factor influence demand directly
Choice variables for profit or welfare maximization:	- flight frequency	- flight frequency	- *regulation:* price and number of firms - *competition:* price	- price, flight frequency and inverse load factor
Main results:	- competition leads to an increase in frequency relative to monopoly supply - increase in price leads to an increase (decrease) in flights when demand is inelastic (elastic)	- increase in price leads to a decrease in load factors - increase in the number of firms leads to an increase in flight frequency, a decrease in profits and a decrease in load factors	- welfare optimal choices of price and number of firms result in non-positive profits - competition leads to higher fares, lower load factors, and more firms compared to the welfare optimum	- time sensitive passengers incur higher fares, flight frequencies and inverse load factors than price sensitive passengers

3. Network Competition

3.1 Introduction

In the following, the model developed in Chapter 2 is extended to the analysis of hub-and-spoke systems and competition. First, network externalities in hub-and-spoke systems are discussed. Then, the size of the network of a monopoly airline is computed, and the additional supply variable ‹network density› is introduced. Again, time sensitivity of passengers influences the monopoly result. Subsequently, it is assumed that firms differentiate products by offering services to different connecting destinations and compete with fares, inverse load factors, schedule and network densities. Comparison of the results for monopoly and competitive networks indicates that competition leads to lower ticket prices, inverse load factors, schedule densities and network densities in city-pair markets. The time sensitivity of passengers influences the free-entry equilibrium number of firms and, therefore, the extent of market power in hub-and-spoke systems. The model predicts that most city-pair markets will be monopolies, and that consumer welfare may be maximized by regulation of a monopoly. However, two alternative interpretations of the model are discussed. First, if we assume that city-pair markets can be divided into a tourist segment and a business segment, the model supports the indication of *Evans* and *Kessides (1993)* that an airline's localized market power may be related to market segmentation. Second, the frequent dominance of hubs by one single airline suggests that instead of competition at hubs, there may be competition between hubs. The simple network model then is extended to a second hub. It is shown that the free-entry equilibrium number of firms for air transport between two regions decreases when the carriers choose a ‹global› network with one hub in each region instead of a ‹local› network with one hub only in the home region. Although an industry with global networks is more concentrated, it may still lead to higher consumer welfare compared to local networks if passengers are sufficiently time sensitive.

3.2 Network Externalities from Connecting Destinations

The models of *Brueckner and Spiller (1991)* and *Hendricks, Piccione and Tan (1995)*, for example, show that airlines develop hub-and-spoke systems in order to exploit economies of density on single routes. The joint use of one single route for air transport services between many indirect city-pairs leads to an increase in market density and, therefore, allows the airline to increase flight frequency. In addition, larger aircraft may be used, which leads to an increase in economies of aircraft size and to a decrease in costs and fares. Therefore, passengers may prefer indirect connections over direct connections because the time lost from changing planes at the hub airport is more than offset by lower fares and higher frequencies. With respect to time costs, *Carlton, Landes and Posner (1980)* found that passengers value *online-flights* (connecting flights with the same airline) higher compared to *interline-flights* (connecting flights with different airlines). This is due to the fact that passengers incur lower time costs from changing planes on online-flights than on interline-flights, because airlines are tempted to improve service to connecting passengers at hub airports. In doing so, they offer through tickets, allocate departures at the same gate, match schedules and try to assure that baggage is reloaded quickly. Thus, interline flights, where passengers do not have these additional services, are bad substitutes for online flights. Moreover, we can assume that in a city-pair market with several competitors offering equal supply variables, passengers to a specific final destination prefer the carrier providing an online flight. The provision of online connections, therefore, may additionally increases the efficiency of hub-and-spoke operations.

However, although the above features help to explain the existence of hub-and-spoke systems, time and transport costs passengers incur from the access to the closest airport may influence the size of the network. In what follows, a model is developed that analyzes network structures, taking access costs of passengers into account. For simplicity, it is assumed that a hub-and-spoke system is always efficient with respect to cost saving. That is, airlines incur lower costs offering a hub-and-spoke system compared to offering only direct flights. Although this assumption may be very restrictive, it is justified by the dominance of indirect connections in the airline industry today, especially with respect to services to local destinations. Starting with this basic notion, the size of a hub-and-spoke network in terms of the number of online connections is calculated.

Taking access costs of passengers into account, it is assumed that the number of online connections influences demand in a single city-pair market. In order to illustrate this type of network externality we may focus on a network structure like in *Figure 3.1.* Suppose there is a region where a monopoly airline offers flights from small cities in this region to a major city **G** in another region. In order to save costs, the airline has a hub-airport at **H**, where all passengers from the small airports around **H** are grouped and jointly transported to **G**. In this situation, we have two kinds of city-pair markets: the main market between **H** and **G** and the connecting markets from **H** to the local destinations. It is assumed that the passengers' homes are equally distributed around the circle, such that at every location on the circle there are an equal number of potential passengers. In order to take a flight to **G**, passengers pick the closest airport to them in order to save access costs in getting to the airport. We can reasonably assume that access costs are composed of costs for taking the car or the train to the airport and opportunity costs for the time needed. Thus, time sensitivity of passengers influences access costs in the same way as costs from frequency and stochastic delay. Access costs decrease when there are flights to an increasing number of small cities in the area, because the average distance from passengers' homes to the closest airport decreases. Thus, with a growing number of destinations, the variety of the services more closely approximates the distribution of consumer preferences. Therefore, it is assumed that demand for flights increases with the number of destinations served, but at a decreasing rate.

Figure 3.1: Hub-and-spoke network of a monopoly

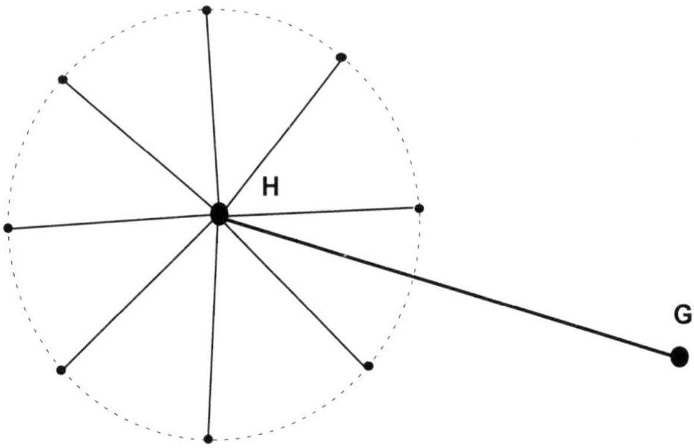

In order to set up a mathematical model, the presumably complex structure of the demand and cost functions for a network like this is simplified by a number of assumptions. First, there is no demand between the connecting destinations, between the connecting destinations and **H**, and between **G** and **H.** Thus all passengers fly from a connecting destination to **G**. Second, the flight distance to the hub airport is the same for all connecting destinations. Third, the cost parameters reflect the respective marginal costs and market distance for the whole trip, that is from the connecting destinations to **G**. Therefore, fares, inverse load factors and schedule densities apply to the entire connection. Following (2.9) and denoting the number of connecting destinations at **H** by *D*, total demand between the two regions is

$$Q = SP^{\varepsilon} X^{\alpha} E^{\beta} D^{\gamma}, \tag{3.1}$$

where $\gamma = (\partial Q/\partial D)(D/Q)$, $0 < \gamma < 1$ is the constant elasticity of demand with respect to the number of connecting destinations, which we call the network elasticity of demand. This parameter increases with increasing access costs to the nearest airport, that is expenses per mile for using the car or the train and opportunity costs for the time needed. When access costs are low, the influence of the number of connecting destinations on demand is small and vice versa. In view of the subsequent analysis, it is assumed that $\alpha + \gamma < 1$.

As is the purpose of hub-and-spoke systems, passengers from the connecting destinations are grouped at **H**, from where they are transported together to their final destination **G**. Therefore, for given supply, demand between one connecting destination and **G** is

$$Q_D = SP^{\varepsilon} X^{\alpha} E^{\beta} D^{\gamma - 1}.$$

The above equation shows that although the total number of passengers traveling between the two regions increases with the number of connecting destinations, the number of passengers for each connecting destination decreases.

The size of the network is limited by the costs airlines incur from establishing a hub airport where passengers change planes for connecting destinations. Thus it is assumed that costs from ‹hubbing› arise when connecting flights are offered out of the same airport. As an increasing number of connecting destinations are offered, the assignment of aircraft and personnel becomes more advanced. In addition, the airline needs to obtain more ground facilities like gates and has to maintain a higher level of ground services like baggage handling for connecting flights. In general, ‹hubbing costs› for providing online connections increase. Assuming that hubbing costs increase linearly with the number of markets served, they increase with the number of connecting destinations. Denoting these costs per connecting destination by h, the profit of the airline now is, like equation (2.11),

$$\Pi = (P - c - gE)Q - fX - hD. \qquad (3.2)$$

The profit function (3.2) shows that there are network externalities. On the one hand, the airline is tempted to increase the network because it increases demand. On the other hand, the firm faces increasing costs from providing online connections. Maximizing the profit function with respect to *D*, an equilibrium number of connecting destinations can be calculated, where net marginal revenue from the number of connecting destinations equals marginal hubbing costs *h*:

$$\frac{\partial Q}{\partial D}\left(P - c - gE\right) = h$$

This condition resembles the corresponding condition for flight frequency, equation (2.16), very closely. According to equations (2.26) and (2.27), the number of connecting destinations of the monopoly airline is

$$D_m = -\frac{\gamma c Q_m}{h\left(\varepsilon + \beta + 1\right)} \tag{3.3}$$

in absolute terms, or

$$B_m \equiv \frac{D_m}{Q_m} = -\frac{c}{h}\frac{\gamma}{\left(\varepsilon + 1 + \beta\right)} \tag{3.4}$$

relative to the number of passengers, where the variable B is called *network density*. Since $0 < \gamma < 1$, equation (3.2) is a concave function at the extremum, which can be demonstrated by the same procedure used for equation (2.11). Equations (3.3) and (3.4) show that the number of connecting destinations and network density increase with access costs γ, increase with passenger specific costs *c*, decrease with hubbing costs *h*, decrease with price elasticity of demand ε, and increase with time sensitivity of passengers with respect to capacity β. As for frequency, the number of connecting destinations increases with Q_m and, therefore, with market size *S*. Moreover, the number of connecting destinations and flight frequency provide externalities to each other, since both variables depend on demand in the equilibrium. Thus, an increase in the size of the network implicitly leads to an increase in flight frequency, and vice versa. The total number of passengers transported by the monopoly airline can be calculated as equation (2.28). Using equations (3.1) and (3.4), the monopoly output is

$$Q_m = SP_m^{\ \varepsilon}(F_m Q_m)^{\alpha} E_m^{\ \beta}(B_m Q_m)^{\gamma},$$

which is equal to

$$Q_m = S^{\left(\frac{1}{1-\alpha-\gamma}\right)} P_m^{\left(\frac{\varepsilon}{1-\alpha-\gamma}\right)} F_m^{\left(\frac{\alpha}{1-\alpha-\gamma}\right)} E_m^{\left(\frac{\beta}{1-\alpha-\gamma}\right)} B_m^{\left(\frac{\gamma}{1-\alpha-\gamma}\right)}. \qquad (3.5)$$

Product Differentiation with Departure Times or Destinations?

The model of *Panzar (1979)* assumes that airlines differentiate their products by offering flights at different departure times during the day. In contrast, the model developed in this chapter assumes that firms have equal departure times but differentiate products by offering connections to different destinations at the hub airport. The question therefore arises as to what extent the two simplifying assumptions correspond to reality. For this reason, city-pair markets of *American Airlines* (AA) and *United Airlines* (UAL), that both use the Chicago O'Hare Airport (Illinois) as one of their major hub airports, are analyzed with respect to departure times and connecting local destinations.

The data for flight frequency were collected from the 1994 timetables of the two airlines and reflect a random selection of seven non-hub destinations in the East and the South of the US that are served by both airlines with direct flights from Chicago. The destinations are Philadelphia, Boston, Atlanta, Harrisburg, New Orleans, Rochester NY and Buffalo. The degree of similarity of departure times (*SIM*) may be defined as the ratio of the average delay in minutes between the direct flights of *American Airlines* and the closest flights of *United Airlines* (*AD*) to the average interval in minutes between the direct flights of *American Airlines* (*IAA*):

$$SIM = \frac{AD}{IAA}.$$

A large degree of product differentiation would imply a value of *SIM* close to 0.5, indicating that on average *United Airlines* offers her flights right between the flights of *American Airlines.* A *SIM* close to zero on the other hand indicates that the competitors provide their flights more or less at the same time. *Table 3.1* presents the results. The last column shows that in all observed markets, the value of *SIM* is below 0.3. This suggests that on average, the two airlines offer flights at similar departure times rather than differentiate their services. Column four indicates that in all markets except Chicago-Harrisburg, the average delay is below 40 minutes. Moreover, a closer look at the timetables reveals that delays are particularly small at peak times. In fact, without going into further detail, it seems that the existence of peak demand periods is the main cause of the small degree of product differentiation with departure times of flights.

Table 3.1: Product differentiation with departure times

Destination	***Daily Flights***	***IAA***	***AD***	***SIM***
Atlanta, GA	6	258	26.7	0.10
Boston, MA	9	103	30	0.29
Buffalo, NY	5	207	38.6	0.19
Harrisburg, PA	3	213	48	0.23
New Orleans, LA	3	290	35	0.12
Philadelphia, PA	7	131	30	0.23
Rochester, NY	5	201	28	0.14

In order to determine whether airlines offer differentiated products with respect to networks rather than similar connecting destinations, local flights of *American Airlines* and *United Airlines* from their hubs at Chicago to destinations in Illinois and to neighboring states of Illinois are examined. The destinations observed are located in Illinois, Missouri, Wisconsin, Indiana, Iowa, Mississippi, and Kentucky. *American Airlines*, together with its commuter carrier *American Eagle*, offers flights to 27 destinations in this area. *United Airlines* and its commuter carrier *United Express* offers flights to 31 destinations. Of the total number of airports either served by *American Airlines* or *United Airlines*, 18 are served by both carriers, whereas 22 destinations are served by only one of the two carriers. Therefore, the majority of local destinations is only served by one of the carriers, which indicates a fair degree of product differentiation with networks. This feature is demonstrated by the *Figure 3.2*, which shows the locations of the airports analyzed above. A closer look indicates that larger cities especially are served by both carriers, whereas smaller cities are often only served by either *American* or *United.*

Figure 3.2: Product differentiation with local destinations

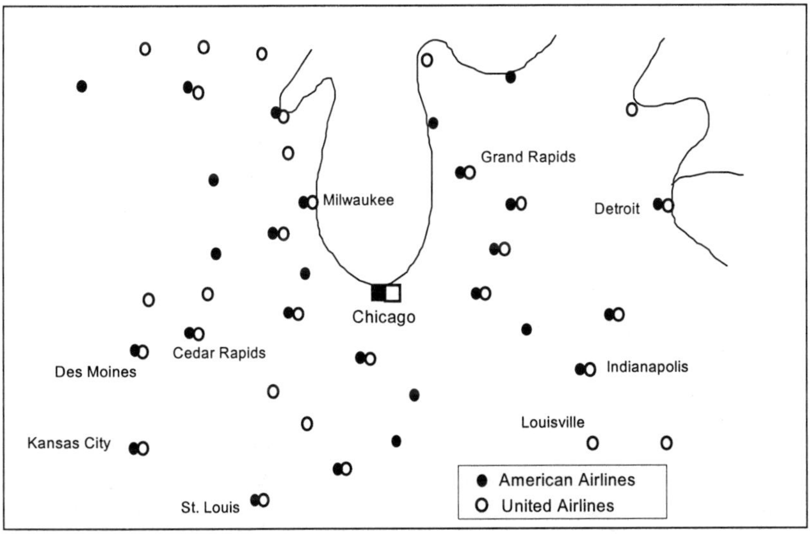

However, it is important to note that the degree of product differentiation may be understated in the above analysis, because Chicago is used as a hub by both carriers. As will be shown in Chapter 4, airlines are also tempted to differentiate products by locating hubs in different regions. In the Mid-South, for example, where *American Airlines* operates a hub at Dallas/Fort Worth, connections with *United Airlines* are virtually non-existent. In the Mountain area, on the other hand, where *United Airlines* operates a hub at Denver, *American Airlines* only offers flights to a few large destinations. Thus, although the assumption that firms offer completely different destinations may be too rigorous, product differentiation with respect to networks in general is a quite realistic assumption for the model.

3.3 Monopolistic Competition

In this section, the above model is extended to a competitive framework. Consider – in a first step – a second airline that also offers services on the main stage **GH**. Based on the analysis in the box above, the two airlines offer differentiated products by providing air transport to different connecting destinations. Although no particular model of location choices is used, it is assumed that the airlines wish to differentiate their products as much as possible.[1] Therefore airlines fly to neighboring airports rather than to the same airports in the region, as it is depicted in *Figure 3.3*. In this situation, we again face two different kinds of markets.

1 Two well-known models in the literature of product differentiation provide the theoretical foundation for the discussion with respect to maximum or minimum product differentiation. Whereas the model of *Hotelling (1929)* advocates minimum product differentiation, the reply of *d'Aspremont, Grabszewicz and Thisse (1979)* shows that the opposite may be true. A summary of the arguments for either maximal or minimal differentiation is found in *Tirole (1988)*, p. 286f.

Figure 3.3: Duopoly of hub-and-spoke networks

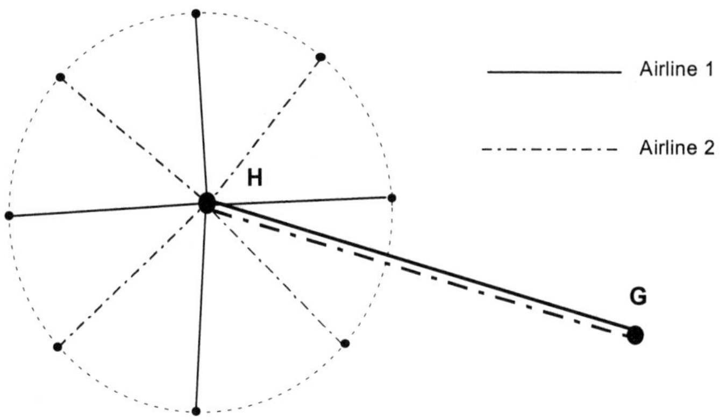

First, there is a main stage **GH**, where we have competition between airlines. Second there are the connecting markets from H to the local destinations, which we assume to be monopoly markets. Like the number of connecting destinations of a monopoly airline, access costs decline as more airlines enter the market, because the total number of small cities served increases and, therefore, approaches the preferences of passengers. In the circular model, passengers choose the airport that offers the ‹best› combination of flight frequency and load factor for the lowest total price that includes the fare and access costs to the airport. Thus, if the two airlines offer the same supply and the same number of connecting destinations, passengers choose the closest airport. But when one airline (for example airline 1) improves its supply relative to the competitor, some passengers are tempted to choose an airport of airline 1 although it is more distant from their location on the circle than the airport of airline 2. This demand shift depends on access costs. When unit access costs are low, even a small change of the supply of airline 1 leads to a relatively large demand shift from airline 2 to airline 1, because a higher distance to the airport only leads to a small increase in total access costs. When access costs are high, the same change of supply only leads to a relatively small demand shift.

In order to apply this concept to the case of n airlines, and with respect to a spatial interpretation, it is necessary to drop the assumption that passengers live on a circle, as was suggested in the monopoly case and the duopoly case. Instead, we assume that the passengers are equally distributed in an area and that more than two firms can compete with each other. Assuming that all destinations have the same size in terms of the population and that the airlines are of equal size in terms of the number of connecting destinations D, demand for air transport in the main city-pair market has the same size for each airline. It is additionally assumed that the airlines have the same departure times for equal flight frequencies on **GH** and that it is not possible to use the tickets of one airline for flights with a competitor.[2] If all firms in the market are of equal size and offer the same supply variables, market demandon the stage **GH** is

$$Q_N = SP^{\varepsilon} X^{\alpha} E^{\beta} (Dn)^{\gamma} . \tag{3.6}$$

The term in the brackets in equation (3.6) accounts for the fact that because firms offer different connecting destinations, the total number of connecting destinations increases linearly with the number of firms n in the market. Demand for one single firm's service is given by

$$Q_i^R \equiv \frac{Q_N}{n} = SP^{\varepsilon} X^{\alpha} E^{\beta} D^{\gamma} n^{\gamma - 1} .$$

The variable Q_i^R denotes the *pro-rata demand* for the service of a single firm, where firms act simultaneously and therefore have equal outputs and supply variables. The pro-rata demand function reflects the notion that for simultaneous actions of all firms in the market, the single airline cannot increase its market

2 This means that there is no *Interlining*. Agreements for *Interlining* regulate the mutual acceptance of tickets between carriers and are administered by *IATA (International Air Transport Association)*; cf. Section 1.2 .

share, although it may have incentives to do so. Whereas total market demand increases with the number of firms, the single airline's pro-rata demand decreases with a growing number of competitors. For convenience, market demand and pro-rata demand can be expressed in terms of the hypothetical monopoly demand of the single firm, which is denoted by $\widetilde{Q}$:

$$Q_N = \widetilde{Q} n^{\gamma} \text{, and} \tag{3.7}$$

$$Q_i^R = \widetilde{Q} n^{\gamma - 1}, \tag{3.8}$$

where $\widetilde{Q} \equiv SP^{\varepsilon} X^{\alpha} E^{\beta} D^{\gamma}$. The incentives of the single firm to change its supply variables are determined by the elasticities of a *perceived* demand function. The perceived demand function reflects the illusion of the single firm that, by changing the price, load factor, flight frequency and/or the number of connecting destinations relative to competitors, it can win customers away from them and thereby increase profit. Thus, the perceived demand function is the single airline's demand for constant supply variables of competitors.[3]

In order to construct a perceived demand function, equations (3.7) and (3.8) are written in terms of market shares, where we assume symmetric firms and equal supply first. Denoting the demand for one single firm by Q_i and the demand for one of the $(n-1)$ other airlines in the market by Q_j, the market share of a representative airline i is

$$s_i = \frac{Q_i}{Q_i + (n-1) Q_j}. \tag{3.9}$$

If all airlines make the same offer, they face equal demand, which implies that $s_i = 1/n$, or $n = 1/s_i$. Replacing n in equation (3.7) by the inverse of the market

3 This approach to monopolistic competition is based on the model of *Chamberlin (1933)*. See, for example, *Hirshleifer (1984)*, pp. 275-279.

share and replacing the market share by equation (3.9), the market demand function may be written as follows,

$$Q_N = \tilde{Q}\left(1+(n-1)\frac{Q_j}{Q_i}\right)^{\gamma}, \tag{3.10}$$

and the pro-rata demand for airline i is

$$Q_i^R = s_i Q_N = \tilde{Q}\left(1+(n-1)\frac{Q_j}{Q_i}\right)^{\gamma-1}.$$

Since it is assumed that the firms are of equal size and have the same cost functions, it must be $\left(Q_j/Q_i\right)=1$ by definition if each firm is on its pro-rata demand curve. Introducing $\Omega=\left(Q_j/Q_i\right)$, any situation where $\Omega \neq 1$ can then be interpreted as a deviation from the pro-rata demand curves. For equal carriers, any deviation from the pro-rata demand curve requires that the firms offer different prices, flight frequencies, inverse load factors and numbers of connecting destinations. In addition, a deviation requires that consumers are willing to switch carriers because of different supply variables. It therefore can be assumed that Ω is a function of the ratio between the supply variables of the representative firm i and competitors j and of the substitutability of services. Since the perceived demand function of a single firm represents deviations from the pro-rata demand function, and taking into account that any deviation from the pro-rata demand function depends on the ratio of supply variables and the substitutability of products, the perceived demand function can be defined as a function of Ω. The perceived demand function of a representative firm i therefore is denoted by

$$Q_i = \tilde{Q}\left[1+(n-1)\Omega\right]^{\gamma-1}, \tag{3.11}$$

where Ω is redefined as follows:

$$\Omega \equiv \left(\frac{P_j^\varepsilon X_j^\alpha E_j^\beta D_j^\gamma}{P_i^\varepsilon X_i^\alpha E_i^\beta D_i^\gamma} \right)^\sigma , \tag{3.12}$$

where we assume
$$\sigma \equiv \frac{n(1-\gamma)}{\gamma} . \tag{3.13}$$

Equations (3.12) and (3.13) reflect the concept of competition between airports introduced above. The functional form of (3.13) is motivated as follows: The passengers' willingness to substitute one airline for another because of changed supply variables mainly depends on the distance between the two airports and access costs. While access costs are expressed by the parameter γ, the distance between airports is determined by the number of competitors.

Since airlines differentiate their networks with connecting destinations, σ actually expresses the homogeneity of the services of the competing firms. When γ approximates 0, e.g. when passengers incur no access costs from getting to the closest airport, competing airlines offer close substitutes, because the passengers do not care which airport they use for departure or arrival. In this case, even a small improvement of an airline's supply leads to a big change in market shares, which is expressed by a σ approaching infinity. When γ approximates 1, that is when passengers face very high access costs, passengers do not substitute the services of competitors for each other even when there is an improvement of an airline's supply, which is expressed by a σ close to 0.

As the number of firms increases, the number of connecting destinations in an area also increases, which implies that the variety of connecting destinations more closely approximates the distribution of passengers in the area. It follows that the average distance between airports and, therefore, access costs decrease. This implies that the demand shift from an improvement of supply increases with the number of firms. Thus, σ decreases with γ and increases with n.

By use of equations (3.11)-(3.13), the perceived demand function can be rewritten as follows:

$$Q_i = \widetilde{Q}\left[1+(n-1)\left(\frac{R_j}{R_i}\right)^{\sigma}\right]^{\gamma-1}, \tag{3.14}$$

where $R_i = P_i^{\varepsilon} X_i^{\alpha} E_i^{\beta} D_i^{\gamma}$ and $R_j = P_j^{\varepsilon} X_j^{\alpha} E_j^{\beta} D_j^{\gamma}$. Taking into account the fact that the market share of one of the other firms in the market is $s_j = Q_j / \left[Q_i + (n-1)Q_j\right]$, the respective residual demand function for the $(n-1)$ other firms in the market is

$$(n-1)Q_j = (n-1)\widetilde{Q}\left[n-1+\left(\frac{R_i}{R_j}\right)^{\sigma}\right]^{\gamma-1}.$$

This function reflects the remaining demand for the services of all the other firms in the market, holding their supply variables constant while firm *i* changes its supply variables. *Figure 3.4* shows simulations of frequency competition for constant prices, inverse load factors, number of connecting destinations and $n = 2$. As can be seen in both panels, the perceived demand function of firm *i*, Q_i, approaches monopoly demand $\widetilde{Q}$ as firm *i* increases the number of flights relative to the (constant) number of flights of firm *j*. Because firm *j* looses demand to firm *i*, the residual demand function of firm *j*, Q_j, approaches zero. Consequently, the market demand function Q_N approaches monopoly demand $\widetilde{Q}$ as firm *i* becomes the only airline selling seats. The same properties apply to changes in prices, inverse load factors and connecting destinations according to the respective elasticities. The system of demand functions, therefore, takes into account the fact that when the improvement of firm *i*'s supply variables relative to the supply variables of competitors is sufficiently high, firm *i* captures the entire market demand. However, this business stealing effect depends on access costs γ.

Figure 3.4: System of demand functions

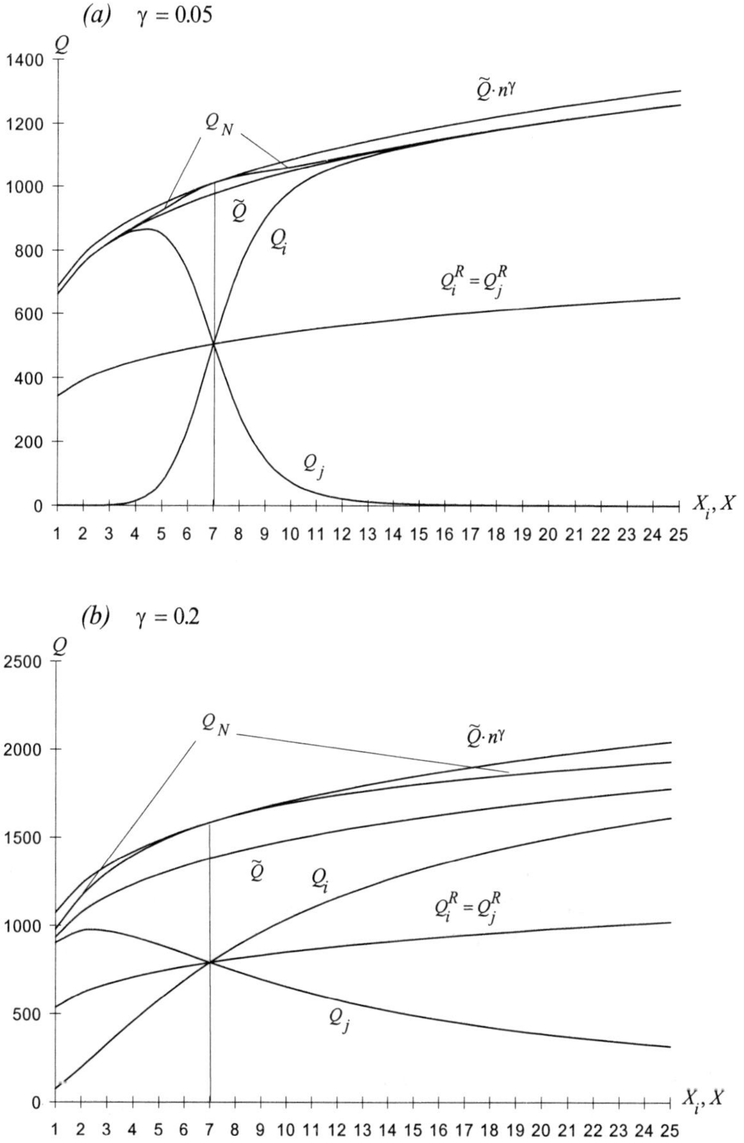

Figure 3.4 shows that when γ is low, the products are easily substituted, which implies that, for example, even a small improvement in carrier *i*'s flight frequency leads to a large increase in demand for carrier *i*, which corresponds to the situation in panel (a). On the other hand, when γ is large, the products are bad substitutes, and only a large improvement of firm *i*'s flight frequency leads to a substantial increase in demand for firm i, which corresponds to panel (b).[4]

Using the above definition of a perceived demand function, the single airline maximizes the profit function

$$\Pi_i = P_i Q_i - (c + gE)Q_i - fX_i - hD_i .$$

Starting with equation (3.14), the elasticities of the perceived demand function can be calculated.[5] For every point on the pro-rata demand function, where we have equal supply variables and market shares, price elasticity of the single firm is

$$\varepsilon_i = \frac{\partial Q_i}{\partial P_i}\frac{P_i}{Q_i} = \varepsilon\theta \text{, with} \tag{3.15}$$

$$\theta = 1 + (n-1)\frac{(\gamma - 1)^2}{\gamma}. \tag{3.15a}$$

Similarly, we have

$$\alpha_i = \alpha\theta,\ \beta_i = \beta\theta, \text{ and } \gamma_i = \gamma\theta .$$

The elasticities of the perceived demand function increase with the number of competitors, increase with market demand elasticities and decrease with access costs, e.g. the degree of diversity between the products.

4 The parameter values for both figures are: $\varepsilon = -1.5, \alpha = 0.2$, $\beta = 0.2$, $S = 1000000$, $P_i = P_j = 150$, $E_i = E_j = 1.5$, and $D_i = D_j = 10$, $X_j = 7$, and X_i variable.

5 See Appendix A.

The increased elasticities imply that the profit maximizing supply of the single firm differ from the monopoly solution. The supply variables of the single firm can be computed according to (2.24)-(2.27) and (3.4) using ε_i, α_i, β_i and γ_i :

$$P_i = \frac{c}{\left(1+\frac{1+\beta_i}{\varepsilon_i}\right)}, \tag{3.16}$$

$$E_i = -\frac{c}{g}\frac{1}{\left(\frac{\varepsilon_i+1}{\beta_i}+1\right)}, \tag{3.17}$$

$$F_i = \frac{X_i}{Q_i} = -\frac{\alpha_i c}{f(\varepsilon_i+1+\beta_i)}, \text{ and} \tag{3.18}$$

$$B_i = \frac{D_i}{Q_i} = -\frac{\gamma_i c}{h(\varepsilon_i+\beta_i+1)}. \tag{3.19}$$

F_i and B_i denote schedule and network densities of the single carrier. If all firms in the market offer these supply variables, incentives to change output variables vanish, because they maximize the private profit of the single airline according to the elasticities of the perceived demand function and firms are on the pro-rata demand curve:

$$Q_i = Q_i^R \quad \forall\, i = 1 \ldots n.$$

The supply variables determined by (3.16) to (3.19) represent the competitive equilibrium for a given number of firms. Because the elasticities of single firms increase with the number of firms *n*, the values of the single firm's supply variables decrease with the number of firms. This result may be demonstrated for the inverse load factor. Equation (3.15a) shows that θ increases with *n*. According to equation (3.17), the inverse load factor is

$$E_i = -\frac{c}{g} \frac{\beta}{\left(\varepsilon + \beta + \frac{1}{\theta}\right)}.$$

Now observe that the denominator is always negative for the restriction imposed on elasticities earlier, $\varepsilon < -(\beta + 1)$. If θ increases, the absolute value of the denominator becomes larger, which leads to a decrease in E_i. The same reasoning applies to the other supply variables. Thus, the ticket price, the inverse load factor, schedule and network density decrease as more competitors enter the market. This implies that competition not only leads to a decrease in fares, but also to a decrease in quality, which raises concern about the effects of competition on consumer welfare. The theoretical results correspond to empirical findings, that demonstrate that quality in terms of load factors and flight frequencies has fallen after deregulation.[6] However, although schedule and network density decrease, the number of flights and the number of connecting destinations may increase when α and γ are sufficiently high and when competition leads to a large increase in demand for the single firm. In order to analyze the problem of consumer welfare in detail, we first calculate the free-entry equilibrium number of firms.

3.4 Free-Entry Equilibrium Number of Firms

One of the most important implications of a growing number of firms in the market is the elimination of monopoly profits. Compared to other models of monopolistic competition, where fixed costs or entry costs determine the equilibrium number of firms in the market, this model predicts that the equilibrium number of firms, and therefore the number of competing networks in a particular region, is determined by passengers' valuation of flight

6 See, for example, *Gaynor and Trapani III (1994).*

frequency and network size. The profit of a single firm and the total profit of all firms in the main market are

$$\Pi_i = \left(P_i - c - gE_i\right)Q_i - fX_i - hD_i \text{, and} \tag{3.20}$$

$$\Pi_N = n\Pi_i = \left(P_i - c - gE_i\right)Q_N - nfX_i - nhD_i . \tag{3.21}$$

Taking into account that the firms have equal departure times, nfX_i in (3.21) indicates that competition leads to a multiplication of the schedule. As will be shown later, this has some interesting implications for the free-entry equilibrium number of firms.

In order to derive the free-entry equilibrium number of firms, where none of the airlines still makes profits, the profit margin – defined as the *profit relative to total revenue* – is calculated according to Appendix B. Using equations (3.16)-(3.20), the profit margin of the single firm, denoted by Φ_i, is

$$\Phi_i = \frac{\Pi_i}{P_i Q_i} = \frac{\alpha_i + \gamma_i - 1}{\varepsilon_i} . \tag{3.22}$$

The profit margin decreases with increasing price, frequency and network elasticities. For constant elasticities of market demand, the profit margin therefore decreases with the number of firms in the market. If incumbent firms have positive profits and if there are no entry barriers, additional firms enter until all (identical) firms have zero profit margins. According to equation (3.22) the profit margin is positive as long as $\alpha_i + \gamma_i < 1$. This condition implies

$$(\alpha + \gamma)\left[1 + (n-1)\frac{(\gamma - 1)^2}{\gamma}\right] - 1 < 0 , \tag{3.23}$$

indicating that the firms still have positive profits as long as

$$n < \frac{\gamma(1 - \alpha - \gamma)}{(\alpha + \gamma)(\gamma - 1)^2} + 1 .$$

Therefore, the free-entry equilibrium number of firms is (the integer part of)

$$n^* = \frac{\gamma(1-\alpha-\gamma)}{(\alpha+\gamma)(\gamma-1)^2} + 1. \tag{3.24}$$

In order to get a free-entry equilibrium number of firms that equals at least one, we have to impose the condition $\alpha + \gamma \leq 1$. It is assumed that this condition holds for all the following results of the model. Inserting the free-entry equilibrium number of firms into the multiplier of market demand elasticities θ [equation (3.15a)] leads to the free-entry equilibrium elasticities.

$$\varepsilon_i^* = \frac{\varepsilon}{\alpha+\gamma}, \; \alpha_i^* = \frac{\alpha}{\alpha+\gamma}, \; \beta_i^* = \frac{\beta}{\alpha+\gamma} \text{ and } \gamma_i^* = \frac{\gamma}{\alpha+\gamma}.$$

The free-entry equilibrium ticket price, inverse load factor, schedule and network densities then are, according to (3.16)-(3.19),

$$P_i^* = \frac{c}{\left(1+\dfrac{\alpha+\beta+\gamma}{\varepsilon}\right)}, \tag{3.25}$$

$$E_i^* = -\frac{c}{g}\frac{1}{\left(1+\dfrac{\varepsilon+\alpha+\gamma}{\beta}\right)}, \tag{3.26}$$

$$F_i^* = \frac{X_i^*}{Q_i^*} = -\frac{c}{f}\frac{1}{\left(1+\dfrac{\varepsilon+\beta+\gamma}{\alpha}\right)}, \text{ and} \tag{3.27}$$

$$B_i^* = \frac{D_i^*}{Q_i^*} = -\frac{c}{h}\frac{1}{\left(1+\dfrac{\varepsilon+\alpha+\beta}{\gamma}\right)}. \tag{3.28}$$

The market output in the free-entry equilibrium is

$$Q_N^* = SP_i^{*\varepsilon} X_i^{*\alpha} E_i^{*\beta} D_i^{*\gamma} n^{*\gamma} . \tag{3.29}$$

This is equal to

$$Q_N^* = SP_i^{*\varepsilon} \left(F_i^* Q_i^*\right)^{\alpha} E_i^{*\beta} \left(B_i^* Q_i^* n^*\right)^{\gamma} .$$

Since $Q_i = Q_N / n$ we have

$$Q_N^* = SP_i^{*\varepsilon} \left[\left(F_i^* Q_N^*\right) / n^*\right]^{\alpha} E_i^{*\beta} \left(B_i^* Q_N^*\right)^{\gamma} ,$$

which finally is equal to the following:

$$Q_N^* = S^{\left(\frac{1}{1-\alpha-\gamma}\right)} P_i^{*\left(\frac{\varepsilon}{1-\alpha-\gamma}\right)} \left(F_i^* / n^*\right)^{\left(\frac{\alpha}{1-\alpha-\gamma}\right)} E_i^{*\left(\frac{\beta}{1-\alpha-\gamma}\right)} B_i^{*\left(\frac{\gamma}{1-\alpha-\gamma}\right)} . \tag{3.30}$$

Looking at the term F_i^* / n^*, equation (3.30) shows that whenever the free-entry equilibrium number of firms exceeds one, a monopoly airline offering the competitive fare, schedule density, inverse load factor and network density would lead to a higher total output. This result can be explained as follows: In the profit maximizing equilibrium of the firm, the number of flights increases with the number of passengers transported, as equation (2.26) shows for the monopoly case and equation (3.18) suggests for the competitive case. Because total demand increases with the number of firms at a decreasing rate, output per firm decreases as more firms enter the market. This leads to a reduction in the equilibrium number of flights of the single firm. The lower flight frequency, in turn, implies a reduction in total demand. However, one has to take into account the fact that this result is due to the assumption that firms have the same departure times, e.g. that they do not compete by offering different departure times. Otherwise, flight frequency and, consequently, total demand would increase with the number of firms, as it is the case for the number of connecting destinations.

Figure 3.5: Free-entry equilibrium number of firms for different time sensitivities

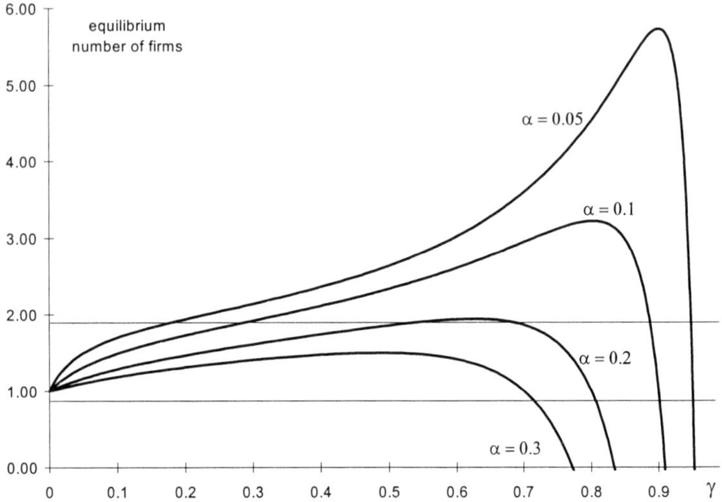

The influence of market demand elasticities on the equilibrium number of firms can be determined by simulation of equation (3.24). In *Figure 3.5*, the equilibrium number of firms is depicted as functions of γ for different values of α. Because large values of α always lead to an equilibrium number of firms below 2 for the whole range of γ, particularly low values of α were chosen for the illustration of the equilibrium number of firms. It can be seen that the equilibrium number of firms first increases with γ before decreasing again. For a constant γ, the equilibrium number of firms decreases as α increases. For high values of α, the free-entry equilibrium number of firms indicates a natural monopoly situation. Moreover, when we assume that α and γ are mainly influenced by the time sensitivity of passengers, we must conclude that city-pair markets are likely to be monopolies. When passengers are time sensitive, both parameters have relatively high values. As can be seen in *Figure 3.5*, respective combinations of elasticities indicate profitable production by only one firm. When passengers are price sensitive, both parameters have relatively low values. This may also lead to a monopoly, although this tendency is not as strong as in the time sensitive case.

The analysis of the profit margin implies that only when frequency elasticity is sufficiently low compared to network elasticity of demand can more than one firm operate at a profit. In other words, competition only exists when the carriers are able to offer sufficiently differentiated products. Thus, the influence of frequency and network elasticities of demand on the equilibrium number of firms requires further attention. In this respect recall that it is assumed that airlines do have equal departure times for their flights. This means that airlines may compete with the density of the schedule, but they do not compete with different departure times. As a result, a growing number of airlines in a city-pair market leads to a multiplication of the schedules, which increases total flight specific costs in the market and the single airline's flight specific costs relative to its demand. Furthermore, if firms have the same departure times, market demand is not related to the total number of flights in the market, but depends on the number of flights of the single firm. If, for example, a monopoly airline with two flights faces a new entrant, the resulting increase in market demand is not due to the additional two flights of the entrant, but is a result of the increase in the number of online connections. Since market demand increases less than proportionately with the number of firms, the single airline's demand and revenue are reduced. Similarly, because the optimal ticket price (3.16) is not influenced by the frequency elasticity of demand, an increase of frequency elasticity and the resulting increase in the number of flights leads, everything else being equal, to an increase in average costs, while the ticket price remains constant. Thus, the margin between price and average costs decreases with increasing frequency elasticity of demand. Therefore, the break-even point of the single firm, where profits are zero, is reached at a lower number of firms if, due to a high time sensitivity of passengers towards frequency, the incumbent monopolist is already offering a dense schedule and, therefore, already incurs high average costs relative to the optimal ticket price.

The influence of network elasticity is twofold. On the one hand, a high γ allows a new entrant to differentiate its product. Firms usually want to differentiate their products in order to soften price competition, or – in our model – to soften competition with fares, flight frequencies, load factors, and the number of online connections. Since a high γ stands for high access costs, the connecting destinations of an entrant are bad substitutes for the airports of the incumbent airlines. Thus, the competitors have local monopoly power on the connecting destinations and competition can be avoided to a certain extent. On the other hand, as with the schedule, a high network elasticity encourages airlines to compete with networks. Therefore, networks are increasingly duplicated as new firms enter the market and the location of connecting destinations increasingly corresponds to the preferences of passengers. As with the schedule, this leads to a reduction of the profit margin. As equation (3.22) shows, this reduction increases with an increasing network elasticity of demand, because a high γ calls for a large network, which leads to relatively high average costs. When network elasticity of demand is sufficiently high, the reduction of the profit margin outweighs the local monopoly power from product differentiation, and monopoly is the only profitable industry structure. Moreover, when $\alpha + \gamma > 1$, scheduled air transport is not profitable even for a monopoly, which means that there will be no scheduled flights to that area at all.

Since the model implies that city-pair markets to hub airports may be monopolies, it can partially explain the structure of today's airline industry in the US, where regions usually are characterized by one hub airport that is dominated by one firm. Because of this natural monopoly characteristic of hub airports, it has to be presumed that today the large airlines rather compete *at* hubs than compete on hubs. In this case, one could imagine a monopolistic competition framework where hubs in different regions are the distinct features of the competing airlines. Passengers face differentiated services in that they can choose between connecting services via different hubs. Competition in specific city-pair markets between hubs then can be viewed as the overlapping of spokes belonging to the different hubs. Similarly, the existence of other firms with lower enplanement shares at a hub airport that is dominated by one firm can be explained. An extension of the present model in that direction will follow in Chapter 4.

However, the above result that major city-pair markets are dominated by monopolies cannot be accepted without reservations. First, there is an integer problem in the model, because there are market conditions where one firm makes a profit but two firms would incur losses.[7] Second, although the model is able to explain concentration of firms at hub airports, it does not account for the fact that there usually is a dominant firm and, at the same time, ‹weak› firms at most hub airports, where the former has larger market shares and has substantial pricing power in markets to that hub compared with the latter. As *Evans and Kessides (1993)* suggest, this may be due to the fact that larger firms attract a different type of traveler. The results of the model support this view, if we assume that there are time sensitive and price sensitive passengers in the same market. In this case, market segmentation in a particular city-pair market may explain differences between airlines with respect to online connections, price, flight frequency and load factors. Assume that a market can be divided into a price sensitive tourist segment and a time sensitive business segment. In this case, airlines offering flights in the business segment offer higher fares, higher schedule densities and lower load factors than airlines in the tourist segment, although they basically operate in the same market. In addition, network externalities imply that for time sensitive passengers airlines offer a denser network than for passengers with a low time sensitivity. Therefore, the ‹business› (or ‹high cost›) airline has a lot of connecting destinations whereas the ‹tourist› (or ‹low cost›) airline offers few connecting destinations at the hub airport. *Figure 3.6* provides an illustration of this industry structure. If airlines operate in different market segments, competition is limited and there is an equilibrium number of firms for each segment, depending on the corresponding

7 For the integer problem in models of product differentiation, see for example *Eaton and Lipsey (1989)*.

elasticities. In the case of natural monopolies, the airlines concerned incur local market power in their segments.

Figure 3.6: ‹High-cost› and ‹low-cost› airline in the same market

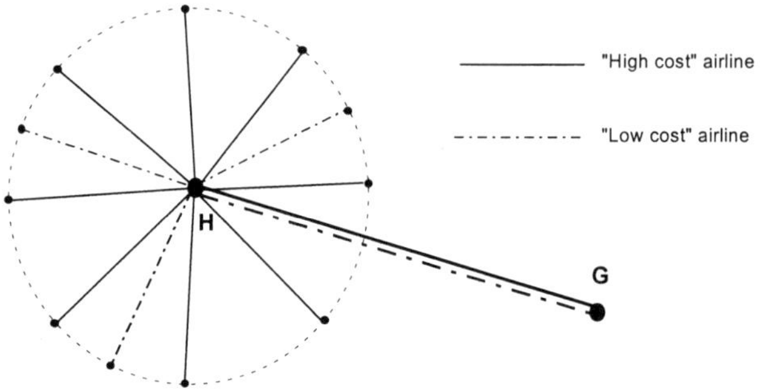

3.5 Consumer Welfare

In the following, the welfare implications of competition are discussed by comparing consumer surplus for different market structures. As *Figure 3.7* shows, consumer surplus is defined by the area under the demand function limited by the ticket price. Schedule density, inverse load factor and network density are accounted for indirectly by shifts in the demand function. A rise in the inverse load factor, for example, shifts the demand curve to the right and thereby increases consumer surplus. Conversely, a decrease in flight frequency shifts the demand curve to the left and thereby reduces consumer surplus. Consumer surplus, therefore, is a function of service quality as well as of the ticket price.

Denoting consumer surplus by V, and assuming that the indefinite integral exists, we have for given values of X, E, D and n,

$$V = \int_{P^*}^{\infty} Q\left(P; \overline{X}, \overline{E}, \overline{D}, \overline{n}\right) dP. \qquad (3.31)$$

For the constant elasticity demand function, this is

$$V = \int_{P^*}^{\infty} \left(S P^{\varepsilon} \overline{X}^{\alpha} \overline{E}^{\beta} \overline{D}^{\gamma} \overline{n}^{\gamma} \right) dP.$$

The value of this integral is given by

$$V = \frac{1}{\varepsilon + 1} S \overline{X}^{\alpha} \overline{E}^{\beta} \overline{D}^{\gamma} \overline{n}^{\gamma} P^{\varepsilon + 1} \Big]_{P^*}^{\infty},$$

Since

$$\lim_{P \to \infty} P^{\varepsilon + 1} = 0,$$

consumer surplus can be approximated by,

$$V = -\frac{1}{\varepsilon + 1} S \overline{X}^{\alpha} \overline{E}^{\beta} \overline{D}^{\gamma} \overline{n}^{\gamma} P^{*\varepsilon + 1}. \qquad (3.32)$$

In the equilibrium, the consumer surplus then is equal to

$$V = \frac{-1}{\varepsilon + 1} Q^* P^*. \qquad (3.33)$$

Figure 3.7: Consumer surplus

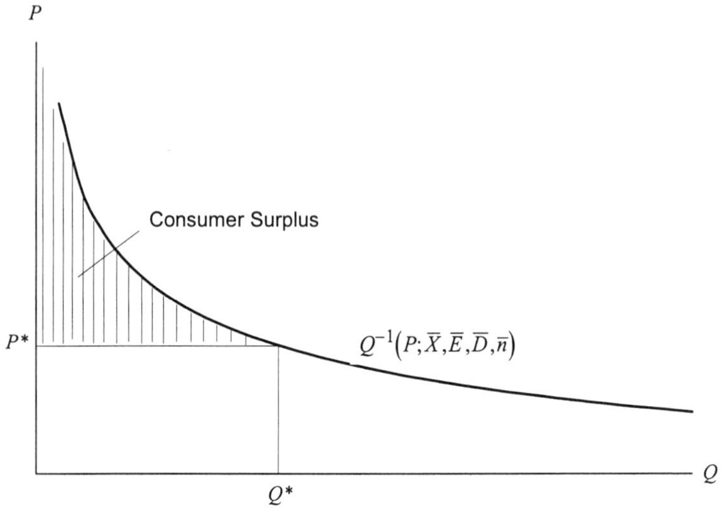

The welfare effects of a change in market structures from monopoly to competitive supply can now be analyzed by comparing the change in consumer surplus. Note that changes in the consumer surplus usually would include an income effect. However, because income does not appear in our demand function, the income effect is neglected. In order to calculate the consumer surplus in the monopoly equilibrium, we write

$$V_m = \int_{P_m}^{\infty} Q dP,$$

with, according to equation (3.5),

$$Q = S^{\left(\frac{1}{1-\alpha-\gamma}\right)} P^{\left(\frac{\varepsilon}{1-\alpha-\gamma}\right)} F^{\left(\frac{\alpha}{1-\alpha-\gamma}\right)} E^{\left(\frac{\beta}{1-\alpha-\gamma}\right)} B^{\left(\frac{\gamma}{1-\alpha-\gamma}\right)}.$$

For the monopoly supply variables, this is

$$V_m = \left[-1\Big/\left(\frac{\varepsilon}{1-\alpha-\gamma}+1\right)\right] Q_m P_m . \tag{3.34}$$

Similarly, the consumer surplus in the free-entry equilibrium is

$$V_N^* = \int_{P_i^*}^{\infty} Q_N dP,$$

with, according to equation (3.30),

$$Q_N = S^{\left(\frac{1}{1-\alpha-\gamma}\right)} P_i^{\left(\frac{\varepsilon}{1-\alpha-\gamma}\right)} \left(F_i / n\right)^{\left(\frac{\alpha}{1-\alpha-\gamma}\right)} E_i^{\left(\frac{\beta}{1-\alpha-\gamma}\right)} B_i^{\left(\frac{\gamma}{1-\alpha-\gamma}\right)} .$$

For the free-entry equilibrium supply variables we have

$$V_N^* = \left[-1\Big/\left(\frac{\varepsilon}{1-\alpha-\gamma}+1\right)\right] Q_N^* P_i^* . \tag{3.35}$$

Competition leads to higher welfare than monopoly supply if

$$\frac{V_N^*}{V_m} = \frac{Q_N^* P_i^*}{Q_m P_m} > 1 .$$

This ‹welfare ratio› can be calculated by using equations (3.5) for the monopoly case and (3.30) for the competitive case. We therefore have

$$\frac{V_N^*}{V_m} = \left(\frac{P_i^*}{P_m}\right)^{\left(\frac{\varepsilon}{1-\alpha-\gamma}+1\right)} \left(\frac{F_i^*}{F_m n^*}\right)^{\left(\frac{\alpha}{1-\alpha-\gamma}\right)} \left(\frac{E_i^*}{E_m}\right)^{\left(\frac{\beta}{1-\alpha-\gamma}\right)} \left(\frac{B_i^*}{B_m}\right)^{\left(\frac{\gamma}{1-\alpha-\gamma}\right)} .$$

Using the respective supply variables from equations (2.24), (2.25), (2.27), (3.4), and (3.25) - (3.28), the welfare ratio can be reduced to

$$\frac{V_N^*}{V_m} = \left(\frac{\varepsilon + 1 + \beta}{\varepsilon + \alpha + \beta + \gamma}\right)^{\left(\frac{\varepsilon+\beta+1}{1-\alpha-\gamma}\right)} \left(\frac{1}{n^*}\right)^{\frac{\alpha}{1-\alpha-\gamma}}. \tag{3.36}$$

As noted above, competition leads to an increase in consumer surplus relative to monopoly supply if the welfare ratio is greater than one. Since

$$0 < \frac{\varepsilon + 1 + \beta}{\varepsilon + \alpha + \beta + \gamma} < 1,$$

$$\text{and } \frac{\varepsilon + 1 + \beta}{1 - \alpha - \gamma} < 0$$

according to the restrictions imposed on the time sensitivity parameters, $\varepsilon < -(\beta + 1)$ and $\alpha + \gamma < 1$, the first term in equation (3.36) exceeds one. But for any $n^* > 1$ the value of the second term lies between zero and one. Therefore, whether or not the welfare ratio exceeds one depends on the values of the elasticity parameters, which implies that, under certain conditions, consumer surplus may be reduced by an increase in the number of competitors. This notion of our model can be illustrated by the empirical results of *Gaynor and Trapani III (1994)*. They demonstrate that for a demand function which is adjusted for quality, the deregulation of the US airline industry led to a lower increase in consumer surplus than for an unadjusted demand function. This result is, as with our model, due to the fact that deregulation was followed by a decrease in quality in terms of the inverse load factor, schedule density, and network density.

Since the parameter combinations necessary for a welfare ratio satisfying $V_N^* / V_m > 1$ are not evident to the author, the welfare ratio was analyzed by simulations. It can be shown that consumer surplus may be higher in the monopoly case than in the competitive case if

a) $|\varepsilon + \beta + 1|$ is very small and

b) $\gamma + \alpha$ is close to 1.

In general, the two conditions are met when passengers are very time sensitive but not price sensitive, because they require relatively high values of α, β and γ, but a relatively low value of $|\varepsilon|$. More specifically, especially when we restrict the analysis to small values of α, condition *b)* implies that a lower consumer surplus may be incurred in the competitive case compared to the monopoly case if γ is large. An increase in γ enlarges scope for product differentiation, which induces entry. But an increase in the number of firms reduces demand for the services of the single firm and, therefore, leads to lower flight frequencies. This implies a relatively large shift in the market demand curve to the left, which reduces consumer surplus. In addition, condition *a)* reflects the notion that a decrease in fares only leads to a small improvement of consumer surplus when price elasticity of demand is small. Thus, the combination of a small increase in consumer surplus due to price competition and a large decrease in consumer surplus due to a large reduction of flight frequency may lead to an overall decrease in consumer welfare as a result of free market entry.

The above result implies that for any combination of values for price, inverse load factor, schedule density and network density, welfare is highest when there is monopoly supply. This is, for example, also true for the competitive equilibrium, as the following equation shows. According to equations (3.30) and (3.35), consumer surplus for the competitive supply is

$$V_N^* = \frac{-1}{\frac{\varepsilon}{1-\alpha-\gamma}+1} S^{\left(\frac{1}{1-\alpha-\gamma}\right)} P_i^{*\left(\frac{\varepsilon}{1-\alpha-\gamma}+1\right)} \left(F_i^* / n^*\right)^{\left(\frac{\alpha}{1-\alpha-\gamma}\right)} E_i^{*\left(\frac{\beta}{1-\alpha-\gamma}\right)} B_i^{*\left(\frac{\gamma}{1-\alpha-\gamma}\right)},$$

which is a decreasing function of the number of firms. In addition, the above equation indicates that if the competitive supply was offered by a monopoly, consumer surplus would always be higher than in the pure competition case, because the second term in equation (3.35) would always be equal to one.

The above results may lead to the hypothesis that welfare is highest if air transport is provided by exactly one firm, as long as the monopoly does not offer the profit maximizing supply. This suggests that time sensitivity of passengers implies a natural monopoly situation for air transport. According to the theory of contestable markets, the welfare maximum in this case can only be achieved either by entry threats of potential competitors or, if there are entry barriers or a high flexibility of prices, by regulation. The discussion in Chapter 1 has shown that scheduled air transport cannot be regarded as a contestable market. Therefore, only regulation of a monopoly airline may lead to the maximum consumer surplus. A ‹good-natured› regulator would maximize consumer surplus subject to the constraint that profit is zero:

$$Z = \frac{-1}{1+\varepsilon} QP + \lambda\left[(P - c - gE)Q - fX - hD\right] \rightarrow \max_{P,X,E,D}, \qquad (3.37)$$

where λ is the Lagrange multiplier. It can be shown that for schedule density, inverse load factor and network density, the welfare maximizing values correspond to the profit maximizing values of the monopoly airline. However, the regulator should require the monopoly to charge the price that is equal to average costs:[8]

$$P = \frac{c(\varepsilon + 1 - \alpha - \beta)}{\varepsilon + 1 + \beta}. \qquad (3.38)$$

The regulation of a monopoly airline assures that quality is increased until marginal consumer surplus from an additional amount of quality is equal to the respective marginal costs. This property is, for example, reflected in the first order conditions for the consumer surplus maximum (B.2)-(B.4) in Appendix C. It shows that in a regulated market, the values for schedule density, inverse load factor and network density reflect the willingness of passengers to pay for quality attributes.

However, one has to take into account the fact that regulation often leads to other inefficiencies. Governments are influenced by interest pressure groups and therefore do not necessarily act in consumers' interest. In addition, regulators may face a variety of empirical problems in connection with the

8 The detailed calculation of optimal supply and average costs is found in Appendix C.

estimation of elasticities and cost parameters, and with respect to the definition of the relevant market, that is the definition of the appropriate region. Thus, although regulation of city-pair markets could theoretically improve consumer welfare, competition may still be the ‹better› solution after all.

3.6 The Global Airline

In the previous sections, we focused on the supply of airlines in single city-pair markets, taking into account the fact that the network – that is the set of connecting destinations – determines the competitive behavior of firms in that particular city-pair market. But, as *Figure 3.8* shows, the previously developed network is incomplete, because it only considers connecting destinations at one endpoint of the main city-pair market GH. The firm basically groups all the passengers from local destinations at a hub in order to provide connecting services to a major city of a neighboring region. But once the passengers arrive in G, they have to change the airline if they want to continue their trip to a local destination in the foreign region. This kind of network is therefore referred to as a *local* network. To illustrate the network of a *local* carrier, we may consider an airline in the United States with a hub in one region – for example the Southwest – offering flights to local destinations within the Southwest and to a major city of another region. As an international example, consider a European national carrier that is not allowed to offer connecting flights within foreign countries. As it is often the case in markets governed by bilateral agreements, the national carrier can only offer international flights to one major city in the foreign country, which it can extend with connecting destinations to local cities in the home country.

In order to complete the model, the extension of an airline's network to local destinations in the foreign country is examined in this section. The resulting larger network improves profits and in some cases also welfare, because it increases the number of online connections, as depicted in *Figure 3.9*. It may be applied to a carrier offering flights from Europe to North-America. The airline groups all the travelers to Europe at a hub in North-America, transports them over the Atlantic to a hub in Europe, from where passengers take connecting flights to their preferred destinations in Europe. We call this type of network a ‹global network›.

Figure 3.8: Network of a local carrier

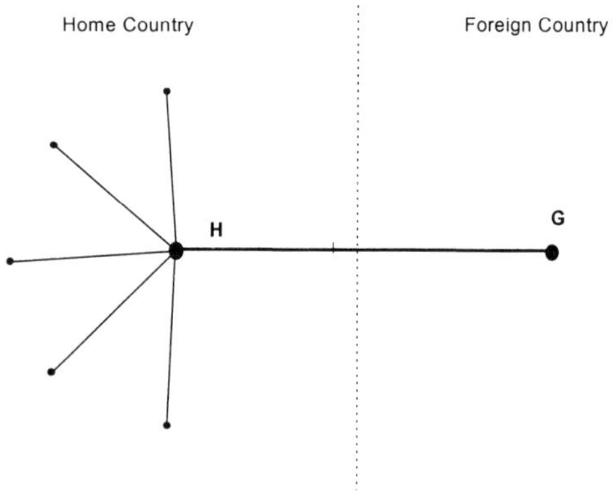

Figure 3.9: Network of a global carrier

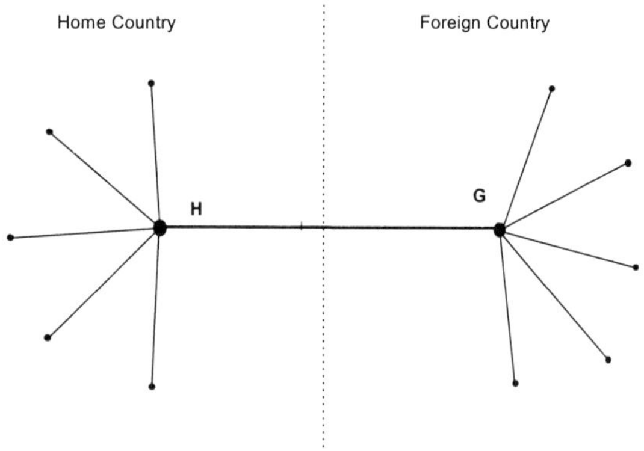

In the global network, demand between the two regions is

$$Q_M = SP^{\varepsilon} X^{\alpha} E^{\beta} D_H^{\gamma} D_G^{\gamma} n^{\gamma}, \tag{3.39}$$

where $D_H \geq 1$ is the number of connecting destinations at **H**, $D_G \geq 1$ is the number of connecting destinations at **G**, and $0 < \gamma < 1$ is the same at both hubs. As we know from the previous sections, the demand between **G** and **H** increases with the number of connecting destinations at **H**. If there additionally is an increasing number of connecting destinations at **G**, demand increases at the same rate as it does for an increasing number of connecting destinations at **H**. A global network, therefore, leads to an increase in the number of online connections. Recalling the assumption that there is no demand between **G** and **H**, the number of online connections between the two countries is $D_H D_G$ per firm and $D_H D_G n$ in total. The linear hubbing costs *h*, which are assumed to be the same as in the local case, are now incurred at both hubs. For a monopoly airline, we therefore have the following profit function:

$$\Pi = (P - c - gE)Q_M - fX - h(D_H + D_G) \tag{3.40}$$

The profit maximizing ticket prices, load factors and schedule densities are the same for the local and the global carriers and therefore correspond to the respective values calculated in the previous sections. Since we have a symmetric problem, the number of connecting destinations at each hub is, according to equation (3.3),

$$D_{m,G} = D_{m,H} = -\frac{\gamma c Q_M}{h(\varepsilon + \beta + 1)}. \tag{3.41}$$

The total number of destinations of a global airline then is

$$D_{m,M} = D_G + D_H = -\frac{2\gamma c Q_{m,M}}{h(\varepsilon + \beta + 1)},$$

and network density is

$$B_{m,M} = \frac{D_{m,M}}{Q_{m,M}} = -\frac{2\gamma c}{h(\varepsilon + \beta + 1)}. \tag{3.42}$$

Thus, the network density of a global carrier is twice as high as network density of a local carrier. Because of the high similarity of the demand and profit functions, the competitive supply variables for the global airline are computed as above and according to those for the local airline. Because the elasticities are the same as in the local case, the global airlines offer the same prices, load factors, and schedule densities as local airlines. However, network densities for global carriers are twice as high as for local carriers:

$$B_{i,M} = -\frac{2\gamma_i c}{h(\varepsilon_i + \beta_i + 1)}.$$

Equation 3.41 implicitly shows that when hubbing costs are equal on both hubs, the single airline rather offers a global network than a local network because of higher profits. This can be illustrated by the following example. Using the notation for the global firm, a local network corresponds to the situation where the number of connecting destinations at one of the two hubs is fixed at 1, for example $\overline{D}_G = 1$. Unless we have a profit maximizing number of connecting destinations for the other hub $D_H = 1$, any profit maximizing value for D_H does not represent a symmetric solution. This means that when the airline has only connecting destinations at one hub, it is tempted to add connecting destinations at the other hub until it offers a symmetric network.

The incentives associated with the change from a local to a global network can be shown graphically. In *Figures 3.10* and *3.11* the development of a global monopoly network with two hubs is depicted in discrete stages, where we look at net revenue and hubbing costs as functions of the total number of connecting destinations. Net revenue is $Q(P - c - gE) - fX$, that is total revenue minus variable costs with respect to capacity and flights. When the airline extends the number of connecting destinations, the resulting increase of passengers and, therefore, the increase in net revenue reflects the gain, whereas the increase in hubbing costs reflects the costs of this extension.

Figure 3.10: Incentives to develop a global network

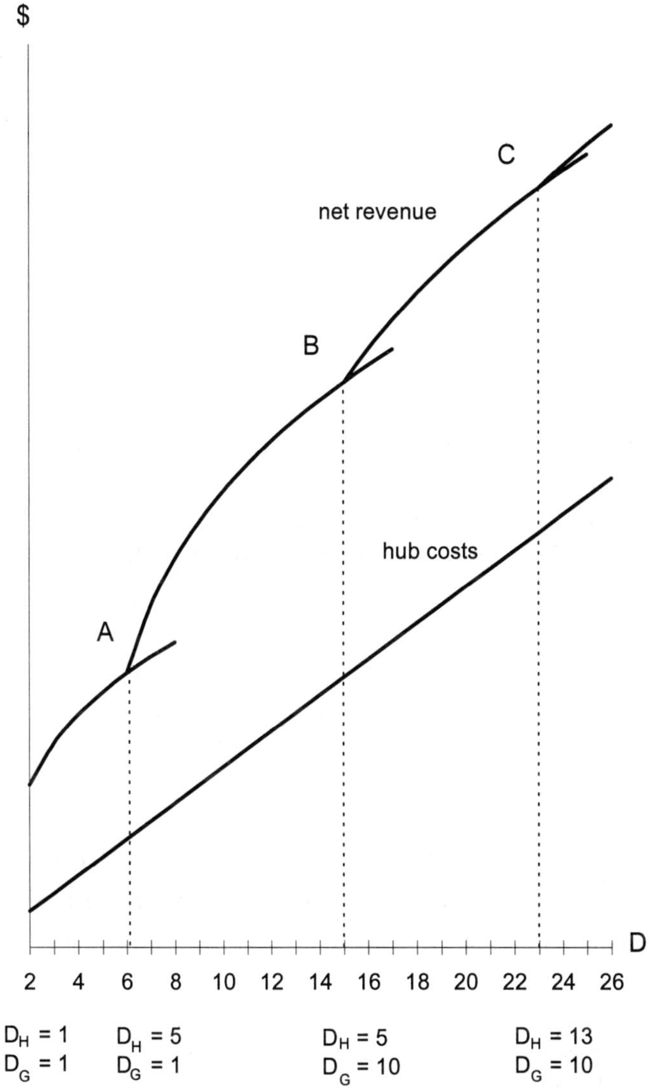

First, it is assumed that the airline operates two hubs in two countries, offering online flights to one connecting destination at each hub. At this first stage, the carrier incurs hubbing costs of $2h$. In a second stage, the airline fixes the number of connecting destinations at **G** at 1 and increases the number of connecting destinations at hub **H** – denoted by D_H – until marginal net revenue equals marginal hubbing costs. Thus it is assumed that the airline first develops a local network. In *Figure 3.10*, this condition is satisfied at point **A**, where the net revenue curve and the hubbing cost curve have the same slope. Point **A** therefore represents the profit maximum of a local network. If the airline would continue to develop additional connecting destinations at **H**, the slope of the net revenue curve and the profit would decrease. But when the airline adds additional connecting destinations at **G** holding the number of connecting destinations at **H** constant, the net revenue curve is kinked at **A** and has a higher slope again. This is due to the increase in network externalities from the growing number of online connections, which increase more than proportionately as connecting destinations are added at the second hub. The airline is tempted to add connecting destinations at the second hub until net marginal revenue equals marginal hubbing costs again at point **B**. However, at this point, the airline is offering more connecting destinations at hub **H** than at hub **G**, which now implies that it starts offering additional connecting destinations at hub **H** again. This procedure continues until the carrier offers the same number of connecting destinations at both hubs. As *Figure 3.10* shows, profit is higher in the global than in the local case.[9] In *Figure 3.11*, the respective equilibrium global network size is shown with intra-firm reaction curves that indicate the profit maximizing number of connecting destinations at one hub for a given number of connecting destinations at the other hub. The dotted line represents the process described above.[10]

9 For the simulations, the following values were used: $P = 70$, $E = 1.5$, $X = 2$, $SP^{\varepsilon}E^{\beta}X^{\alpha} = 100$, $c = 20$, $g = 20$, $f = 100$, $h = 200$, and $\gamma = 0.3$.

10 In order to determine the curves in *Figure 3.11*, note that as with equation (2.23), we can write

Figure 3.11: Equilibrium global network size

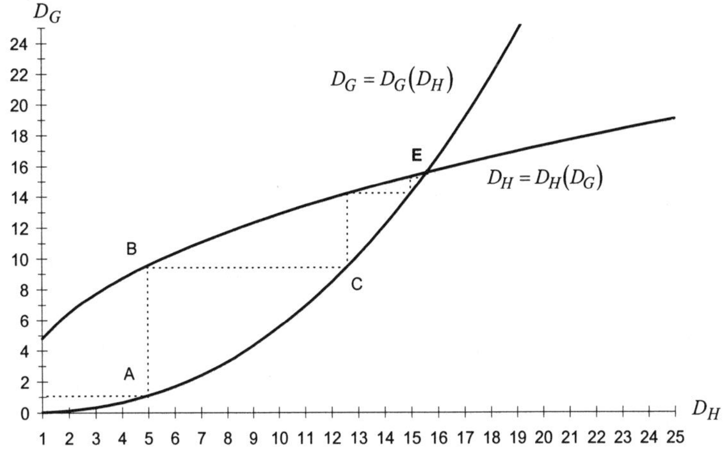

To get back to the main analysis, it is important to note that because the global carrier has doubled hubbing costs due to the operation of two hubs, it has a

$$D_G = \frac{\gamma Q(P - c - gE)}{h}.$$

Using the value set above, this is equal to

$$D_G = \frac{0.3}{200} \cdot 20 \cdot 100 \cdot {D_H}^{0.3} \cdot {D_G}^{0.3}.$$

Solving for D_G leads to

$$D_G = \left[\frac{0.3}{200} \cdot 20 \cdot 100 \cdot {D_H}^{0.3}\right]^{\frac{1}{0.7}},$$

which is the reaction function $D_G = D_G(D_H)$ shown in *Figure 3.11*. The second curve is determined accordingly.

lower profit margin compared to the local carrier, although profit may be higher. According to equation (3.22), and using the respective monopoly supply, the profit margin of a local monopoly network is

$$\Phi_m = \frac{\Pi_m}{Q_m P_m} = \frac{\alpha + \gamma - 1}{\varepsilon}, \tag{3.43}$$

whereas for the global carrier, this profit margin is only

$$\Phi_m = \frac{\alpha + 2\gamma - 1}{\varepsilon}. \tag{3.44}$$

For the competitive case, note that the single firm additionally competes with the connecting destinations at the second hub. It follows that the profit margin of the global firm in competition is

$$\Phi_{M,i} = \frac{\alpha_i + 2\gamma_i - 1}{\varepsilon_i}. \tag{3.45}$$

Because the elasticity multiplier θ is the same in the global case as in the local case, the free-entry equilibrium number of firms is

$$n_M = \frac{\gamma(1 - \alpha - 2\gamma)}{(\alpha + 2\gamma)(\gamma - 1)^2} + 1. \tag{3.46}$$

In the two-hub case, it is assumed that $\alpha + 2\gamma \leq 1$, such that $n_M \geq 1$. As in the one-hub case, this indicates that competition is restricted to relatively small α. Comparison of equation (3.46) with equation (3.24) shows that the free-entry equilibrium number of firms is lower for global carriers than for local carriers. The trade-off between the two equilibrium numbers of firms can be shown by simulation. In *Figure 3.12*, the equilibrium number of firms in the global case is depicted as functions of γ for different values of α. Compared to *Figure 3.5*, the curves for a fixed α are below the respective curves in the local case, which indicates that the global equilibrium number of firms is lower for any combination of time sensitivity parameters. Moreover, because the free-entry equilibrium number of firms is below 2 for even small α, a global network between two regions is likely to be a natural monopoly. This feature of the model is due to the large network externalities a carrier incurs from offering a global network.

Figure 3.12: Free-entry equilibrium number of firms for global networks

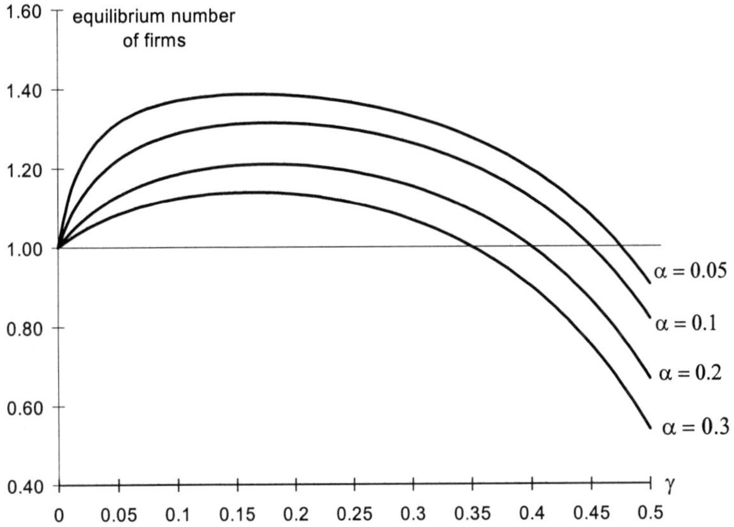

The lower equilibrium number of firms implies lower values for the free-entry demand elasticities, as the following equations show:

$$\varepsilon_{i,M}^{*} = \frac{\varepsilon}{\alpha+2\gamma},\ \alpha_{i,M}^{*} = \frac{\alpha}{\alpha+2\gamma},\ \beta_{i,M}^{*} = \frac{\beta}{\alpha+2\gamma} \text{ and } \gamma_{i,M}^{*} = \frac{\gamma}{\alpha+2\gamma}.$$

As a result, all the supply variables take higher values in the global case compared to the local case. According to equations (3.25)-(3.28),

$$P_{i,M}^{*} = \frac{c}{\left(1+\frac{\alpha+\beta+2\gamma}{\varepsilon}\right)}, \tag{3.47}$$

$$E_{i,M}^{*} = -\frac{c}{g}\frac{1}{\left(1+\frac{\varepsilon+\alpha+2\gamma}{\beta}\right)}, \tag{3.48}$$

$$F_{i,M}^{*} = -\frac{c}{f}\frac{1}{\left(1+\frac{\beta+2\gamma+\varepsilon}{\alpha}\right)}, \text{ and} \tag{3.49}$$

$$B_{i,M}^{*} = -\frac{c}{h}\frac{1}{\left(1+\frac{\alpha+\beta+\varepsilon}{\gamma}\right)}. \tag{3.50}$$

The lower number of firms in a ‹global› industry compared to a ‹local› industry raises concern about the implications of a global network for social welfare. On the one hand, consumer welfare is increased when passengers face a higher number of online connections. On the other hand, welfare decreases because of a lower number of firms. Only when the welfare gain from additional online connections exceeds the loss from industry concentration, a global network is preferred to local networks.

Using the equilibrium *flight frequency* and the *number of connecting destinations*, the output in a global network is,

$$Q_M = S\left(P_{i,M}^{*}\right)^{\varepsilon}\left(X_{i,M}^{*}\right)^{\alpha}\left(E_{i,M}^{*}\right)^{\beta}\left(D_{i,G}^{*}D_{i,H}^{*}n_m^{*}\right)^{\gamma}.$$

In this case, consumer surplus is calculated according to equation (3.33). We therefore have $V_N = \left[-1/(1+\varepsilon)\right]Q_N P_i^{*}$ for local carriers and $V_M = \left[-1/(1+\varepsilon)\right]Q_M P_{i,M}^{*}$ for global carriers. Assuming that welfare increases with the total number of passengers transported in the industry, the relative welfare increase from a change from local to global networks can be denoted by

$$\nu \equiv \frac{V_M - V_N}{V_N}. \tag{3.51}$$

The consumer surplus increases with the change from local to global networks when $\nu > 0$, which is equal to the condition $V_M / V_N > 1$. Taking the free-entry equilibrium supply variables for the local and the global case, this ratio is

$$\left(\frac{P_{i,M}^*}{P_i^*}\right)^{\varepsilon+1}\left(\frac{X_{i,M}^*}{X_i^*}\right)^{\alpha}\left(\frac{E_{i,M}^*}{E_i^*}\right)^{\beta}\left(\frac{D_{i,G}^* D_{i,H}^* n_M^*}{D_i^* n^*}\right)^{\gamma} > 1, \tag{3.52}$$

according to the equilibrium demand functions (3.29) and Q_M above. The last term on the left hand side of the above condition denotes the ratio between the total equilibrium number of online connections in the local and the global industry. Therefore,

$$\left(\frac{P_{i,M}^*}{P_i^*}\right)^{\varepsilon+1}\left(\frac{X_{i,M}^*}{X_i^*}\right)^{\alpha}\left(\frac{E_{i,M}^*}{E_i^*}\right)^{\beta}\left(\frac{Y_M^*}{Y^*}\right)^{\gamma} > 1, \tag{3.53}$$

where $Y_M^* = D_{i,G}^* D_{i,H}^* n_M^*$ is the total number of online connections in the global industry and $Y^* = D_i^* n^*$ is the total number of online connections in the local industry. After taking logs, the condition is

$$\alpha\left(\ln X_{i,M}^* - \ln X_i^*\right) + \beta\left(\ln E_{i,M}^* - \ln E_i^*\right) + \gamma\left(\ln Y_M^* - \ln Y^*\right) > -(\varepsilon+1)\left(\ln P_{i,M}^* - \ln P_i^*\right). \tag{3.54}$$

Taking into account that the development of global networks always leads to an increase in prices relative to local networks, this condition shows that welfare increases when the overall elasticity weighted quality improvements exceed the elasticity weighted increase in prices. Quality improvements are a higher frequency, a higher availability of seats and an increase in online connections.

Since the sign of ν, and therefore the validity of the above condition, depends on any elasticity and cost parameter in the model, we cannot draw more detailed conclusions. The change from local to global networks can lead to an increase as well as to a decrease in consumer welfare. However, as a qualitative result, a change from a local to a global network structure is likely to increase consumer surplus when there is only a slight increase in prices, a large increase in online connections, increasing flight frequencies and decreasing load factors, and when passengers are more time sensitive than price sensitive. In a special case, if schedule and network elasticities are such that we have natural monopolies in the local and the global case, and when we assume that an unregulated natural monopoly offers the monopoly supply, the change from a local network to a global network always leads to an increase in welfare. This is due to the fact that for a monopoly, the change in the route structure does not lead to an increase in the ticket price and the inverse load factor, but – as a result from higher network externalities – to an increase in the profit maximizing number of online connections, which in turn leads to an increase in the number of passengers and flight frequency. In Chapter 4, it will be shown that the welfare implications of global networks also depend on the geographical size of the market.

3.7 Summary

In order to extend the basic model to competitive situations, a model of monopolistic competition was used, where the distinct features of the firms are different sets of connecting destinations for a major city-pair market. In addition, it was assumed that demand for the main market increases with the number of connecting destinations, because access costs for the closest airport in a given area are reduced. Therefore, an increasing number of identical firms leads to an increase in demand due to an increase in the number of total connecting destinations. The model shows that load factors increase, whereas fares, schedule densities and network densities decrease with an increasing number of firms in the market. This indicates that with an increasing number of competitors, fares but also quality with respect to time saving decline. Because of the multiplication of schedules, the free-entry equilibrium number of firms is very low, that is in most cases we expect a natural monopoly situation. For the same reason, consumer welfare is maximized if air transport is provided by a regulated monopoly. However, taking into account difficulties with respect to the collection of data and the allocation of property rights involved with regulation, competition between a small number of firms may still be more efficient.

In a second step, it was shown that an airline offering connecting destinations at one endpoint of a city-pair market is tempted to increase the size of its network by offering additional connecting destinations at the other endpoint. This further extension of the model was interpreted as a change from a local to a global network structure. With respect to the whole industry, the change from local to global network structures reduces the free-entry equilibrium number of firms, which implies a rise in ticket prices, schedule densities and network densities, and a reduction in load factors. However, if the increase in the number of online connections is sufficiently high, the decline in the number of firms still leads to an increase in consumer surplus.

The local network as well as the global network model show that competition in a major city-pair market may lead to natural monopoly situations. This does not always correspond to reality, where we can often find a lot of firms competing in the same city-pair markets, especially in main markets between large hubs. However, there are two possible interpretations that would still support the model in this respect. First, we can assume that every carrier operates in a different passenger segment. This means for example that one airline may provide ‹high cost› services with a great number of connecting destinations, high frequencies, low load factors and high fares, while another carrier provides ‹low cost› services with few connecting destinations, low frequencies, high load factors and low fares. Whereas the first carrier would suit time sensitive business passengers, the second would be more attractive to price sensitive consumers. Second, it can be presumed that airlines compete *with hubs* rather than at hubs. Products then would be differentiated by developing hubs in different regions. In this case, a single city-pair market may be the main market for one firm, but may be ‹only› a spoke for other firms. This second idea of competition between hubs will be further developed and illustrated in the following chapter.

Appendix A

In this appendix, the elasticities of the perceived demand functions on the pro-rata demand curves are derived. Since the mathematics is the same for all four elasticities, price elasticity is used as an example. Recall that the single airline's perceived demand is

$$Q_i = \tilde{Q}\left[1+(n-1)\left(\frac{R_j}{R_i}\right)^{\sigma}\right]^{\gamma-1} \tag{3.14}$$

The first derivative with respect to the single firm's fare is

$$\frac{\partial Q_i}{\partial P_i} = \frac{\partial \tilde{Q}}{\partial P_i}[\,\cdot\,]^{\gamma-1} - \tilde{Q}(\gamma-1)[\,\cdot\,]^{\gamma-2}(n-1)\sigma\left(\frac{R_j}{R_i}\right)^{\sigma-1}\frac{R_j}{R_i^2}\frac{\partial R_i}{\partial P_i},$$

which is equal to

$$\frac{\partial Q_i}{\partial P_i} = \frac{\partial \tilde{Q}}{\partial P_i}[\,\cdot\,]^{\gamma-1} - \tilde{Q}(\gamma-1)[\,\cdot\,]^{\gamma-2}(n-1)\sigma\left(\frac{R_j}{R_i}\right)^{\sigma}\frac{\partial R_i}{\partial P_i}\frac{1}{R_i}.$$

Multiplication by P_i/Q_i, and taking into account that $Q_i = \tilde{Q}[\,\cdot\,]^{(\gamma-1)}$, leads to

$$\varepsilon_i = \frac{\partial Q_i}{\partial P_i}\frac{P_i}{Q_i} = \frac{\partial \tilde{Q}}{\partial P_i}\frac{P_i}{\tilde{Q}[\,\cdot\,]^{\gamma-1}}[\,\cdot\,]^{\gamma-1} - \frac{\tilde{Q}}{\tilde{Q}[\,\cdot\,]^{\gamma-1}}(\gamma-1)[\,\cdot\,]^{\gamma-2}(n-1)\sigma\left(\frac{R_j}{R_i}\right)^{\sigma}\frac{\partial R_i}{\partial P_i}\frac{P_i}{R_i}.$$

Since $\tilde{Q}$ is the demand if firm i would be a monopoly, $\left(\partial\tilde{Q}/\partial P_i\right)\left(P_i/\tilde{Q}\right) = \varepsilon$ for constant elasticities. Furthermore $\left(\partial R_i/\partial P_i\right)\left(P_i/R_i\right) = \varepsilon$,

$$\varepsilon_i = \varepsilon - \varepsilon\frac{1}{[\,\cdot\,]}(n-1)(\gamma-1)\sigma\left(\frac{R_j}{R_i}\right)^{\sigma}.$$

Because $R_j/R_i = 1$ when firms act simultaneously and are on the pro-rata demand curve, we have

$$\left[1+(n-1)\left(\frac{R_j}{R_i}\right)^{\sigma}\right]=n.$$

Taking into account that, according to (3.13),

$$\sigma=\frac{n(1-\gamma)}{\gamma}$$

the single carrier's price elasticity of demand is

$$\varepsilon_i=\varepsilon\left[1+(n-1)\frac{(\gamma-1)^2}{\gamma}\right].$$

Appendix B

In this appendix, the profit margin for the single firm is calculated. Note that according to equation (3.20)

$$\frac{\Pi_i}{Q_i}=P_i-c-gE_i-fF_i-hB_i$$

Inserting equations (3.16)-(3.19) this equals

$$\frac{\Pi_i}{Q_i}=\frac{c(\varepsilon_i+\beta_i+\alpha_i+\gamma_i)}{\varepsilon_i+1+\beta_i}-c,$$

which can be changed to

$$\frac{\Pi_i}{Q_i} = \frac{-c(1-\alpha_i - \gamma_i)}{\varepsilon_i + 1 + \beta_i}.$$

Using the ticket price given by equation (3.16) we then have

$$\frac{\Pi_i}{P_i Q_i} = \frac{-c(1-\alpha_i - \gamma_i)}{\varepsilon_i + 1 + \beta_i} \cdot \frac{\varepsilon_i + 1 + \beta_i}{\varepsilon_i c},$$

which straightforwardly leads to the profit margin (3.22).

Appendix C

In this appendix, the ticket price, schedule density, inverse load factor and network density that maximize consumer surplus subject to the condition that profit is zero, are calculated. The respective Lagrange function is given by equation (3.37):

$$Z = \frac{-1}{\varepsilon + 1} QP + \lambda\left[(P - c - gE)Q - fX - hD\right] \tag{3.34}$$

First order conditions for a consumer surplus maximum are obtained by setting the first partial derivatives of the Lagrange function with respect to price, inverse load factor, flight frequency, number of connecting destinations and the Lagrange multiplier equal to zero. Assuming an interior solution:

$$\frac{\partial Z}{\partial P} = \frac{-1}{(\varepsilon + 1)}\left(\frac{\partial Q}{\partial P} P + Q\right) + \lambda(P - c - gE)\frac{\partial Q}{\partial P} + \lambda Q = 0 \tag{B.1}$$

$$\frac{\partial Z}{\partial E} = \frac{-1}{(\varepsilon + 1)}\left(\frac{\partial Q}{\partial E} P\right) + \lambda(P - c - gE)\frac{\partial Q}{\partial E} - \lambda g Q = 0 \tag{B.2}$$

$$\frac{\partial Z}{\partial X} = \frac{-1}{(\varepsilon+1)}\left(\frac{\partial Q}{\partial X}P\right) + \lambda(P - c - gE)\frac{\partial Q}{\partial X} - \lambda f = 0 \tag{B.3}$$

$$\frac{\partial Z}{\partial D} = \frac{-1}{(\varepsilon+1)}\left(\frac{\partial Q}{\partial D}P\right) + \lambda(P - c - gE)\frac{\partial Q}{\partial D} - \lambda h = 0. \tag{B.4}$$

$$\frac{\partial Z}{\partial \lambda} = (P - c - gE)Q - fX - hD = 0. \tag{B.5}$$

Equations (B.1)-(B.4) can be changed to

$$\frac{\partial Z}{\partial P} = \frac{-1}{\lambda(\varepsilon+1)}\left(\frac{\partial Q}{\partial P}P + Q\right) + (P - c - gE)\frac{\partial Q}{\partial P} + Q = 0 \tag{B.6}$$

$$\frac{\partial Z}{\partial E} = \frac{-1}{\lambda(\varepsilon+1)}\left(\frac{\partial Q}{\partial E}P\right) + (P - c - gE)\frac{\partial Q}{\partial E} - gQ = 0 \tag{B.7}$$

$$\frac{\partial Z}{\partial X} = \frac{-1}{\lambda(\varepsilon+1)}\left(\frac{\partial Q}{\partial X}P\right) + (P - c - gE)\frac{\partial Q}{\partial X} - f = 0 \tag{B.8}$$

$$\frac{\partial Z}{\partial D} = \frac{-1}{\lambda(\varepsilon+1)}\left(\frac{\partial Q}{\partial D}P\right) + (P - c - gE)\frac{\partial Q}{\partial D} - h = 0. \tag{B.9}$$

In order to simplify the following analysis, we define

$$u \equiv 1 - \frac{1}{\lambda(\varepsilon+1)}. \tag{B.10}$$

The first order conditions for the welfare maximum then change to

$$\frac{\partial Z}{\partial P} = (uP - c - gE)\frac{\partial Q}{\partial P} + uQ = 0 \tag{B.11}$$

$$\frac{\partial Z}{\partial E} = \left(uP - c - gE\right)\frac{\partial Q}{\partial E} - gQ = 0 \tag{B.12}$$

$$\frac{\partial Z}{\partial X} = \left(uP - c - gE\right)\frac{\partial Q}{\partial X} - f = 0 \tag{B.13}$$

$$\frac{\partial Z}{\partial D} = \left(uP - c - gE\right)\frac{\partial Q}{\partial D} - h = 0 \tag{B.14}$$

After multiplication of equation (B.11) by P/Q the following expression is obtained:

$$uP = \frac{c + gE}{1 + \frac{1}{\varepsilon}}. \tag{B.15}$$

The subsequent analysis follows the procedure elaborated in Appendix C of Chapter 2: Equation (B.12) can be changed to

$$gE = \frac{\beta\left(uP - c\right)}{\left(1 + \beta\right)}. \tag{B.16}$$

which then is inserted into equation (B.11). This leads to

$$uP = \frac{c}{1 + \frac{1+\beta}{\varepsilon}}, \tag{B.17}$$

which is equivalent to the monopoly ticket price. Replacing uP in equation (B.16) by equation (B.17) leads to inverse load factor that maximizes consumer welfare:

$$E = -\frac{c}{g}\frac{1}{\left(1 + \frac{1+\varepsilon}{\beta}\right)}. \tag{B.18}$$

Comparison with equation (2.25) shows that this is exactly the inverse load factor that maximizes profit. Equations (B.17) and (B.18) then are used to calculate schedule density and network density, which also turn out to be equal to the respective values of the profit maximizing monopoly:

$$F = -\frac{c}{f}\frac{\alpha}{1+\varepsilon+\beta}, \tag{B.19}$$

$$B = -\frac{c}{h}\frac{\gamma}{1+\varepsilon+\beta}. \tag{B.20}$$

The zero-profit condition (B.5) may be rewritten as follows:

$$P - c - gE - fF - hB = 0. \tag{B.21}$$

From (B.18) we know that

$$P = \frac{c\varepsilon}{u(1+\varepsilon+\beta)}. \tag{B.22}$$

The supply variables in (B.21) now are replaced by their equilibrium values (B.18)-(B.20) and (B.22). Solving for u leads to

$$u = \frac{\varepsilon}{\varepsilon-\alpha-\gamma+1}. \tag{B.23}$$

Inserting this equation into (B.22) directly leads to the welfare maximizing ticket price:

$$P = \frac{c(\varepsilon-\alpha-\gamma+1)}{(1+\varepsilon+\beta)}. \tag{B.24}$$

It can be shown that this price is equal to average costs. According to equation (3.2), total costs are

$$C = (c+gE)Q + fX + hD,$$

Average costs are

$$AC = c + gE + fF + hB,$$

because $X/Q = F$ and $D/Q = B$. In the equilibrium, the supply variables in the average cost function then can be replaced by their equilibrium values (B.18)-(B.20). We therefore have

$$AC = \frac{c(\varepsilon - \alpha - \gamma + 1)}{(1 + \varepsilon + \beta)},$$

which is equal to the ticket price obtained in (B.24).

Since Z is concave in the extremum and the constraint function is linear, we face a unique absolute constrained maximum. The concavity of Z at the extremum can be shown according to the same procedure and using the same conditions as demonstrated for the monopoly profit function in Appendix B of Chapter 2. In order to derive the equations considered, we take into account the fact that according to equation (B.23) and because of the restriction $\alpha + \gamma < 1$, u is a positive constant in the extremum. The first and second order partial derivatives for a welfare maximum then can be determined using equations (3.1) and (B.11)-(B.14).

$$\frac{\partial^2 Z}{\partial X^2} = \alpha(\alpha - 1)\Gamma_1 X^{\alpha-2},$$

with $\Gamma_1 = (uP - c - gE)SP^{\varepsilon} E^{\beta} D^{\gamma}$, and

$$\frac{\partial^2 Z}{\partial E^2} = \beta(\beta - 1)\Gamma_2 E^{\beta-2} - (\beta + 1)\beta\Gamma_3 E^{\beta-1}$$

with $\Gamma_2 = (uP - c)SP^{\varepsilon} X^{\alpha} D^{\gamma}$ and $\Gamma_3 = gSP^{\varepsilon} X^{\alpha} D^{\gamma}$. Finally,

$$\frac{\partial Z}{\partial P} = (\varepsilon + 1)\Gamma_4 P^{\varepsilon} - \varepsilon\Gamma_5 P^{\varepsilon-1}, \text{ and}$$

$$\frac{\partial^2 Z}{\partial P^2} = (\varepsilon+1)\varepsilon\Gamma_4 P^{\varepsilon-1} - \varepsilon(\varepsilon-1)\Gamma_5 P^{\varepsilon-2},$$

where $\Gamma_4 = uSX^{\alpha}E^{\beta}D^{\gamma}$ and $\Gamma_5 = (c+gE)SX^{\alpha}E^{\beta}D^{\gamma}$. Since $0<\gamma<1$, we additionally have

$$\frac{\partial^2 Z}{\partial D^2} = \gamma(\gamma-1)\Gamma_6 D^{\gamma-2} < 0,$$

with $\Gamma_6 = (uP - c - gE)SP^{\varepsilon}E^{\beta}X^{\alpha}$.

4. Global Deregulation

4.1 Introduction

The monopolistic competition model derived in the previous chapter led to the result that city-pair markets are likely to be monopolies, because competition implies a costly multiplication of the optimal schedule. However, the low number of firms does not seem to correspond to reality, where there is often more than one carrier operating in a city-pair market. One possible solution to the problem is the assumption that city-pair markets with more than one firm operating may be spokes of different hubs belonging to different airlines. In this case, the deregulated airline industry is not characterized by competition at hubs or in single markets, as it was assumed in the previous chapter. Instead airlines may offer differentiated products in that they operate indirect flights via different hubs. This seems to correspond to the development in the US after deregulation, where carriers concentrated operations on different hubs. Whereas *American Airlines*, for example, has concentrated its operations in the South and in the East of the US, *United Airlines* is more dominant in the West and in the North. Another indication for competition with hubs is the fact that some hub airports are dominated by single airlines. The large shares of enplanements of single firms supports the proposition that often only one firm uses a large airport as a main hub, whereas the other firms use the airport as a connecting destination or, in other words, as an endpoint of a spoke to its own hub.

In the following, the network model is extended to global competition with hubs. Two different cases are examined, reflecting the different institutional conditions in a partially regulated industry on the one hand and a completely deregulated industry on the other hand. In Chapter 1 it was shown that the regulated markets in the US and the international markets governed by bilateral agreements prevented airlines from establishing global networks. During the period of air transport regulation in the US, firms were subdivided into local and trunk carriers, where the local carriers operations were restricted to city-pair markets in one specific region. In the international air transport industry, the restrictions are similar. Because airlines are often not allowed to offer flights within a foreign country, and because the number of destinations into the foreign country is limited, global networks are also prevented. Therefore we can assume that the airline industry in the US shortly after deregulation was and in Europe still is characterized by local networks. After deregulation of the US airline industry, competition led to the development of global networks, because airlines were tempted to increase the number of connecting destinations in order to increase their market shares. Numerous strategic alliances between airlines from different areas indicate that deregulation of air transport in the EU and international liberalization may lead to similar results.

After the discussion of hub competition with local and global networks, the model is used to describe a deregulation process of an economic area in three stages. In the first stage, airlines cooperate and behave like a monopoly airline for the whole area. In the second stage, regulatory authorities introduce competition between the carriers and open markets for new entrants. The model shows that the industry incurs lower ticket prices, lower network and schedule densities and higher load factors. In the third stage, the airlines start extending their networks to a global structure. Because of the higher network externalities, the number of carriers is reduced. Additionally, ticket prices increase and load factors decrease again. The increasing industry concentration in the US underpins the theoretical results.

4.2 Local and Global Airlines

In the following model it is assumed that the world consists of two large geographical areas, the East and the West. The world can be further divided into a fixed number of regions of equal geographical size that are equally distributed over the areas. As areas we may consider the US and the EU, and as regions the states of the US or the member countries of the EU. Another example may be the Eastern states of the US as one area and the Western states as the second area. In reality, the areas and regions of course are of different size in terms of population, production and geographical extent. For convenience they are assumed to be homogenous in the model. It is further assumed that the structure of demand is such that consumers want to fly from local cities in one region in one area to local cities in another region in the other area. In order to provide air transport between the two areas, each airline, therefore, develops a hub airport in one region of each area. Thus, every firm transports passengers between the two regions in which it operates a hub. In this respect, it is assumed that airlines differentiate products by developing hubs in different regions. However, carriers may have overlapping networks in order to capture passengers living close to the border of the regions. In addition, it is assumed that there is consumer mobility between the regions. Passengers living in one region, therefore, may take a carrier operating a local destination in a neighboring region.

First, only local networks are considered because of restrictive bilateral agreements or regulation. Carriers are only allowed to offer connecting flights to local destinations from their hub in the home area, but they are not allowed to offer connecting flights from the second hub in the second area. Thus, the carriers group passengers from local destinations in the home area at its hub, transports them to the hub in the other area, from where they have to change airlines in order to reach their final destinations.

The concept is illustrated in *Figure 4.1*, where two areas with two regions each are depicted. The regions are indicated by the numbers 1.1 to 2.2. Airline 1, for example, basically offers connections between regions 1.1 and 2.1.

Passengers looking for transport between regions 1.1 and 2.2 may take a local flight with airline 1 from the closest airport to hub A, take an international flight with the same airline (online connection) to hub C, from where they use a local flight with airline 3 to travel to their final destination. However, because of overlapping networks, these passengers can choose from alternative connections. They may as well take airline 1 to get to hub A, but from here they choose an online connection with airline 4 via hub D, especially if their destination in region 2.1 is located close to the border of region 2.2. Where they live close to the border of region 1.2, they may also take airline 2 to hub B, from where they take airline 3 over hub C. However, for passengers located at the edge of the two areas, only one combination of local networks may be feasible, which implies that the dominant carriers in the respective regions have local monopoly power.

Figure 4.1: Air transport between two areas with local carriers

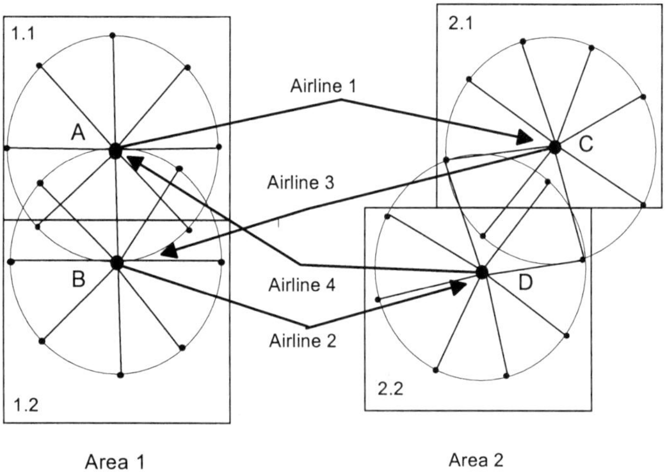

As for the model developed in Chapter 3, it is assumed that airlines are tempted to differentiate their products as much as possible. Therefore, each firm tries to offer flights between different regions and to different connecting destinations than its competitors. This has two main implications for competitive behavior. First, substantial competition only occurs when there is a sufficiently large number of airlines in the world, that is if the local networks overlap such that they include some connecting destinations close to each other or even in the same regions. The extent to which networks overlap then influences the substitutability of networks because of passengers' access costs. Second, the hubs in different regions determine local monopoly power and are the distinct features for monopolistic competition. This implies that competitive pressure increases with the number of airlines and decreases with the size of the world, which is determined by the total number of regions. Since the airlines are eager to differentiate their products as much as possible, an entering firm basically chooses a hub in a region where none of the competitors is already offering connecting destinations. As more airlines enter the world market, the industry gets more ‹crowded› and the possibility that the networks will overlap increases, which in turn increases competition. In contrast, when the size of the world market, e.g. the number of equally sized regions, increases, there is more space for product differentiation, and the possibility of overlapping networks decreases. In the model, it is assumed that the number of firms is determined endogenously, whereas the size of the world is exogenous, reflecting the given geographical extension of an area.

The demand function is adapted from Chapter 3, where demand between two regions was derived. Since we assume that regions are of equal size in terms of population, production and geographic extent, the world demand function differs from the one in the previous model in that market size increases linearly with the number of regions. For a world with only local networks, total demand between two areas then is

$$Q_L = SWP^{\varepsilon} X^{\alpha} E^{\beta} (Dn)^{\gamma}, \tag{4.1}$$

where W is the total number of regions in the world. It is assumed again that demand increases with the number of firms, but at a decreasing rate, because passengers can choose from a larger variety of products. The pro-rata demand for the single firm then is

$$Q_{i,L}^{R} = SWP^{\varepsilon} X^{\alpha} E^{\beta} D^{\gamma} n^{\gamma-1}. \tag{4.2}$$

For the analysis of competition, the same procedure as in Chapter 3 is applied. Therefore, according to (3.11), the perceived demand function for a representative airline i is

$$Q_{i,L} = \tilde{Q}_L \left[1 + (n-1)\Omega\right]^{\gamma-1}, \tag{4.3}$$

where $\tilde{Q}_L = SWP^{\varepsilon} X^{\alpha} E^{\beta} D^{\gamma}$ is the hypothetical demand for the service of a monopoly airline. It is assumed that competitors are composed of airlines of the same area as well as of airlines from the other area, since all the firms in the world basically offer differentiated air transport services between the two areas. Again we define

$$\Omega \equiv \left(\frac{P_j^{\varepsilon} X_j^{\alpha} E_j^{\beta} D_j^{\gamma}}{P_i^{\varepsilon} X_i^{\alpha} E_i^{\beta} D_i^{\gamma}} \right)^{\sigma}. \tag{4.4}$$

But in contrast to the situation for competition in the two-region case, we assume that

$$\sigma \equiv \frac{n(1-\gamma)}{W\gamma}, \tag{4.5}$$

which indicates that the number of regions W influences the substitutability of the firms' products. This notion of the model takes into account the fact that product diversity increases with the number of regions. The passengers' willingness to substitute one airline for another because of changes in supply variables mainly depends on the distance between destinations and access costs.

Whereas access costs are captured by the parameter γ, the distance between competitive airports is determined by the number of competitors *and*, in contrast to the one-region model, also by the number of regions. Whereas the number of competitors increases the substitutability of products, the number of regions decreases it. If $W = 1$, the situation is equivalent to the case of competition at hubs discussed in Chapter 3, since the airlines compete with connecting destinations in the same region. If $W > 1$, every newly entering airline is tempted to choose a region with no incumbent. As hubs and connecting destinations are located more distant, competitive pressure is reduced and regional monopoly power is strengthened.

Because of the similarity of the extension of the model to the basic model presented in the previous chapter, the calculation of elasticities and the supply variables is carried out in the same way. For every point on the pro-rata demand function, where we have equal supply variables and market shares for equally sized firms, the elasticities of the single carrier are, according to (3.15),

$$\alpha_i = \alpha\theta_W,\ \beta_i = \beta\theta_W,\ \gamma_i = \gamma\theta_W,\ \text{and}\ \varepsilon_i = \varepsilon\theta_W,\ \text{with} \tag{4.6}$$

$$\theta_W = 1 + (n-1)\frac{1}{W}\frac{(\gamma-1)^2}{\gamma}. \tag{4.6a}$$

Equations (4.6) show that the single carriers' elasticities for a given number of airlines decrease with the number of regions or, in other words, with the geographic size of the areas. The values of price, inverse load factor, schedule and network densities of the local competitors correspond to equations (3.16) to (3.19) in Chapter 3, using the respective elasticities determined according to equation (4.6).

The main influence the number of regions has is on the equilibrium number of firms. Referring to equation (3.24) in Chapter 3, we have for the local airline

$$n_L^* = \frac{\gamma(1-\alpha-\gamma)}{(\alpha+\gamma)(\gamma-1)^2}W + 1, \tag{4.7}$$

which indicates that the free-entry equilibrium number of firms increases linearly with the number of regions. Depending on α and γ, the number of firms can be below or above the number of regions. As a general rule, the number of firms exceeds the number of regions when network elasticity of demand γ is high relative to frequency elasticity of demand α, or in other words, when there is room for more than one competitor in at least one region.

Figure 4.2: Air transport between two areas with global carriers

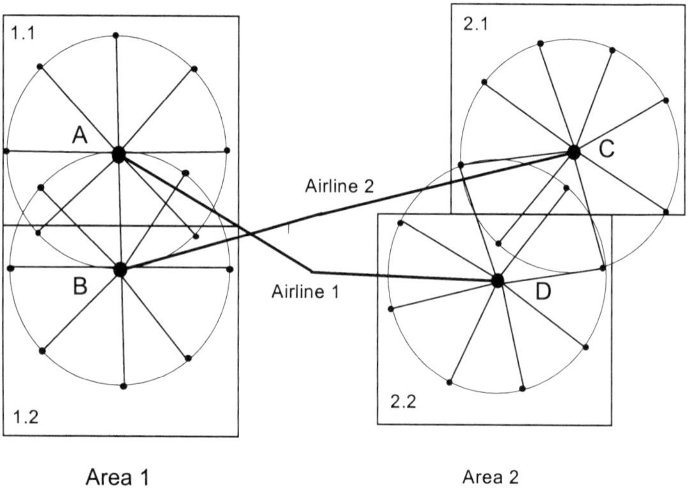

If there are no entry restrictions between the two areas, firms build global networks by operating one hub with an equal number of connecting destinations in each area, as is depicted in *Figure 4.2*. The concept of competition is the same as introduced above for the local case, except that passengers may choose from a smaller number of alternative connections. However, they now enjoy online connections for the whole trip. For a world with global airlines, total demand between the East and the West is

$$Q_U = SWP^{\varepsilon} X^{\alpha} E^{\beta} D_G^{\gamma} D_H^{\gamma} n^{\gamma} . \tag{4.8}$$

Because of increased network externalities from online connections, the free-entry equilibrium number of firms decreases relative to a world with local networks, as was shown in equation (3.46) in Chapter 3 for the one-region case. We therefore have

$$n_U^* = \frac{\gamma(1-\alpha-2\gamma)}{(\alpha+2\gamma)(\gamma-1)^2} W + 1. \tag{4.9}$$

The pattern of equilibrium number of firms for different combinations of α and γ correspond to *Figures 3.5* and *3.12* except for $n_U^* - 1$ being increased by the factor W. We therefore focus on the influence of the number of regions on the equilibrium number of firms in the local and the global case. *Figure 4.3* indicates two main implications of the extended model. First, it can be seen that for the local and the global case, the equilibrium number of firms increases with the number of regions. Second, for any ‹size of the world›, the number of firms decreases when airlines replace local with global networks.

Unlike the equilibrium number of firms, the free-entry equilibrium supply variables for a given set of market demand elasticities and cost parameters are independent of the number of regions and therefore correspond to equations (3.25)-(3.28) and (3.47)-(3.50) respectively in Chapter 3. This is due to the fact that the free-entry demand elasticities are independent of W, as the insertion of (4.7) or (4.9) into (4.6) shows. Therefore, as in the one region case, a change from local to global networks leads to an increase in prices, inverse load factors, schedule and network densities.

Figure 4.3: Equilibrium number of firms as a function of the number of regions

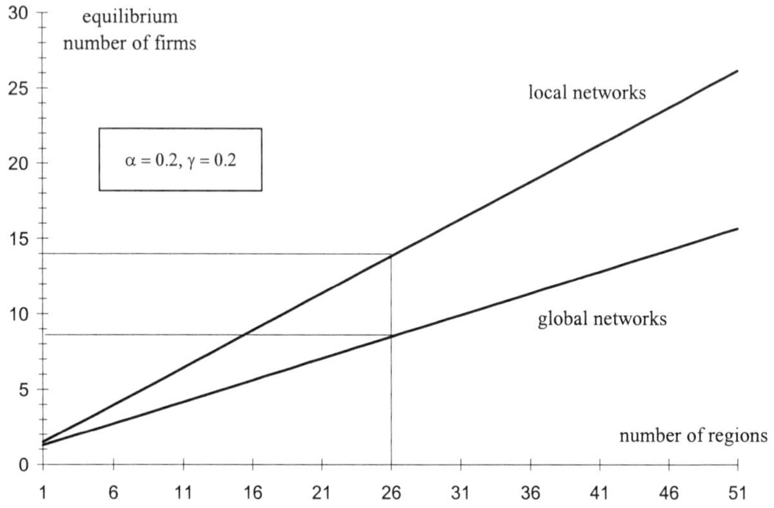

The welfare implications of a change from a local industry to a global industry are also similar to the case of one region developed in Chapter 3. But welfare is more likely to improve as a result of change in network structures when the number of regions is high. The change of the industry structure towards global networks increases consumer surplus if

$$\omega \equiv \frac{V_U^*}{V_L^*} > 1, \tag{4.10}$$

where V_U^* and V_L^* denote the consumer surplus in the global and in the local case respectively. As shown in the Appendix

$$\frac{d \ln \omega}{dW} > 0, \tag{4.11}$$

which implies that ω also increases with W. Therefore, for given elasticities and cost parameters, an increase in the number of regions increases the ratio between consumer surplus in global networks to consumer surplus in local networks. This result does not necessarily mean that the development of global networks is always beneficial to consumers for a sufficiently high number of regions, but it indicates that when the area is large in terms of regions, it is more likely that the development of global networks will increase consumer welfare.

The above property is not due to a greater extent of competition, as one would expect from a larger number of firms, since the free-entry equilibrium values of supply do not depend on the number of regions. An increase in the number of firms raises consumer welfare because passengers can choose from a larger variety of products. But this welfare enhancing influence decreases with the number of firms, because demand increases with the number of firms at a decreasing rate. This implies that when the number of regions is high and therefore the number of firms for local and global networks is also high, a decrease in the number of firms only leads to a small decrease in welfare with respect to product diversity. In contrast, for relatively low numbers of regions and firms, a similar decrease in the number of firms leads to a relatively high decrease in welfare with respect to product diversity.

4.3 Deregulation and the Change of Industry Structure

The results derived in Chapter 3 and Section 4.2 predict that an industry with global networks is characterized by a lower number of firms than an industry with local networks. This feature of the model can be used to describe a deregulation process. In a completely regulated industry, as is often the case in international markets governed by bilateral agreements and pool arrangements, firms form a cartel and therefore offer the monopoly supply variables maximizing joint profit. In addition, the number of firms is determined politically. The national governments are eager to guarantee a certain market share to their flag carriers, which, besides their main duty of transporting passengers to foreign countries, represent the home country all around the world.

After a partial deregulation, airlines may be allowed to offer connecting destinations in the home area, or at least connecting destinations in the home country. But the regulatory framework may still prevent carriers from offering connecting destinations in foreign countries. Except for those European countries that have signed open-sky agreements with the US, this corresponds to the present situation in the North-Atlantic market between the EU and the US. Within these two ‹areas›, airlines based in one area enjoy complete freedom to offer flights from their hubs to any destination, but they are usually not allowed to offer flights within the foreign area. Thus, EU carriers can offer flights between the EU and the US, but they can only develop a network with connecting destinations in Europe. For US carriers in turn the development of a European hub is restricted by entry barriers for city-pair markets inside the EU. In this second stage, the carriers now compete with local networks, which leads to a decrease in prices, inverse load factors, schedule and network densities. With respect to the change in the number of firms no clear statement is possible, since during regulation, the number of carriers was determined politically. Therefore, partial deregulation can lead to an increase or a decrease in the number of firms.

Complete deregulation – as a third step – implies that airlines would start building a second hub in the foreign area in order to develop a global network. Since the global industry has a lower equilibrium number of firms, there would be too many firms in the market shortly after deregulation. It follows that some firms eventually would be forced to exit until the new equilibrium number of firms is reached. However, the decrease in the number of firms need not necessarily be achieved by exits. As will be shown later in a case study, the number of networks may as well be reduced by mergers or strategic alliances. As global networks are developed, prices, inverse load factors, schedule densities and network densities increase again.

The decrease in the number of firms as a result of deregulation may be described by the concept of the *war of attrition*.[1] This model was originally introduced in theoretical biology to explain the fight between two animals for prey. Fighting is costly to the animals because they forgo the opportunity of other activities and get exhausted. For the single animal, the object of the fight is to induce the other animal to give up the whole prey. As *Tirole (1985)* notes, this situation requires that the outcome of the fight is not deterministic. Each player must see at least some chance of winning the fight, otherwise it would not participate. The animals' fight can be compared to two firms in an industry with economies of scale fighting for the natural monopoly position. The existence of two firms in the industry is costly to both firms because they both incur a loss. But the firms see some chance that after a while the competitor will give up and exit the market. The firm left in the market then attain monopoly power and the respective profits.

In the case of our model, the war of attrition is not fought in order to gain monopoly power, but in order to be among the firms that can operate profitably with global networks after complete deregulation. The concept is especially useful since the equilibrium number of firms in monopolistic competition models usually is not an integer, which implies that the firms in the market incur at least some small monopoly rents. Therefore, these rents are the objective of the fight. It can be assumed that the firms do not give up their fights at the same time. As in the animal world, there are stronger and weaker firms. Whereas the weak firms exit the market shortly after deregulation, stronger firms can hold on although they incur losses over a certain period of time. The longer a firm is able to operate with losses, the higher is its chance of being one of the firms left in the global industry. Of course, at the beginning most firms believe in their chance of staying in the industry, expecting that future profits from global networks will exceed the losses during the fight.

1 See *Tirole (1985)*, pp. 311-314.

The drop out of firms and the respective changes from negative to positive profits are best shown with the profit margin. The profit margins for a given number of regions and firms are, according to equations (3.22) and (3.45) respectively,

$$\Phi_{i,L} = \frac{\alpha_i + \gamma_i - 1}{\varepsilon_i}$$

for local airlines, and

$$\Phi_{i,U} = \frac{\alpha_i + 2\gamma_i - 1}{\varepsilon_i}$$

for global airlines. The elasticities equal the respective market demand elasticities multiplied by θ_W. The comparison between the two profit margins shows that for a given number of firms and regions, the profit margin is always lower for global networks than for local networks. Therefore, if an industry with local networks is in its zero profit equilibrium, deregulation and the development of global networks first leads to negative profit margins until a sufficiently high number of firms exit the market.

Although this simple model illustrates possible outcomes of dynamic processes with respect to deregulation and industry concentration, it leaves open the question why firms have different financial means in order to survive losses over several periods. Two reasons may be of importance. First, in a world or economic area with several states, governments may subsidize their flag carrier in order to increase its probability of staying in the market, especially if the carrier concerned is state owned. The government expects its national carrier to gain the monopoly rents if the carrier stays in the market for a sufficiently long time. Otherwise, when the carrier has to exit the market, workers will have to be laid off and people will ‹import› services in that they use a foreign carrier. This argument is similar to the theory of strategic trade policy.[2] Thus, if governments

2 See, for example, *Krugman (1987)*.

cannot agree on not subsidizing national carriers, deregulation may lead to socially too many firms as governments vie with each other in subsidizing. Second, some airlines' financial record may be improved by monopoly rents from protected markets. In this case, carriers cross-subsidize the deregulated markets with profits earned from monopoly markets, which increases the chances of survival relative to other carriers not having this opportunity. In addition, one has to take into account the fact that the number of firms, or networks, can be reduced by mergers and strategic alliances instead of bankruptcies. As the history of the US airline industry shows, deregulation was followed by both, mergers and bankruptcies. The following section illustrates the model with the change in the US airline industry half a decade after deregulation.

4.4 Case Study: Deregulation in the US Airline Industry and Market Concentration

4.4.1 Regulation: Capacity and Schedule Competition

In the previous sections it was shown that for a given number of firms with free market entry, the single airline is tempted to establish a global network in order to increase its market share and profit. In what follows, it is shown that this model may help to explain the concentration process in the US airline industry after deregulation. The development of today's industry structure occurred in basically two steps. First, the formerly regulated local carriers started to operate hub-and-spoke systems in their designated areas shortly after deregulation. Besides offering flights from their traditional destinations to the hub, they became affiliated with commuter carriers and started to offer flights to long-distance destinations. In the mid 80s, a number of mergers and bankruptcies reduced the number of competitors and established multiple-hub networks. In this respect, it can be observed that the airlines differentiate their products by offering online connections between different regions and via different hubs.

In Chapter 1, the regulatory framework before the implementation of the Airline Deregulation Act in 1978 was described. Property rights theory, e.g. *Stigler (1971)*, suggests that under regulation airlines are able to seek economic rents. Therefore, one would assume that the regulated period of the US airline industry was characterized by high profits. However, several empirical studies found that despite the protection from competitive forces, the regulated airlines did not maintain excess rates of return. *Jordan (1970),* for example, found that the non-regulated intra-state carrier *Pacific Southwest Airlines* had been more profitable than any trunk-carrier over the regulatory period, although it had charged lower fares. *Keeler (1972)* showed that the trunk carriers earned ‹normal› profits compared to the non-regulated intra-state carriers in California, because they incurred higher costs due to excess capacity. The trunk carriers had lower load factors and higher flight frequencies compared to intrastate carriers, indicating that while prices were set at high cartel levels, airlines competed profits away with capacity. *De Vany (1975)* and *Schmalensee (1977)* provided theoretical support for the hypothesis that under a regime that fixes fares and restricts entry while not imposing any restraints on schedules and capacity utilization, competition with schedules tends to erode carrier profits. Since the model developed here belongs to the same ‹family› of models, it leads to similar results.

In order to account for price and entry regulation, we assume that the regulator fixes the monopoly price P_m and the total number of connecting destinations D_m. The number of connecting destinations per firm then is D_m/n. The use of the monopoly values is based on the assumption that regulation is more beneficial to the regulated firms than to consumers, because regulators are influenced by firms through the political process.[3] Thus, we assume that the regulated airlines are able to achieve the monopoly price and network size.

3 See, for example, *Stigler (1971)*.

Therefore, whereas fares and network densities are constant, the carriers are free to compete with load factors and schedule densities.

According to equation (2.22) in Chapter 2, the inverse load factor of the monopoly airline is

$$E = \frac{\beta(P - c - gE)}{g}.$$

Assuming that firms compete with the inverse load factor, but are restricted to the monopoly ticket price, we can assume that the single firm determines its inverse load factor according to the elasticities of its perceived demand function. We therefore write

$$E_i = \frac{\beta_i(P_m - c - gE_i)}{g}, \qquad (4.12)$$

where $\beta_i = \theta\beta$ with, analogous to (3.14),

$$\theta = 1 + (n-1)\frac{(\gamma - 1)^2}{\gamma}$$

for a local network in the one region case. The inverse load factor then is, solving (4.12) for E_i,

$$E_i = \frac{1}{\left(1 + \frac{1}{\beta_i}\right)} \frac{P_m - c}{g}, \text{ or} \qquad (4.13)$$

$$E_i = \frac{1}{\left(1 + \frac{1}{\beta\theta}\right)} \frac{P_m - c}{g}. \qquad (4.14)$$

Since θ increases with the number of firms, the inverse load factor increases with the number of firms as well. Similarly, according to (2.23) but taking frequency competition into account, schedule density may be written as follows:

$$F_i = \frac{X_i}{Q_i} = \frac{\alpha_i(P_m - c - gE_i)}{f}, \tag{4.15}$$

where $\alpha_i = \alpha\theta$. For the constant (regulated) monopoly fare and the competitive inverse load factor E_i, schedule density for a given number of firms is

$$F_i = \frac{P_m - c}{f} \frac{\alpha}{\left(\frac{1}{\theta} + \beta\right)}. \tag{4.16}$$

As the influence of θ on F_i is positive, schedule density also increases with the number of firms. Therefore, assuming the price and the number of destinations as the regulated variables, the model shows that monopoly rents decrease as a result of increasing competition with capacity and the schedule. This result is in line with *Schmalensee (1977)*.[4]

4 Cf. Chapter 2, Section 2.3.3 and Appendix D.

Figure 4.4: Western Airlines' route structure before and after deregulation

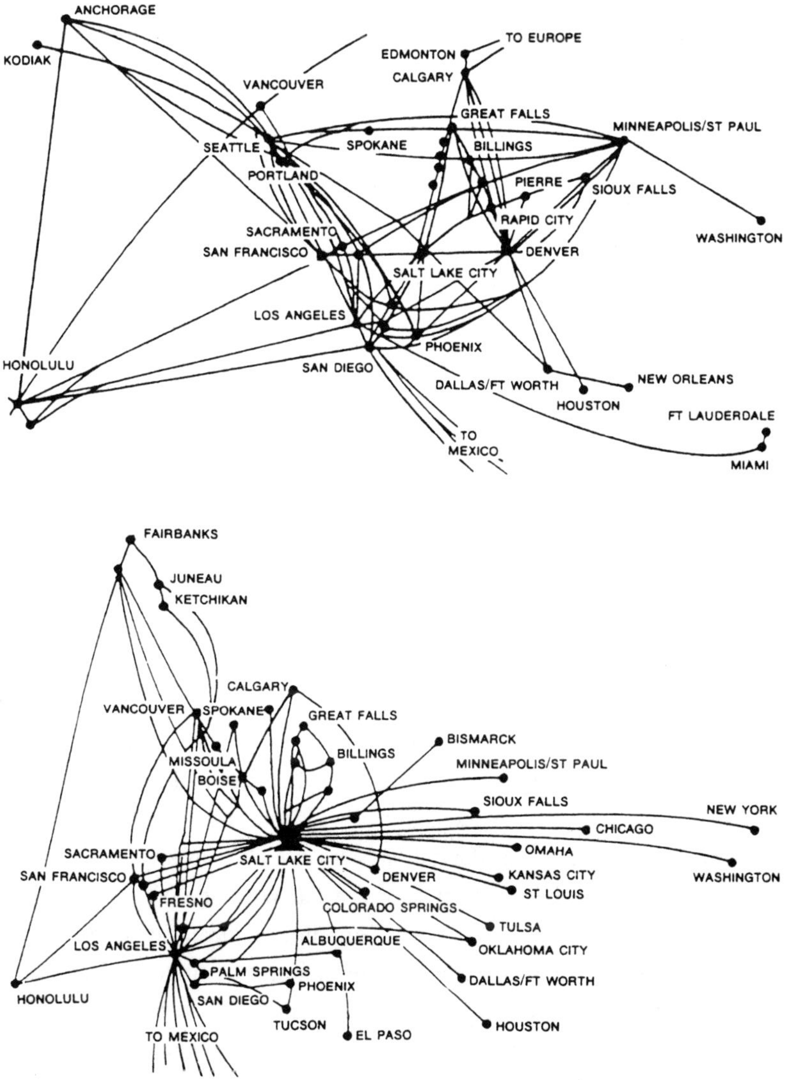

4.4.2 Deregulation: Network Consolidation and Hub-and-Spoke Systems

With the Airline Deregulation Act of 1978 the US airlines gained the freedom to enter any US market without any restrictions on fares, capacities and schedules. In order to increase the efficiency of their operations, the trunk carriers developed hub-and-spoke networks. The local airlines, which were restricted to offering flights in one specific region during regulation, increasingly entered long-haul markets to destinations outside their original areas of operation. Most of them developed a hub in their home region, where they grouped the passengers from the local destinations in order to offer connecting services to some major cities in the US. In order to use the newly established hubs more effectively, several airlines became affiliated with commuter carriers. The commuters originally were exempted from CAB regulation and provided services from major airports to small communities with small propeller aircraft. Whereas in the first years of deregulation, locals and commuters cooperated by code sharing and interlining agreements, the commuters were often purchased by the larger airlines in the late 80s. Many renamed their companies according to their large partners, like *United Express, Continental Express* or *American Eagle.*

The hub-and-spoke networks the local airlines developed in the first years after deregulation resembled the theoretically predicted network of a local airline, at least for domestic flights. *Figure 4.4* displays the network of *Western Airlines* before and after deregulation. As a local carrier, *Western Airlines* was operating in several city-pair markets in the West and Midwest of the US. After deregulation, *Western* developed a hub in Salt Lake City, from where it offered services to a large number of destinations in the West and Midwest, to some destinations in the East, and to Alaska. For international flights to Mexico, *Western Airlines* developed a second smaller hub in Los Angeles. Because the local carriers rarely were operating in the same areas as a result of the former entry regulation, products were differentiated after deregulation in that the carriers mainly created hubs in different regions, as *Figure 4.5* shows.

Figure 4.5: Leading hub cities of selected US airlines in 1983.

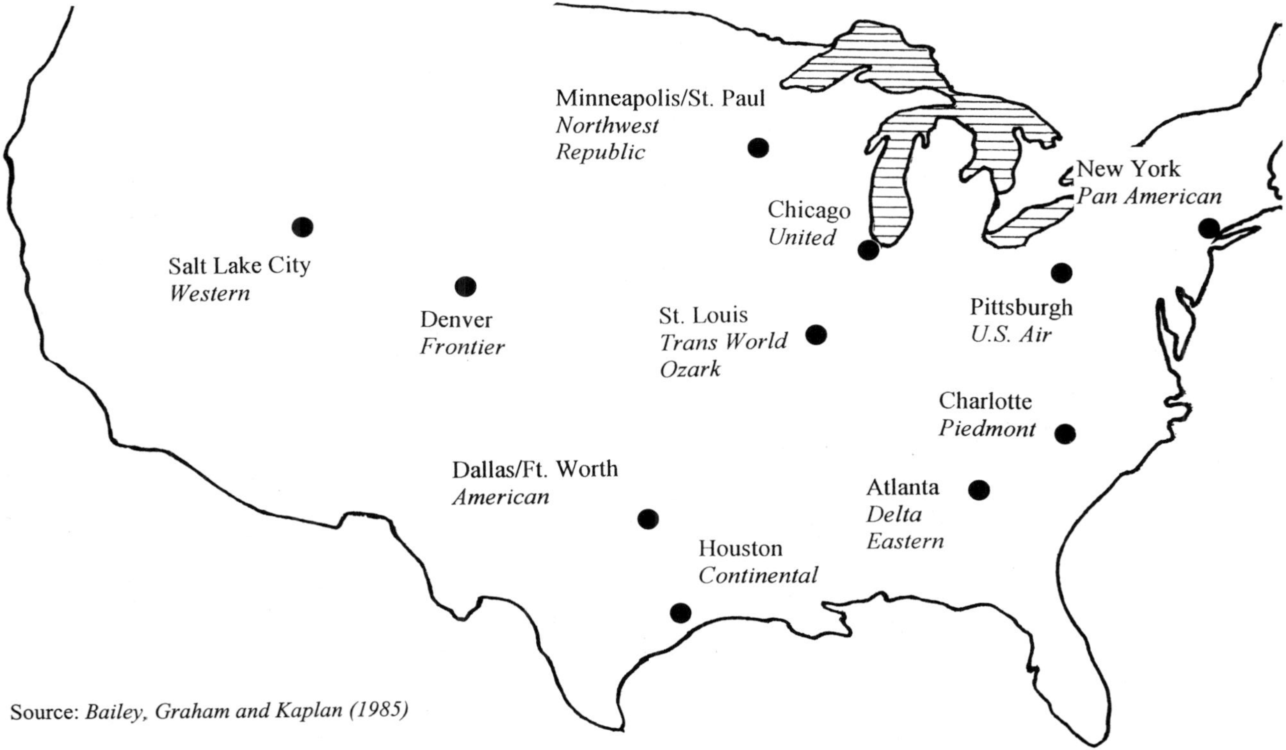

Source: *Bailey, Graham and Kaplan (1985)*

Figure 4.6: Location of the two major hubs of selected US airlines in 1991

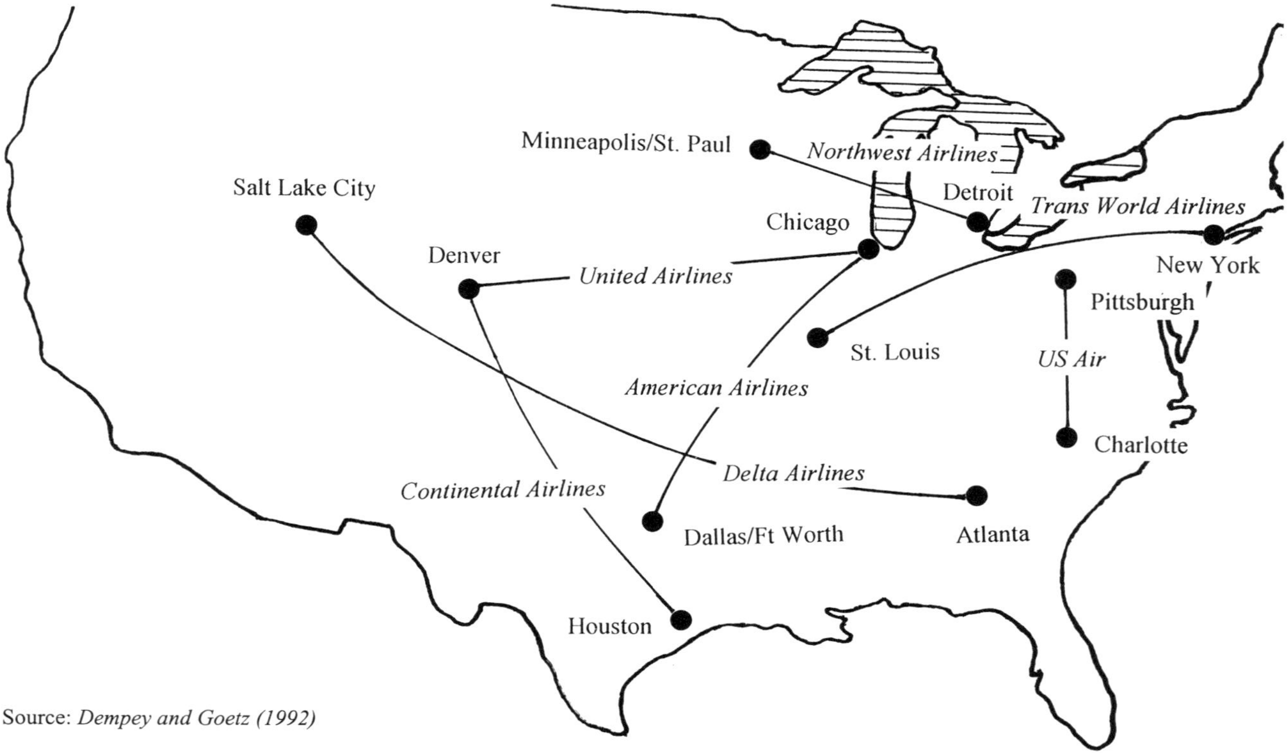

Source: *Dempey and Goetz (1992)*

4.4.3 Mergers

Whereas the large trunk carriers like *American Airlines* and *United Airlines* already operated all over the United States at the beginning of deregulation, the other trunk and local carriers usually dominated one specific area and only offered a small number of flights to destinations outside the home region. Consequently, the smaller carriers had some disadvantages compared to the two larger airlines because they were not able to offer a nationwide network at similar costs. This was especially important with respect to Frequent Flyer Programms (FFPs) and Travel Agent Commission Override Programs (TACOs), which are provided more effectively when there is a large network with many destinations. Furthermore the locals and small trunks were not able to provide as many online connections as the large trunk carriers. Thus, in the mid 80's, a series of mergers between smaller carriers occurred.

The mergers of local carriers and smaller trunk carriers usually increased the number of online connections, but some mergers led to an unusually high concentration at hub airports. In the following, a selection of mergers and their effects on network structures and dominant positions at hubs are briefly discussed.[5] *Figure 4.6.* provides an illustration of the resulting networks by depicting the major hubs of the largest carriers.

- *Delta Airlines' Acquisition of «Western Airlines»:*

  Before the merger, *Delta* was mainly operating from its hub in Atlanta. After the acquisition of *Western Airlines* and its hub in Salt Lake City, *Delta* was

5 The following information mainly stems from *Dempsey and Goetz (1992)*. For a more detailed analysis and econometric surveys of specific mergers, see, for example, *Carlton, Landes and Posner (1980), Fisher (1987),* and *Borenstein (1990). Carlton, Landes and Posner (1980)* predict welfare effects of the merger of *Southern Airways* and *North Central Airlines* in 1979. *Fisher (1987)* investigates the purchase of *Pan American's* transpacific routes by *United Airlines. Borenstein (1990)* analyzes the effects of the merger of Northwest Airlines and Republic Airlines and the merger of *TWA* and *Ozark Airlines* on fares in markets to the respective major hubs.

able to extend its network towards the West. Because the networks of *Delta* and *Western* did not overlap prior to the merger and Salt Lake City was already dominated by *Western*, the acquisition did not lead to an increase in concentration on hub airports but established a large number of new online connections between the East and the West of the United States.

- *Trans World Airlines' Acquisition of «Ozark Airlines»*

  Ozark was a small carrier that concentrated its operations around a hub in St. Louis. *Trans World Airlines* (*TWA*) had a hub at the New York Kennedy airport, from where most of its international flights started. *TWA's* purchase of *Ozark* in 1986 was part of a strategic plan to develop a major hub in St. Louis for domestic operations. After the merger, *TWA* dominated St. Louis airport and fares for connections through the St. Louis hub slightly increased on average. But, as with the *Western Airlines* case, the merger led to a large increase in the number of online connections.

- *Merger Between «Northwest Airlines» and «Republic Airlines»*

  This merger also took place in 1986. *Republic Airlines* itself was the result of the merger between *Southern Airways* and *North Central Airlines* in 1979. The 1979 merger was regarded as very beneficial for consumers because the two local carriers *Southern* and *North Central* did not serve any common markets. Therefore, the merger between the two led to a large increase in connecting destinations between the South and the North of the US. Whereas *Southern Airways* brought in a small hub at Memphis, *North Central* had small hubs in Minneapolis/St. Paul and Detroit. *Northwest Airlines* was a trunk carrier, that also established a hub in Minneapolis/St. Paul and had a large market share in air transport between the US and Asia, mainly Japan and South Korea. Since *Northwest* and *Republic* both were providing numerous flights to and out of Minneapolis/St. Paul, the merger led to a large increase in the new *Northwest's* market share and to fare increases above the national average at Minneapolis/St. Paul, as *Table 4.1* shows. The fare increases were highest relative to the national average fare increases in those markets where

Northwest and *Republic* were the only competitors prior to the merger (type 2a) and which, therefore, became monopoly markets after the merger. The second highest fare increase can be observed in markets that were already monopolies before the merger (type 2b). In these markets, the fare increases may be due to the decrease in potential competition. In third place are markets with competition remaining after the merger, but where the number of competitors decreased (type 1a). The lowest fare increases can be observed in competitive markets where the merger between *Northwest* and *Republic* did not affect the number of competitors (type 1b). However, the merger led to a large increase in the number of online connections through Minneapolis/St. Paul, Detroit and the third hub at Memphis. The local network of *Republic Airlines* in the East and South completed *Northwest's* network of Western destinations and international connections to Asia.

Table 4.1: Average fare changes in markets to Minneapolis/St. Paul after the merger of Northwest Airlines and Republic Airlines

type of market	airlines operating in markets			number of markets	average fare changes (percentage above national average fare changes)
	*NW**	*RC***	others		
1a	•	•	•	16	6,7%
1b	•		•	41	6,0%
		•	•		
2a	•	•		11	22,5%
2b	•			16	12,0%
		•			

* *Northwest Airlines* prior to the merger
** *Republic Airlines* prior to the merger
Source: *Borenstein (1990)*

– «*Continental Airlines*»

Continental airlines today is the result of a series of mergers of one trunk carrier (*Continental*), two former local airlines (*Texas International* and *Frontier*) and two airlines that started operation shortly after deregulation (*New York Air* and *People's Express*). The first step was the hostile takeover of the former trunk carrier *Continental Airlines* by *Texas International* in 1981. The new company was then named *Continental Airlines* and had its major hub in Houston and a minor hub in Denver. The second step was the acquisition of *Frontier Airlines* by *People's Express* in 1985. *Frontier* was the largest carrier at Denver's Stapleton International Airport, but faced heavy competition from *United Airlines* and *Continental. People's Express* was based in New York Newark and was lacking a nationwide network. With the purchase of *Frontier*, *People's Express* was able to offer an increased number of online connections. However, two years later *People's Express* and *New York Air* were bought by *Continental Airlines*. As in the case of the mergers mentioned above, the location of *Continentals'* hubs can be derived from the merged companies. Besides the two major hubs in Denver (*Frontier*) and Houston (*Texas International*), post-merger *Continental* has smaller hubs in Newark (*People's Express*) and Cleveland. Later in 1987, *Continentals* mother company *Texas Air* also bought the troubled *Eastern Airlines*, which was driven into bankruptcy in 1989.

– «*US Air*»

Before deregulation, *US Air* was named *Allegheny Airlines* and was a local carrier with its primary hub in Pittsburgh. Since *US Air*'s operations were concentrated in the East, increasing competition forced the carrier to expand westward. In 1987, therefore, *US Air* bought *Pacific Southwest Airlines* and one year later *Piedmont Airlines,* which enabled it to develop two major hubs in Pittsburgh and Charlotte. Both hubs are dominated by *US Air* today, which became the largest carrier in the East of the United States.

While the local and smaller trunk carriers were eager to correct the shortcomings of their local networks by mergers, the larger trunk carriers, which were already operating all over the US, focused on internationalization. *United Airlines*, for example, purchased *Pan American's* trans-pacific routes and *Pan American's* authority to London Heathrow and beyond. Due to the mergers in the mid 80s, route structures in the US airline industry changed dramatically. The development of multiple hub networks and the increasing concentration of the industry is in accordance with the theoretical model.

As the theoretical analysis in the previous chapter and sections has shown, there is no unique prediction with respect to net benefits of mergers to consumers. *Morrison and Winston (1989)* estimated the welfare effects of six post deregulation mergers of US carriers, taking into account price and non-price variables. As a measure of welfare changes the authors calculated compensating variations.[6] They found that for all mergers, the implications of the mergers consist of a welfare loss from increased fares and a welfare gain from increased frequent flier mileage and cities served. The mergers also changed welfare through schedule delays, but these effects are very small compared to the price and network effects. Thus, these empirical findings are consistent with the predictions of the model that the change in consumer welfare from a merger depends on the net quality improvements relative to the price increase.[7] In addition, *Morrison and Winston (1989)* found that half the mergers reduce welfare, and half increase it. Cumulatively, the mergers have a modest positive effect on annual consumer welfare. Assuming that the concentration process in the US airline industry was completed by 1989, this result indicates that welfare increased from the change from a local to a global industry structure in the USA.

6 Compensating variation as a measure for welfare change is, for example, explained in *Varian (1992)*, pp. 160ff.

7 See equation (3.54) in Section 3.6.

4.5 Summary and Conclusions

In this chapter the model of local and global networks was extended to a framework that takes the geographical extent of the market into account. In doing so it was assumed that airlines compete with networks using different hubs instead of competing at the same hubs. First, it was shown that the number of firms increases with the number of geographical regions in the local as well as in the global case. Second, when a local industry changes to a global industry, this change is more likely to lead to net welfare benefits for passengers when the number of deregulated regions is high, e.g. when the geographical extent of the liberalized area is sufficiently large.

Deregulation and the decrease in the number of firms can be described by the theory of the war of attrition, where carriers fight for a position in the global industry. As with to the game theoretical solution for industrial policy, one can argue that it may be beneficial to a country to be in possession of one of the future global carriers and, therefore, to subsidize the national carrier. But it is important to note that attempts of national governments to protect national airlines are harmful to the industry and the firm in the long run. First, it is questionable whether or not the subsidization of a national carrier over a long period of time will improve its position relative to competitors. As X-efficiency and property rights theory suggest, a lack of competitive pressure leads to inefficient production. One can presume that profitable carriers are more likely to be among the future global carriers than unprofitable carriers with large debts. Second, the reduction in the number of carriers in a deregulated area and the development of global networks is likely to lead to an increase in consumer welfare, if the deregulated area is sufficiently large. Thus, governments that impede the concentration process may not be acting in the consumers' interest.

The theoretical model was illustrated by the mergers that took place in the US airline industry in the mid 80s. In order to increase the number of online connections within the US, and to implement FFPs and TACOs more effectively, small trunk and local airlines extended their networks by mergers and acquisitions. As a result, multiple-hub networks were developed and the number of carriers decreased considerably. Although the mergers sometimes led to an increase in fares at concentrated hub airports, empirical results suggest that the net effect of this concentration process was a slight increase in consumer welfare because of a higher number of online connections.

Appendix

In this appendix, the welfare ratio ω as a function of the number of regions W is calculated. In order to simplify the notation, the sub- and superscripts of the supply variables have been eliminated in the following analysis. The supply variables all represent the respective equilibrium values. The total demand functions for the local and the global cases are

$$Q_L = SWP^{\varepsilon} X^{\alpha} E^{\beta} (Dn)^{\gamma} \text{ and}$$

$$Q_U = SWP^{\varepsilon} X^{\alpha} E^{\beta} D_G^{\gamma} D_H^{\gamma} n^{\gamma} .$$

Because flight frequency and the number of connecting destinations depend on the single firms outputs, we can write

$$Q_L = SWP^{\varepsilon} \left(FQ_{i,L}\right)^{\alpha} E^{\beta} \left(BQ_{i,L} n\right)^{\gamma} \text{ and}$$

$$Q_U = SWP^{\varepsilon} \left(FQ_{i,U}\right)^{\alpha} E^{\beta} \left(B_G Q_{i,U}\right)^{\gamma} \left(B_H Q_{i,U}\right)^{\gamma} n^{\gamma} .$$

Since $Q_{i,L} = Q_L / n$ and $Q_{i,U} = Q_U / n$,

$$Q_L = SWP^{\varepsilon} \left(F \frac{Q_L}{n} \right)^{\alpha} E^{\beta} \left(BQ_L\right)^{\gamma} \text{ and}$$

$$Q_U = SWP^{\varepsilon} \left(F \frac{Q_U}{n} \right)^{\alpha} E^{\beta} \left(B_G \frac{Q_U}{n} \right)^{\gamma} \left(B_H Q_U\right)^{\gamma} .$$

Solving for outputs leads to

$$Q_L = (SW)^{\frac{1}{1-\alpha-\gamma}} P^{\frac{\varepsilon}{1-\alpha-\gamma}} E^{\frac{\beta}{1-\alpha-\gamma}} \left(\frac{F}{n}\right)^{\frac{\alpha}{1-\alpha-\gamma}} B^{\frac{\gamma}{1-\alpha-\gamma}} \text{ and}$$

$$Q_U = (SW)^{\frac{1}{1-\alpha-2\gamma}} P^{\frac{\varepsilon}{1-\alpha-2\gamma}} E^{\frac{\beta}{1-\alpha-2\gamma}} \left(\frac{F}{n}\right)^{\frac{\alpha}{1-\alpha-2\gamma}} \left(\frac{B_G}{n} B_H\right)^{\frac{\gamma}{1-\alpha-2\gamma}}.$$

As in section 3.5, consumer surplus is

$$V_L^* = \left[-1\Big/\left(\frac{\varepsilon}{1-\alpha-\gamma}+1\right)\right](SW)^{\frac{1}{1-\alpha-\gamma}} P^{\frac{\varepsilon}{1-\alpha-\gamma}+1} E^{\frac{\beta}{1-\alpha-\gamma}} \left(\frac{F}{n^*}\right)^{\frac{\alpha}{1-\alpha-\gamma}} B^{\frac{\gamma}{1-\alpha-\gamma}}$$

for local airlines and

$$V_U^* = \left[-1\Big/\left(\frac{\varepsilon}{1-\alpha-2\gamma}+1\right)\right](SW)^{\frac{1}{1-\alpha-2\gamma}} P^{\frac{\varepsilon}{1-\alpha-2\gamma}+1} E^{\frac{\beta}{1-\alpha-2\gamma}} \left(\frac{F}{n^*}\right)^{\frac{\alpha}{1-\alpha-2\gamma}} \left(\frac{B_G}{n^*} B_H\right)^{\frac{\gamma}{1-\alpha-2\gamma}}.$$

Now observe that except for the equilibrium number of firms no free-entry supply variable depends on W. Therefore, in the ratio $\omega = V_U^* / V_L^*$, the terms independent of W can be aggregated to a constant M. Thus

$$\omega = M \frac{W^{\frac{1}{1-\alpha-2\gamma}} n_L^{*\frac{\alpha}{1-\alpha-\gamma}}}{W^{\frac{1}{1-\alpha-\gamma}} n_U^{*\frac{\alpha+\gamma}{1-\alpha-2\gamma}}},$$

where,

$$M = \frac{\left[-1\Big/\left(\frac{\varepsilon}{1-\alpha-2\gamma}+1\right)\right] S^{\frac{1}{1-\alpha-2\gamma}} P^{\frac{\varepsilon}{1-\alpha-2\gamma}+1} E^{\frac{\beta}{1-\alpha-2\gamma}} F^{\frac{\alpha}{1-\alpha-2\gamma}} (B_G B_H)^{\frac{\gamma}{1-\alpha-2\gamma}}}{\left[-1\Big/\left(\frac{\varepsilon}{1-\alpha-\gamma}+1\right)\right] S^{\frac{1}{1-\alpha-\gamma}} P^{\frac{\varepsilon}{1-\alpha-\gamma}+1} E^{\frac{\beta}{1-\alpha-\gamma}} F^{\frac{\alpha}{1-\alpha-\gamma}} B^{\frac{\gamma}{1-\alpha-\gamma}}}.$$

The welfare ratio ω can be rewritten as

$$\omega = M \cdot \frac{W^{\frac{1-\alpha-\gamma}{1-\alpha-2\gamma}} \cdot \left(\frac{n_L^*}{W}\right)^{\frac{\alpha}{1-\alpha-\gamma}}}{W^{\frac{1-\alpha}{1-\alpha-\gamma}} \cdot \left(\frac{n_U^*}{W}\right)^{\frac{\alpha+\gamma}{1-\alpha-2\gamma}}}.$$

Taking logs we have

$$\ln\omega = \ln M + \left(\frac{1-\alpha-\gamma}{1-\alpha-2\gamma} - \frac{1-\alpha}{1-\alpha-\gamma}\right)\ln W + \frac{\alpha}{1-\alpha-\gamma}\ln\left(\frac{n_L^*}{W}\right) - \frac{\alpha+\gamma}{1-\alpha-2\gamma}\ln\left(\frac{n_U^*}{W}\right).$$

The welfare ratio ω increases with the number of regions provided that $d\ln\omega/dW > 0$. Note that

$$\frac{d\ln\left(n_L^*/W\right)}{dW} = \frac{W}{n_L^*} \cdot \frac{d\left(n_L^*/W\right)}{dW}, \text{ and}$$

$$\frac{d\ln\left(n_U^*/W\right)}{dW} = \frac{W}{n_U^*} \cdot \frac{d\left(n_U^*/W\right)}{dW}.$$

Because, according to equations (4.7) and (4.9),

$$\frac{n_L^*}{W} = \frac{\gamma(1-\alpha-\gamma)}{(\alpha+\gamma)(\gamma-1)^2} + \frac{1}{W}, \text{ and}$$

$$\frac{n_U^*}{W} = \frac{\gamma(1-\alpha-2\gamma)}{(\alpha+2\gamma)(\gamma-1)^2} + \frac{1}{W},$$

we have

$$\frac{d\left(n_L^*/W\right)}{dW} = -\frac{1}{W^2}\text{, and}$$

$$\frac{d\left(n_U^*/W\right)}{dW} = -\frac{1}{W^2}.$$

Therefore

$$\frac{d\ln\left(n_L^*/W\right)}{dW} = -\frac{1}{n_L^* W}\text{, and}$$

$$\frac{d\ln\left(n_U^*/W\right)}{dW} = -\frac{1}{n_U^* W}.$$

Thus, the first derivative of the log welfare ratio with respect to the number of regions is

$$\frac{d\ln\omega}{dW} = \frac{1}{W}\left(\frac{1-\alpha-\gamma}{1-\alpha-2\gamma} - \frac{1-\alpha}{1-\alpha-\gamma} + \frac{\alpha+\gamma}{1-\alpha-2\gamma}\cdot\frac{1}{n_U^*} - \frac{\alpha}{1-\alpha-\gamma}\cdot\frac{1}{n_L^*}\right).$$

The term in the brackets is always positive because for any α and γ,

$$n_U^* < n_L^*,$$

$$\frac{\alpha+\gamma}{1-\alpha-2\gamma} > \frac{\alpha}{1-\alpha-\gamma}\text{, and}$$

$$\frac{1-\alpha-\gamma}{1-\alpha-2\gamma} > \frac{1-\alpha}{1-\alpha-\gamma}.$$

Therefore, the welfare ratio ω always increases as W increases.

5. Policy Implications

5.1 Introduction

Starting with the deregulation in the US, the structure of the international airline industry has been changing rapidly. Whereas in the 70s almost all airline markets were still regulated by national authorities or restrictive bilateral agreements between countries, an increasing proportion of air transport takes place in a liberalized environment today. The liberalization process in the EU and the recent attempts to sign open-sky agreements between European countries and the US point to the continuation of deregulation in international markets. In Europe, where the majority of carriers is still state-owned or at least controlled by governments, politicians increasingly advocate the privatization of airlines, since the profitability of 100% private *British Airways* outdoes the poor performance of state-owned companies.

However, several observers consider deregulation of the US airline industry as a failure rather than a success, and therefore propose re-regulation. They point to several developments in fares and market structures that seem to be negative with respect to consumer welfare. The dominant position of large carriers at hub airports, the increased concentration of firms at the national as well as at the city-pair market level, and higher fares in some markets are the main deficiencies of deregulation in the view of the critics. They also complain about the large losses incurred by several carriers in recent years, and about the following mergers, takeovers and bankruptcies. Although these doubts about the merits of free markets in scheduled air transport are in line with several market failure arguments, they may be weakened by the results of the monopolistic competition model developed here. If it is true that airlines not only compete with fares but also with hubs, connecting destinations, frequencies and capacities, several ‹deficiencies› mentioned above are in accordance with competition. Furthermore, the model predicts that the decrease in the number of firms, which explains the concentration process, losses and bankruptcies of previously well established independent firms, may lead to an increase in welfare in the long run. Although most of the results of the model are in favor of deregulation, it is important to note that mergers and oligopolies still have to be analyzed thoroughly with respect to market power and collusive behavior.

In this chapter, a summary of the model results is first presented by developing major propositions. In view of the deregulation process in Europe, the propositions are used to explain presumable implications of ‹open skies› and differences to the US experience. This analysis is completed by corresponding implications for international markets. Finally, some features of competition policy are presented, including topics like market definition, the role of elasticities for the determination of market power and the possibility of collusive behavior.

5.2 Propositions

Empirical investigations have shown that scheduled air service is not contestable. One reason for the ineffectiveness of potential competition are large entry costs with respect to scarce airport facilities, scarce slots and the development of large hub-and-spoke networks. In addition, the Bertrand-Nash condition of quasi fixed prices is violated in scheduled air transport. Whereas fares are changed quickly in today's airline industry, entry takes time and can easily be observed by competitors and the public, which prevents hit-and-run entry strategies. Thus, incumbent firms may charge monopoly fares until actual entry occurs. However, at least in this respect, it is presumed that charter services may be more contestable. Charter services rely on private contracts between suppliers (airlines) and customers (travel agencies) for which potential entrants can effectively bid against incumbents. Furthermore, charter airlines provide relatively homogenous products, because they are able to offer or withdraw services to any destination in the world in the short run. In contrast, airlines providing scheduled services are bound to the schedule and, at least in the short run, a finite number of destinations. Moreover, since firms basically are tempted to offer distinct products in order to capture monopoly rents, airlines offering scheduled services do not develop identical networks and, therefore, provide differentiated rather than homogenous products. In this respect, the model developed here, considering schedules, networks and product differentiation, provides further insight into the market structures of scheduled air transport.

In developing the model, the trade off between time sensitive and price sensitive passengers is used. It is assumed that the ‹actual price› a consumer faces is composed of the selling price and time costs. For example, different passenger segments have different preferences with respect to a low fare, seats available on demand and frequency of service. Assuming that production costs are composed of passenger, flight and capacity related costs, a model is developed where a monopoly airline in a city-pair market maximizes profit by offering a ticket price, flight frequency and inverse load factor according to the time sensitivity and price elasticity of passengers. The comparative static analysis of the results for different types of passengers leads to the following first proposition:

Proposition 1:

In markets where passengers have a high time sensitivity but a low price sensitivity, the monopoly carrier offers a relatively high ticket price, high flight frequency and high inverse load factor. In markets where passengers have a low time sensitivity but a high price sensitivity, it offers a relatively low ticket price, low flight frequency and low inverse load factor.

Attempts to test this basic model revealed some difficulties with respect to the collection of the data. First, marginal costs corresponding to the specification of the model are usually not available. Second, the passenger segment of single city-pair markets is hard to determine for Europe, because most business markets are also tourist markets. Nevertheless, OLS regressions support the predicted influences of market distance and time sensitivity of passengers on the supply variables.

In order to extend the model to a competitive framework, it is assumed that airlines differentiate services for a city-pair market by offering different sets of connecting destinations on a hub. The optimal number of connecting destinations is also influenced by the time sensitivity of consumers. Passengers face access costs, including time opportunity costs, from getting to the closest airport for departure. As the number of connecting destinations in a well defined region increases, the average distance between airports decreases. This leads to a reduction in access costs and, therefore, to an increase in demand. But the provision of connecting destinations is costly. For the monopoly airline, this means that in markets with time sensitive passengers, a denser network is offered than in markets with price sensitive passengers.

When competitors enter the market, firms compete with the supply variables price, inverse load factor, flight frequency and the number of connecting destinations. Taking into account the assumption that airlines differentiate their products by offering flights to different connecting destinations, demand increases with the number of firms in the market, because passengers can choose from a higher number of connecting destinations. However, it was shown that the free-entry equilibrium number of firms in a city-pair market is rather small for two reasons. First, since it is assumed that firms do not differentiate their services with respect to departure times, more than one firm in the market leads to a multiplication of the schedule. Second, because firms differentiate their services with respect to connecting destinations, the extent of local monopoly power depends on the time sensitivity of passengers with respect to access to the closest airport. Therefore, when passengers are time sensitive, there may be a large scope for product differentiation with connecting destinations, which would increase the free-entry equilibrium number of firms. But firms offering services to time sensitive passengers are also tempted to use a dense schedule, which reduces the equilibrium number of firms because of the costly multiplication of the schedule. In contrast, when passengers are price sensitive, the costs from the multiplication of the schedule are lower, which would increase the free-entry equilibrium number of firms. But because of low access costs, there is little scope for product differentiation, which reduces the free-entry equilibrium number of firms again. This leads to the second proposition, that is derived from the results obtained in Chapter 3:

Proposition 2:

The free-entry equilibrium number of firms in single city-pair markets depends on time sensitivity of passengers with respect to flight frequency and access time to the closest airport. Because of the multiplication of the schedule, the number of firms is low for a large variety of combinations of these parameters.

Further analysis shows that for the same reason, consumer welfare is maximized by a regulated monopoly. However, without taking into account incentive problems with respect to managers in regulated firms, this result may not be used as a proposition of this model. But it indicates that competition in air transport services may lead to inefficiencies.

So far, the monopolistic competition model has investigated supply and demand in a city-pair market, where firms have connecting destinations only at one endpoint of this market. This type of network is referred to as *local*, because it can be interpreted as a network that basically provides air transport services from local destinations in one specific region to a large airport of another region. A local network corresponds to the situation in many international markets governed by bilateral agreements. National carriers may be able to offer local flights within the home country to its major airport, from where passengers are transported to international destinations. But because of entry restrictions, the national carrier may not be allowed to offer connecting destinations within foreign countries (8th freedom rights).

The model developed in Chapter 3 further shows that in the absence of entry restrictions, airlines are tempted to offer connecting destinations at both endpoints of city-pair markets. This type of network is called a *global network.* The comparison between local and global networks leads to *Propositions 3 to 5.*

Proposition 3:

In the absence of entry restrictions for air transport between two regions, airlines develop global networks with a hub and connecting destinations in both regions.

The main reason for the development of global networks is economies with respect to the number of online connections. Passengers value online connections (e.g. connections with the same carrier) higher than interline connections (e.g. connections with a change of carrier), because time costs for changing planes at airports and the possibility of lost baggage are lower. When there is a hub at one endpoint of a city-pair market, the addition of connecting destinations at the other endpoint increases the number of online connections more than proportionately. If costs for connecting destinations are equal at both hubs, this implies that each airline is tempted to offer a symmetrical network.

The development of global networks also influences the other supply variables and the free-entry equilibrium number of firms:

Proposition 4:

For a given set of elasticity and cost parameters, the change from a local to a global network structure leads to an increase in fares, inverse load factors, schedule densities, and network densities. In addition, the free-entry equilibrium number of firms is reduced.

This result first suggests a reduction in consumer welfare, because competition in the respective city-pair markets is reduced. However, a global network leads to a higher number of online connections between the two regions compared to a local network. With respect to consumer welfare, this means that the development of a global network is characterized by a trade off between higher fares on the one hand and a higher quality of service on the other hand:

Proposition 5:

Consumer welfare increases from the development of global networks if the elasticity weighted increase in flight frequency, inverse load factor and online connections exceeds the elasticity weighted increase in prices.

It follows from *Proposition 5* that the change from local to global network structures will more likely be beneficial to consumers if they are time sensitive rather than price sensitive.

The analysis of free-entry equilibrium number of firms in the local and global network models implies natural monopoly situations for a large variety of parameter combinations, which does not seem to correspond to reality.

However, it can be assumed that airlines do not compete *at* hubs but compete *with* hubs. In other words, although firms may compete in transporting passengers between two regions, they do not use the same pair of hubs. In order to adjust the model in this respect, product differentiation with connecting destinations is completed by product differentiation with hubs in different regions. Here it is assumed that airlines transport passengers between two *large areas* consisting of an equal number of regions. Because firms are tempted to differentiate their products in order to gain local monopoly power, it is assumed that they develop hubs in different regions. The effectiveness of competition then is determined by the extent the respective networks overlap. If there are many regions, airlines may enjoy local monopoly power because there are many ways to differentiate products and, therefore, the chance of overlapping networks is very low. This induces entry of additional firms. In contrast, when there is only a small number of regions, there is little space for product differentiation, which implies a high chance of overlapping networks and low local monopoly power. In this case only a small number of firms can operate profitably. As a result the following proposition holds:

> *Proposition 6:*
>
> *For air transport between two large areas composed of several regions, the free-entry equilibrium number of firms increases with the number of regions for local and global networks.*

Note that *Proposition 4,* according to which a change from local to global networks reduces the free-entry equilibrium number of firms, is still valid for this extended version of the model. The same is true for *Proposition 5*. Moreover, it can be shown that the development of global networks is more likely to lead to an increase in consumer welfare if the number of regions is high. This feature of the model is due to decreasing economies of a large number of firms. Demand increases when passengers can choose from a larger variety of products, but at a decreasing rate. Therefore, if the number of firms is reduced from a relatively high level, demand decreases only slightly, whereas a reduction from a relatively low level leads to a large decrease in demand. This leads to the following final proposition:

Proposition 7:

When airlines change their networks between two areas from local to global structures, consumer surplus is more likely to be increased for large areas than for small areas.

This proposition has to be further discussed in the context of deregulation. In most cases, international regulatory constraints prevent airlines from establishing global networks, but tolerate local networks. In addition, regulation often also prevents competition with hubs. Since deregulation would not be advisable when the development of global networks leads to a decrease in consumer welfare, the effect of the size of the area on the outcome of liberalization has to be taken into account. In this respect *Proposition 7* implies that deregulation should not only guarantee free-entry, but should also affect as large a geographic area as possible.

The case study on the deregulation of the US airline industry shows that the model helps to explain the concentration process in the mid 80s. As follows from *Propositions 3 and 4*, the deregulation process led to the development of multiple-hub networks and to a decrease in the number of firms, which was mainly achieved by mergers. The empirical results of *Morrison and Winston (1989)* show that the welfare effects of six post deregulation mergers in the US are composed of losses from increased fares and gains from increased frequent flier milages and cities served. With respect to the model derived here, these results show that the concentration of firms and the development of multiple-hub networks improve consumer welfare if quality improvements exceed price increases.

5.3 Deregulation of European and Intercontinental Airline Markets

Differences with respect to geographical, institutional and political characteristics between the US on the one hand and the EU and intercontinental markets on the other hand may lead to different effects of deregulation. In order to get some ideas for the presumed further development of market structures in

Europe and intercontinental markets, the different market conditions have to be accounted for when interpreting the model. With respect to market definition, it is important to see that while Europe is larger than the US in terms of population, it is geographically much smaller. In addition, the major heavily populated areas in the EU are located relatively close together in the center of the continent, whereas in the US, the largest cities are located at the edge of the country (for example Los Angeles, New York, Chicago). With respect to intercontinental traffic, it has to be remembered that most markets are still regulated by restrictive bilateral agreements. In addition, there is no large deregulated geographical area outside of the EU and the US. Therefore, the freedom rights granted for air transport to respective countries are still of major importance.

With respect to the development of global networks, the smaller geographical size of the EU and the location of large cities in the center of the EU may prevent airlines from developing multiple-hub networks for inter-European traffic. Unlike the EU, the US consists of several heavily populated regions located in different parts of the country. Thus, a large proportion of the total number of US passengers is transported between these regions. US airlines, therefore, are tempted to have a hub in at least two regions, because long-distance direct flights between several destinations in two regions would be too costly. In Europe, the dense regions are located much closer together, which favors direct flights, especially if we take the competition from the railway system into account. It can therefore be presumed that the deregulated airline industry in the EU will be characterized by a larger proportion of direct flights than in the US. In addition, the main airports of European carriers may primarily serve as international hubs. This may be partially due to the low percentage of inter-European traffic of European carriers compared to inter-US traffic of US airlines, which was already discussed in Section 1.4.

Proposition 6 implies that the equilibrium number of firms increases with the geographical size of the area. Thus, the smaller geographical size of the EU compared to the US indicates that the deregulated airline industry in the EU may be characterized by a smaller number of firms compared to the US. This may also be due to a higher frequency elasticity of demand. The smaller geographical size of the EU and the central location of major cities indicate that average market distance is smaller for inter-EU traffic than inter-US traffic.

Therefore, inter-EU air transport faces more intensive competition from ground transport like the railway system, which increases elasticities. Furthermore, due to ground transport competition, it can be presumed that inter-EU traffic will continue to play only a minor role for European carriers compared to the intercontinental services. Therefore, a large proportion of inter-European flights of the large carriers will predominantly serve as connecting flights for international destinations. This may lead to additional opportunities for numerous small regional carriers providing short-distance scheduled services with small aircraft. Regional airlines, *Crossair* and *Air Engadina* are Swiss examples, often use small airports that are less congested than the large hubs. This puts them in a more favorable position with respect to competition from the railway system compared to the large national carriers. *Crossair,* for example, is offering flights from Zurich to the London City Airport, which is located closer to the City and may be more convenient than the large congested airports Heathrow or Gatwick. Similarly, *Air Engadina* offers flights from the small airport of Bern to the London City Airport. However, the question has to be raised whether or not the regional carriers can survive as independent firms. When market structures in Europe change according to the US pattern, where most commuter carriers were acquired by the large trunk carriers within a decade after deregulation, we may expect several similar mergers in Europe too. *Crossair*, for example, has already been bought by *Swissair* a few years ago.

Restricted by bilateral agreements and pool arrangements, which have only allowed direct flights from the home country to foreign destinations, European carriers usually have developed hubs in their home countries. These hubs are mainly used to group or distribute intercontinental passengers to or from other cities in the EU. Despite the deregulation of European air transport, numerous entry restrictions for markets outside of Europe still prevent the development of global networks in the sense of this model. US carriers face similar problems. Whereas they enjoy complete freedom in developing efficient multiple-hub networks for inter-US traffic, restrictive bilateral agreements still prevent the development of international multiple-hub networks. Therefore, carriers based in the EU or the US may only offer local networks for intercontinental traffic, although they face liberal home markets. However, especially in the North-Atlantic market, carriers are beginning to form strategic alliances composed of interlining and code sharing agreements for intercontinental flights. For these agreements, the US usually grants anti-trust immunity. The strategic alliance between *Swissair, Sabena, Delta Airlines* and *Austrian Airlines*, for example, has a code sharing agreement for flights between Austria, Switzerland and the US. In addition, the airlines use the same airport facilities at their hubs in Atlanta and Zurich. Thus, Atlanta has become a US hub for *Swissair*, whereas *Delta* uses Zurich as its European hub. Similar agreements exist between *United Airlines* and *Lufthansa*, *Northwest Airlines* and *KLM*, and soon there will be one between *American Airlines* and *British Airways*. Strategic alliances that develop global networks do not necessarily lead to a decrease in competition, since passengers often benefit from a large choice of online connections. Thus, the modern strategic alliances between carriers from different continents go beyond the former pool arrangements between national carriers. Whereas the latter basically were designed to capture monopoly rents in single markets under the protection of restrictive bilateral agreements, strategic alliances as described above are designed to develop global networks and increase online connections in an increasingly deregulated environment.

However, although air traffic over the North-Atlantic is already partially deregulated by several more liberal bilateral agreements between some European countries and the US, an open-sky agreement between the EU and the US is desirable in view of the development of efficient multiple-hub networks and consumer welfare. Taking into account the fact that welfare is likely to increase from the development of global networks if the deregulated area is sufficiently large, European governments should no longer prevent such an agreement. However, since the development of global networks leads to a reduction in the number of firms, a lot of European national carriers would no longer be able to exist as independent firms. Incentives to form intercontinental global networks would lead to additional strategic alliances and even mergers between US and EU firms.

With respect to air transport outside of the EU and the US, the development of global networks is even more difficult, because there is no larger area with a completely deregulated airline industry. According to the majority of the traditional bilateral agreements, airlines are not allowed to offer connecting flights *within* a foreign country or *between* foreign countries. But the development of a hub in a foreign continent is only useful when the airline is able to serve connecting destinations from this hub. For a European carrier transporting passengers to South-East Asia, for example, this means that they should have 5th freedom rights with all the countries in this area in order to develop global networks. Unless carriers are able to obtain these rights or to sign code sharing and interlining agreements with carriers from foreign countries, a major proportion of intercontinental traffic from Europe and the US to Asia, Africa, South America and Australia will continue to have a local structure.

5.4 Competition Policy

5.4.1 Object

The model results and the case study in Chapter 4 on the concentration process in the US airline industry indicate that deregulated international air transport markets will be characterized by a small number of large firms in the future. As in other concentrated industries, mergers, strategic alliances and collusive behavior of firms raise concern about their effects on consumer welfare. Therefore, competition law in many countries and in the EU requires that mergers of large firms be investigated if they meet certain requirements with respect to revenue and market shares. Since airlines usually are relatively large firms, competition policy will play a major role in the development of future market structures in the airline industry.

The primary object of competition policy is to prevent firms from the exerting market power. The problem of market power is closely related to market structures, especially economies of scale and scope, that lead to a small number of firms or even a natural monopoly in the equilibrium. On the one hand, a small number of firms facilitates cartel agreements or tacit collusion, which may reduce consumer welfare. On the other hand, a small number of firms may be efficient because of economies of scale and scope. The traditional solution to this dilemma was regulation. But since regulation is biased with agency problems arising from different utility functions of consumers, regulators and firms, monopoly rents may not be avoided but are only redistributed through government control. However, as the theory of contestable markets shows, marginal cost – or at least average cost – pricing may persist if there are potential competitors and if entry barriers are absent. This means that the capture of monopoly rents is interfered with by firms that theoretically could offer the same good at a lower price or a higher quality than the incumbent firms. Thus the restriction of market power does not necessarily correspond to the maintenance of a high number of firms or the prohibition of mergers, takeovers and strategic alliances. Furthermore, the models in this work show that high prices do not necessarily indicate a lack of competition, since airlines may also compete with frequencies, seats available on demand and connecting destinations. The need for competition policy crucially depends on the existence of entry barriers, that is on the possibility of quick and costless entry of potential competitors. In other words, the most effective ‹competition policy› would be the elimination of entry barriers. However, this is not always possible.

For international airline markets, the above proposition indicates that in order to restrain market power of firms, governments should abolish any legal restriction of market entry in the first place. However, as has been discussed in Section 1.3.4., scheduled air transport markets are not perfect contestable, even in the absence of regulatory entry barriers. Entrants may face sunk costs at large airports and from the development of a sufficiently large network. In addition, because the development of a new service and network takes time, incumbents may offer the monopoly supply variables until they face actual competition. Therefore, even if institutional entry barriers are eliminated, some markets may still be characterized by market structures that presumably are harmful to consumers and should be watched closely.

Market power may arise from integration or collusion. In the airline industry, integration includes attempts by firms to offer joint services as is the case in mergers, takeovers, and strategic alliances. Collusion means that firms offer independent services but secretly cooperate in order to capture monopoly rents. With respect to the models developed in this work, collusion may cover the fixing of fares as well as the coordination of other supply variables. In the next section, integration and collusion in airline markets are discussed.

5.4.2 Integration

According to *Scherer and Ross (1990)*, the first step in merger analysis is to identify the relevant product market and the relevant geographical market. In general, this includes the consumers of a specific good or service, the firms offering the product or a near substitute, and the firms that could offer the product or a close substitute without large entry costs if there is an increase in the price of that product. Here, the relevant product market and the relevant geographical market are considered to be the same, since the product of airlines and product differentiation with hubs are based on geographic terms.

Markets may be defined according to the *U.S. Department of Justice Merger Guidelines*.[1] Accordingly, the relevant market is the smallest group of producers that could, if integrating, profitably exert market power. The delineation of the market is carried out by the following procedure. First, the production plants of the integrating firms are located and the cities concerned are considered as the market. Second, it is assumed that a hypothetical monopolist produces the good instead of the integrating firms, and the question is asked whether a price increase for the good initiated by the monopolist would lead to the substitution of the goods of firms located in cities outside the market for the monopolist. If there presumably is substitution, the market will be completed by the location of those firms that offer the best substitutes. Then, a hypothetical monopolist for the enlarged market is assumed and the substitutability of the respective products is checked again. The procedure is repeated until a market can be defined where a price increase of the hypothetical monopolist will no longer lead to substitution. The firms included in the relevant market then are used as references for the calculation and the judgment of concentration indices and market shares.

A similar procedure may be applied to airline markets. Neighboring city-pair connections are close substitutes if competitors offer similar fares, frequencies, inverse load factors and network sizes. *Figure 5.1* provides an

1 See *Scheffman and Spiller* (1987).

illustration of air transport between two regions, where the services of all three carriers A, B and C may be considered as close substitutes.[2]

Figure 5.1: Neighboring city-pair markets as substitutes

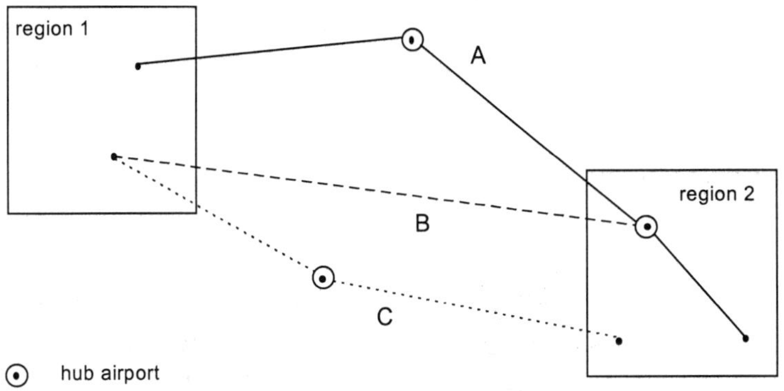

As a first step in market definition in airline markets, the direct and indirect city-pair connections of the integrating firms are located. Subsequently, it is assumed that these city-pair connections are provided by a monopoly airline, and the question is asked whether or not passengers have the opportunity of substituting the services of the hypothetical monopoly in case of a fare increase. When there are substitution opportunities, the respective competitors and city-pair connections are added to the market, a monopoly carrier for the enlarged

2 Such market structures seem to develop increasingly in European air transport, as the following example shows: Today, passengers can travel from Zurich to London with six different carriers using different airports. They either take a flight of *British Airways*, *British Midland* or *Swissair* from Zurich to London Heathrow or Gatwick, a *Crossair* flight from Zurich to London City Airport, or a flight with *Air UK* from Zurich to London Stansted. As a last alternative, they may consider the connection of *Air Engadina* from Bern to London City Airport.

market is assumed and the search for substitutes is continued. The process of market definition ends when no additional firm and city-pair market, that presumably are good substitutes, can be located. In this respect it is important to note that outside competitors may only enter city-pair markets served by incumbents after the incumbents have integrated their operations. Integrated firms (the insiders) usually produce a lower output than the pre-merger joint output, which leaves some residual demand to the remaining firms (the outsiders). If it is likely that competitors will enter additional city-pair markets after the merger, they also should be included within the relevant market.

Figure 5.2: Competition of global carriers

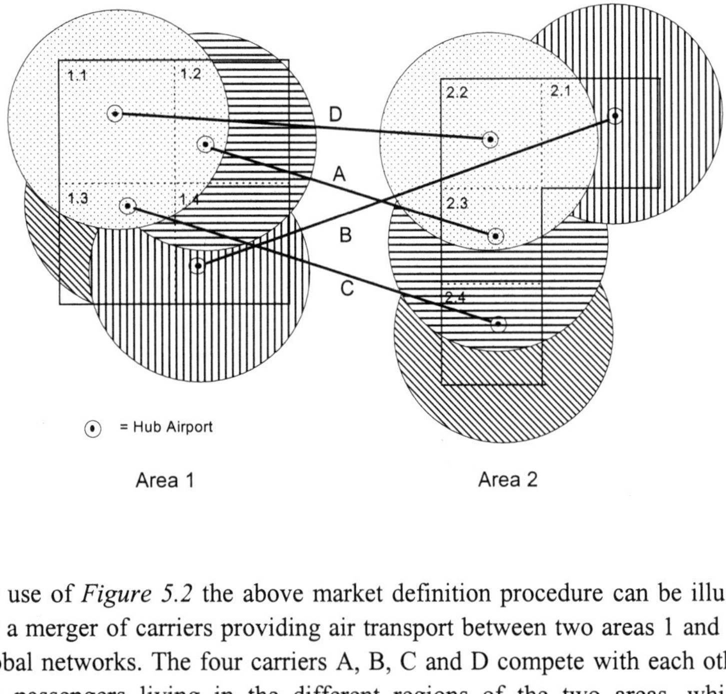

By use of *Figure 5.2* the above market definition procedure can be illustrated for a merger of carriers providing air transport between two areas 1 and 2 with global networks. The four carriers A, B, C and D compete with each other for the passengers living in the different regions of the two areas, which are indicated by the numbers 1.1 to 2.4. According to the monopolistic competition model developed in the previous chapter, it is assumed that airlines differentiate their products by offering flights over different hubs. The circle around each hub airport represents the geographical area within which a carrier offers connecting flights, which may be called the ‹commuter-belt› of the hub. Thus, carriers may offer local connections across regional borders in the home area. As can be seen in *Figure 5.2*, some passengers living in the commuter-belts of more than one hub can choose from different carriers, whereas others, mainly those living at the edge of the two areas, have to take the carrier nearest to them. This underlines the local monopoly characteristics of the model. However, since the greatest proportion of both areas is covered by two or more commuter-belts, the majority of passengers may choose from at least two products.

Figure 5.3: Post-merger competition of global carriers

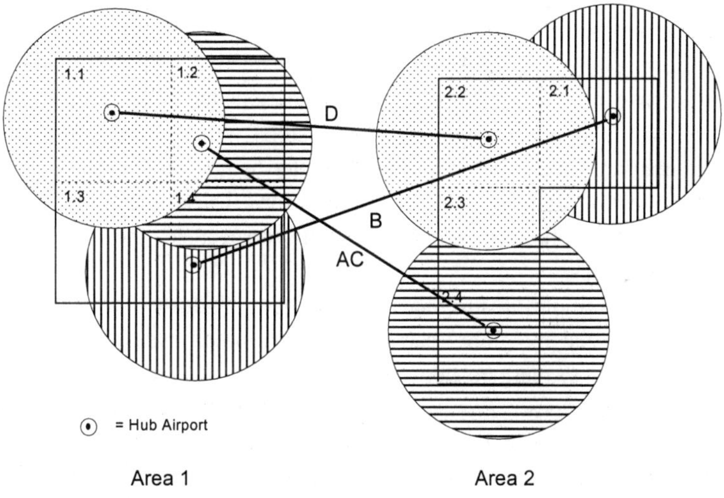

Now let us assume that two carriers apply for merger, which would have to be approved by a competition authority. For convenience, it is assumed that the merging firms keep two of their four hubs and that the remaining carriers keep all their hubs in the short run, e.g. there is no development of new hubs. Therefore, the passengers will incur a reduction of the variety of products after the merger. Should the merger be approved or not, and what may be the criteria for the judgment of possible welfare effects? The answer to these questions crucially depends on the geographic distribution of the regions, as *Figure 5.3* shows. Here, a possible post merger situation is illustrated for the integration of airlines A and C to firm AC. Assuming that the new firm is eager to differentiate its product from competitors' services as much as possible, it probably chooses to keep the hub of former carrier A in region 1.2, which was already predominantly served by A before the merger, and the hub of former carrier C in 2.4, which was already predominantly served by C. As a result, passengers living in region 2.4 face monopoly supply by AC after the merger, and competition is reduced considerably in region 2.3. In terms of the above market definition procedure, this means that the relevant market for this merger is composed of airlines A and C. In area 1, where the geographic location of the regions is more compact, the post-merger situation is not as dramatic. Nevertheless, for many passengers, the number of competitors has decreased and the proportion of passengers facing monopoly supply has increased. Therefore one may conclude that the merger between A and C should not be approved. However, without knowledge of the actions the other carriers outside the merger will take, no final judgment is possible. Will airlines B and D enter additional markets and enlarge their commuter-belts? Will they be able to change the location of their hubs in the long run? These questions show the limits of market definition procedures with respect to the judgment of integration strategies.

The above example is designed to describe an industry structure that is already characterized by global carriers. In a regulated industry or during a deregulation process, mergers between carriers that still have local networks may be of greater interest. *Figure 5.4* illustrates the same geographic areas as *Figures 5.2* and *5.3*, but it is assumed that areas 1 and 2 represent two large economic areas that have just signed an open-sky agreement. Because of the former entry restrictions from bilateral agreements, the carriers offering air transport between the two areas still have local networks. For convenience, the reader has to imagine the commuter-belt around each hub in *Figure 5.4* and it is assumed that each carrier uses a hub of a foreign carrier as its only foreign destination, from where it cannot offer connecting services. Because of the large number of carriers offering services between the two areas, the majority of the passengers in both areas benefit from a high level of competition. However, unless they live or visit close to a hub, passengers are forced to change carriers either in the home or the foreign country, because the regulatory constraints prohibit feasible online connections.

Figure 5.4: Competition of local carriers

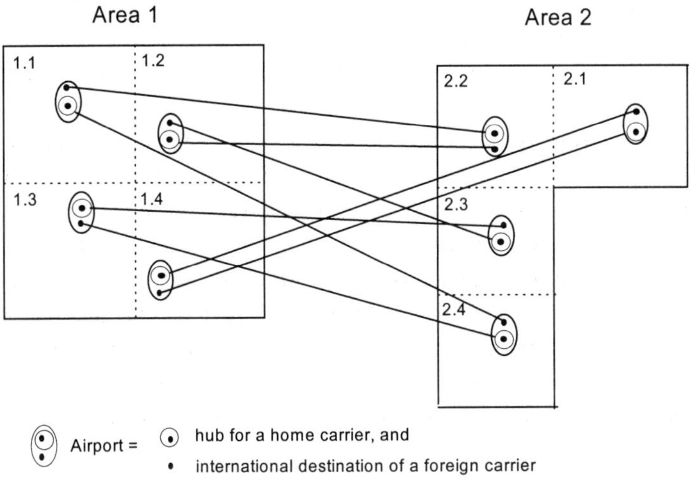

The carriers start to develop global networks after an open-sky agreement has been implemented. It is assumed that the airlines achieve this goal by integration, e.g. mergers and takeovers, rather than by a war of attrition, which would lead to bankruptcies. As in the case of integrating global carriers, the questions have to be raised whether or not the mergers should be approved, and what may be the criteria for the judgment of possible welfare effects? The integration process leads to a reduction in the number of firms and reduces competition in both areas. After the restructuring to global networks, we may get a situation resembling *Figure 5.2*, where there are only four carriers left. But if the net quality improvements exceed price increases, any merger between two carriers *from different areas* increases consumer welfare and therefore should be approved. As *Figure 5.2* shows, carriers A, B, C, and D compete almost in the whole area after the development of global networks. This leads to the conclusion that mergers across areas do not lead to increased market power of single firms if consumers benefit from the development of a large number of additional online connections, a higher schedule density and a higher availability of seats

The examples illustrated in *Figures 5.2* to *5.4* indicate that welfare effects of mergers in the airline industry crucially depend on the industry structure. Besides this, the examples also show that market definition hardly provides a clear answer with respect to welfare implications of mergers, since all the observations and suggestions are rather of qualitative nature. In addition, the above examples show two extreme cases: the integration of two global networks serving the same two areas on the one hand and the development of a global network out of two local networks in two different areas on the other hand. In reality, most cases probably represent a situation somewhere in between, which complicates the analysis.

Furthermore, one cannot generalize from the above result by judging the merger of local carriers to be strictly beneficial to consumers and mergers of global carriers to be strictly harmful. Suppose there is a merger between two local carriers with the majority of connecting destinations in the same area, or a merger of two global carriers with only one common area of operation. Whereas the former probably will reduce competition in the area and only lead to a small number of additional online connections between areas, the latter extends the global structures of the merging firms to a ‹superglobal› network over three areas, which further increases the number of online connections.[3] On the other hand, even if a merger corresponds to one of the potential extreme cases – for example a merger of two global carriers over the same areas – we do not know for sure that this particular merger will be harmful. The integration of two global carriers could still be the long-run result of the change from local to global networks that has led to a too large number of firms in the short run. Similarly, the merger of two local carriers from different areas is not always

3 For example, the alliances between *Lufthansa*, *SAS*, *United Airlines*, and *Thai Airways International* as well as the alliance between *Swissair*, *Austrian Airlines*, *Sabena, Delta Airlines* and *Singapore Airlines* cover the three areas North-America, Europe and South-East Asia.

beneficial to consumers. If the deregulated area is not sufficiently large and if passengers are not sufficiently time sensitive, the welfare loss from higher fares may not be offset by a higher quality. For competition policy, a general recommendation may be that the integration of airline networks should only be approved when it leads to a considerable number of additional online connections. Otherwise one can reasonably expect that the primary goal of the parties is to obtain market power.

The limited scope of market definition procedures may be enlarged by using a more precise economic definition of market power, as for example provided by demand elasticities. Following *Landes and Posner (1981),* a firm incurs market power if it is able to set its price above marginal cost. A profit maximizing monopolist – for example – chooses the price/output combination for which marginal costs equal marginal revenue while not taking the market price as given, as is the case under perfect competition. A measure for market power as the setting of price in excess of marginal costs is provided by the *Lerner index*, which is the proportional deviation of price at the profit-maximizing output from marginal costs at that output. As was already shown in Chapter 2 (2.20), the *Lerner index* is inversely proportional to the price elasticity of demand. Market power of a single airline can therefore be denoted by

$$LI_i \equiv \frac{P_i - c - gE_i}{P_i} = -\frac{1}{\varepsilon_i}, \tag{5.1}$$

where LI_i is the *Lerner index* for firm *i*. Equation (5.1) shows that by use of the *Lerner index*, market power of a single firm is determined by its price elasticity. However, as *Landes and Posner (1981)* note, the estimation of a firm's elasticities is characterized by empirical difficulties, especially when the elasticity of demand and the elasticity of supply are being estimated for the same market. To moderate these problems, they show that the single firms demand elasticity – and therefore the *Lerner index* as well – may be determined indirectly by the analysis of the market demand elasticity, the fringe supply elasticity and the market share of the analyzed firm.

While the *Lerner index* may be a useful measure of market power in various markets, its utility is rather limited in the case of this model, since profit maximization includes the simultaneous determination of more than one variable. Market power is not only reflected by a price that exceeds marginal cost, it can also lead to non-optimal values of capacity, flight frequency and network size. As equation (5.1) shows, marginal costs depend on the inverse load factor. Therefore the Lerner index may understate the extent of market power because marginal costs are also increased relative to the competitive level. The profit margin of the single firm, as was defined in Chapter 3, provides an alternative measure of market power in airline markets. Taking the case of global carriers, the profit margin is, according to equation (3.45),

$$\Phi_i = \frac{\Pi_i}{P_i Q_i} = \frac{\alpha_i + 2\gamma_i - 1}{\varepsilon_i}. \tag{5.2}$$

A profit margin of zero corresponds to the free-entry equilibrium level of supply, which indicates that no firm has positive profits and, therefore, market power. The profit margin decreases with increasing price elasticity, frequency elasticity and network elasticity of the single firm. In order to avoid the determination of single firms' elasticities, they may be replaced. According to equation (4.6) in Chapter 4, the single firms' price elasticity is

$$\varepsilon_i = \varepsilon \theta_W,$$

with

$$\theta_W = 1 + (n-1)\frac{1}{W}\frac{(\gamma - 1)^2}{\gamma}$$

The values for the frequency and network elasticities of demand are calculated accordingly by multiplying the respective market demand elasticities by θ_W.[4] Therefore, we have for the profit margin of the single firm:

4 Note that the use of the number of firms is only correct if we assume equally sized airlines. Otherwise, the demand elasticities of a single firm depend on its market share. Because the calculation of single firms elasticities in the monopolistic competition model derived in Chapter 3 has some close similarities to the approach of *Landes and Posner (1981)*, their concept theoretically may be fully applied. However, to facilitate the comparison with the results of our model, it is not used here. In order to derive single firm elasticities with market shares, the number of firms n would simply have to be replaced by the inverse of firm i's market share $1/s_i$.

$$\Phi_i = \frac{\alpha + 2\gamma}{\varepsilon} - \frac{1}{\varepsilon\theta_W}. \tag{5.3}$$

Since θ_W increases with the number of firms. the profit margin - and therefore market power - decreases with the number of competitors, increases with access cost to airports (that is network elasticity of demand γ), and increases with the number of regions W. This indicates that market power is positively correlated with the possibility to differentiate products. In addition, everything else being equal, market power is lower in markets with price sensitive passengers than in markets with time sensitive passengers, as the influence of the respective market demand elasticities show.

Figure 5.5 depicts profit margins for an increasing number of firms in the local and the global case for constant demand elasticities and number of regions. The profit margin curves show that - in contrast to the *Lerner index* - the profit margin not only indicates market power due to a lack of competitors, it also illustrates the case of too many firms in the market. Since mergers towards the free-entry equilibrium number of firms are desirable from a welfare point of view, efficient integration can be distinguished from attempts to gain market power. In addition, *Figure 5.5* confirms the previously found notion that the free-entry equilibrium number of competitors is lower for global carriers as compared to local networks. It also shows that deregulation, which leads to mergers between local carriers to form global networks, may as well lead to mergers between global carriers later on. Suppose a regulated airline industry between two areas is characterized by 14 local carriers, as is assumed in *Figure 5.5*. After deregulation, pairs of local carriers from different areas develop global networks. If there is originally an equal number of carriers in both areas, the industry structure changes to seven airlines offering global services between the two areas. But as *Figure 5.5* shows, only five firms can operate profitably with global networks. Therefore, two additional mergers between global carriers occur on the adjustment path to the global free-entry equilibrium. From this point, any further attempt at integration would lead to market power.

Although the use of elasticities for the determination of market power is more precise than market definition procedures, its utility crucially depends on the estimation of elasticities and problems associated with the methods. However, as the model results and the elaboration of the profit margin above have shown, market power in air transport markets cannot be investigated relying on market shares and the number of competitors alone. In this respect, the influence of time sensitivity of passengers on industry structures and market power has to be emphasized. Therefore, it is desirable that courts and enforcement agencies devote resources to the analysis of elasticities or, at least, to the determination of time sensitivity parameters.

Figure 5.5: Profit margins for local and global carriers

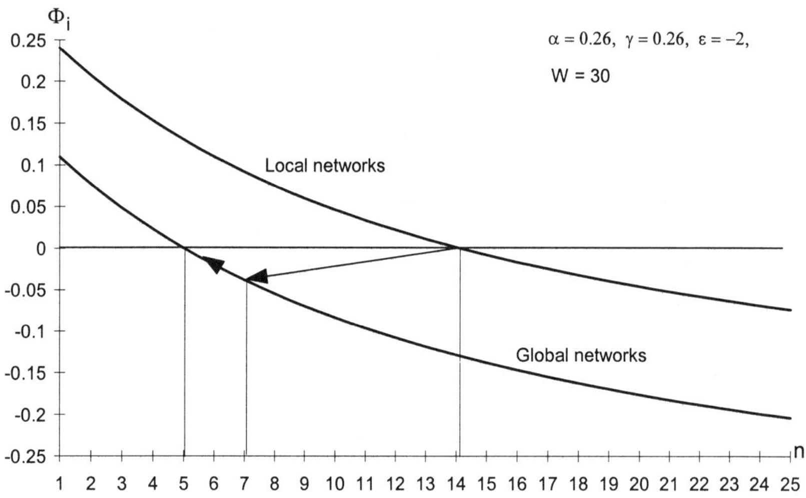

5.4.3 Collusion

The joint determination of supply variables poses one of the most serious threats to competition in deregulated airline markets. This presumption may be underlined by the fact that within the framework of the restrictive bilateral agreements, cooperation has persisted for a long period of time. Because of the rather complicated structure of supply which is determined by the price as well as by non-monetary supply variables, competition authorities face several problems with respect to the detection of collusive behavior and the collection of feasible data. However, as several historical examples show, cartel agreements are not always stable for various reasons. Therefore, one has to pay considerable attention to the stability of collusion in airline markets in the first place. If collusion is not stable in the long run, the problem may be regarded as not important with respect to consumer welfare. On the other hand, if collusion is stable, measures should be taken to avoid it.

Using the monopolistic competition model introduced in Chapter 3, we know that in a market with more than one firm, the single airline faces a *perceived demand* function, whose elasticities reflect the incentive to choose different supply variables than a monopoly airline. The same is true in the case of colluding firms; the single airline faces a perceived demand function reflecting the illusion that it can win customers away and thereby increase its private profit at the cost of its partner by cheating on the collusive supply. The incentives to cheat may be illustrated within the framework of game theory. In order to demonstrate the payoffs, a simple game is first introduced. However, as will become clear later on, only repeated games may provide suitable models of collusion in international air transport.

Suppose there is a secret cartel between two airlines operating in a market with a free-entry equilibrium number of firms $n^* = 2$. It is assumed that the actions of the two airlines take place in two periods. At ‹time $t = 1$›, a contract is signed in which the two airlines i and j agree to maximize joint profit by offering the monopoly supply together as a cartel.[5] At ‹time $t = 2$›, the airlines start operating and selling tickets. Because it is assumed that the airlines act simultaneously, a single airline doesn't observe the action of the other airline before deciding on its own action.

The single airline can choose from two different combinations of supply variables, e.g. two different strategies: The first strategy, $a_i^1 = C$, means that

5 Taking the efficiency loss from the multiplication of the schedules, the highest profit would be obtained if the colluding firms additionally integrate their schedules. But this action would clearly indicate cooperation to the public and to the competition authorities. The integration of schedules therefore is not feasible for secrete collusion. However, within the regulatory framework of bilateral agreements, joint scheduling agreements are quite common. Cf. Section 1.2.

airline i cooperates at ‹time $t = 2$› by choosing the monopoly level of supply. The second strategy, denoted by $a_i^2 = D$, is defection from the cartel agreement, where airline i chooses the supply variables that maximize private profit. The respective strategies for airline j are denoted by $a_j^1 = C$ and $a_j^2 = D$. The strategies and the payoffs for this game are given in *Figure 5.6.*

Figure 5.6: Normal form of airline-game

Airline j / Airline i	$a_j^1 = C$	$a_j^2 = D$
$a_i^1 = C$	*1* $\Pi_i^{C,C}, \Pi_j^{C,C}$	*3* $\Pi_i^{C,D}, \Pi_j^{C,D}$
$a_i^2 = D$	*2* $\Pi_i^{D,C}, \Pi_j^{D,C}$	*4* $\Pi_i^{D,D}, \Pi_j^{D,D}$

If it is assumed that the airlines have the same cost functions and that cooperation leads to the same output for both airlines, the profits obtained from choosing the different strategies have the following properties:

$$\Pi_i^{C,C} = \Pi_j^{C,C} \quad ; \quad \Pi_i^{D,C} = \Pi_j^{C,D} \quad ; \quad \Pi_i^{C,D} = \Pi_j^{D,C} \quad ; \quad \Pi_i^{D,D} = \Pi_j^{D,D}.$$

From our model it follows that the combination of strategies

$$a_i^2, a_j^2$$

leads to a Nash equilibrium, because the combination of payoffs

$$\Pi_i^{D,D}, \Pi_j^{D,D}$$

corresponds to the monopolistic competition equilibrium of two firms, where no firm has further incentives to alter supply variables.[6] It can be shown that this Nash equilibrium is unique.[7] Thus, strategy a^2 always dominates strategy a^1 for both airlines. This leads to the conclusion that any collusive arrangement that fixes supply variables is not stable in the first place, although both parties would be better off cooperating. We therefore face a prisoners' dilemma situation, which implies that

$$\Pi_i^{C,D} < \Pi_i^{D,D} < \Pi_i^{C,C} < \Pi_i^{D,C}.$$

Looking at European city-pair markets, where regulation tolerated cartels, the result just stated is contrary to the fact that numerous cartel arrangements still exist, or at least existed for a long period of time. Thus, the two period model is a weak theory to explore collusive behavior of airlines. In order to explain the long term stability of collusion and to deepen the analysis, we assume an infinitely repeated game where each airline is allowed to change its own strategy in every period. In such a *supergame* framework, the present value of future profits determine the payoffs of the game.[8] For constant profits per time unit, we may have

6 A Nash equilibrium is a set of actions such that no firm, taking the other firms' actions as given, wishes to change its own action.

7 In *Figure 5.6*, the combinations of payoffs are numbered from 1 to 4. In order to prove that payoff combination 4 constitutes a unique Nash equilibrium, we have to show that the airlines always have incentives to change supply variables if the payoff combination corresponds to either 1, 2 or 3. The payoffs in 1 correspond to the cooperative solution, where both airlines have incentives to defect. Depending on the different combinations of strategies, the airlines either "move" to 2, 3 or 4 after choosing the actions. Thus 1 cannot be a Nash-equilibrium. If the airlines act according to payoffs 2, which means that airline *i* chooses to defect whereas airline j chooses to cooperate, airline *j*'s market share and profit decreases, because airline *i* has „stolen" passengers away according to its perceived demand function. However, airline *j*, being confronted with a very low market share, has strong incentives to increase its profit by also changing supply variables and steeling passengers. In doing so, *j*'s market share increases until both firms have the same market shares again, which finally leads to the payoff combination 4. Therefore, combinations 2 and 3 are not Nash-equilibria either.

8 For the theory of supergames see, for example, *Tirole (1988)*, pp. 239-276.

$$\Pi \int_0^\infty e^{-rt} dt = \frac{\Pi}{r}, \tag{5.4}$$

where r is the interest rate, which is assumed to be constant, and t is time.[9] Therefore, in an infinitely repeated game, the payoffs in *Figure 5.6* would have to be adjusted according to equation (5.4). Given these payoffs, the single airline maximizes future profits if it cooperates as long as the partner cooperates and defects the moment it learns about defection of the partner. Assuming that each airline learns about the partner's strategy immediately and reacts in the following period, cooperation is an equilibrium solution of the game. Because the airlines cooperate at ‹time $t = 2$›, they both cooperate in the next period and, therefore, in all future periods.

However, this result may no longer be valid in the following two cases. First, if we face a finitely repeated game, defection in every period is the only equilibrium solution.[10] Second, in an infinitely repeated game, cooperation may not persist if the values of supply variables of each airline stay hidden for a certain time, that is, if there is a sufficiently long *information* or *detection lag*. In the following, we first discuss the problem of a finitely repeated game, while the role of detection lags will be discussed later.

The solution to a finitely repeated game stated above can be obtained by backwards induction. In the final stage of the game, defection dominates collusion for the same reason discussed above in the two period game. Therefore, the decision taken by the two players in the last period is independent of any outcome in preceding periods. Then, in the penultimate period, defection dominates collusion in terms of the current period, while decisions in this period do not affect the outcome in the subsequent (last) period. Thus, the two players also chose defection in this period, and so on in all preceding periods. As a result, defection of both firms at any stage is the unique perfect Nash equilibrium of this game.

However, experiments of games that were designed as repeated prisoner's dilemmas have shown that a strategy known as ‹Tit-for-Tat› was most

9 For the feasibility of the assumption of a constant interest rate, see *Strotz, H. (1956).*

10 See, for example, *Tirole (1988)*, pp. 245.

successful. The Tit-for-Tat strategy requires the player using it to cooperate in the first period and then to cooperate at each of the subsequent stages if and only if the opponent cooperated at the respective preceding stage. If, at one stage, the opponent defects, Tit-for-Tat always defects at the following stage. But if the opponent goes back to cooperation again, Tit-for-Tat will also cooperate again in the subsequent period. Therefore, the Tit-for-Tat player does punish the opponent for defection but does not prevent a successful return to cooperation later on. Thus, in view of this strategy, the Nash equilibrium of defection at every stage of the game is not very plausible. *Kreps, Milgrom, Roberts and Wilson (1982)* show that in the finitely repeated prisoner's dilemma, cooperation may occur if at least one party plays the Tit-for-Tat strategy with a certain probability. Specifically, *Kreps et. al. (1982)* provide an upper bound on the number of periods in which either one of the players defects. This bound is independent of the total number of repetitions and includes, among others, the last few periods of the game. Thus, for a sufficiently large number of repetitions of the game, there are periods in which both parties cooperate.

We now turn to the problem of detection lags in infinitely repeated games. In a first step, it is assumed that each player cooperates as long as the partner cooperates and defects the moment it learns about defection of the partner. If there is a detection lag associated with the supply variables of the players, the single firm can defect and capture the higher profit $\Pi^{D,C}$ for a certain period of time until the partner learns about it and also defects. Of course, after defection is detected by the competitor, both airlines incur the competitive profit $\Pi^{D,D}$. This can be modeled as follows: suppose there is an airline deciding whether to cooperate or defect given a detection lag of τ. If the airline defects and the opponent cooperates, the present value of future profits is

$$\Pi^{D,\tau} = \Pi^{D,C} \int_0^{\tau} e^{-rt} dt + \Pi^{D,D} \int_{\tau}^{\infty} e^{-rt} dt$$

$$= -\frac{1}{r}\left[\Pi^{D,C}\left(e^{-r\tau} - 1\right) + \Pi^{D,D}\left(-e^{-r\tau}\right)\right] \quad , \qquad (5.5)$$

which indicates that the defecting airline incurs excessive profits until the partner detects the cheating and gets the competitive profit thereafter. If both airlines cooperate forever, the present value of future profits for a single firm is

$$\Pi^{C,\tau} = \Pi^{C,C} \int_0^{\infty} e^{-rt} dt = \frac{\Pi^{C,C}}{r}. \qquad (5.6)$$

Comparison between (5.5) and (5.6) yields the result that defection is only profitable relative to perpetual cooperation if

$$\Pi^{C,C} < \Pi^{D,C} - e^{-r\tau}\left(\Pi^{D,C} - \Pi^{D,D}\right), \text{ or} \qquad (5.7)$$

$$\tau > \frac{1}{r} \ln\left(\frac{\Pi^{D,C} - \Pi^{D,D}}{\Pi^{D,C} - \Pi^{C,C}}\right).^{11} \qquad (5.8)$$

Thus, for given payoffs, an increasing detection lag intensifies the temptation to defect, because future costs and benefits are valued lower for more distant time periods. With an increasing detection lag, the cheater faces a decreasing ‹punishment› by the partner, which is given by the difference between the collusive profit and the competitive profit, while the total of excess profit from cheating increases. Therefore, if there are sufficiently long detection lags, cooperation may not occurs.

However, the punishment strategy of perpetual defection assumed above is very restrictive. To solve this problem, we may again consider a game where the players can use the Tit-for-Tat strategy. In this case, it can be presumed that collusion is more stable than in the above model. Whereas in the above model players punish the opponent for defection with perpetual competition, even if it occurs only in one period, the Tit-for-Tat player allows the return to collusion later on. Therefore, we can expect a larger number of periods of cooperation if

11 Note that

$$\frac{\Pi^{D,C} - \Pi^{D,D}}{\Pi^{D,C} - \Pi^{C,C}} > 1,$$

because the collusive profit is higher than the profit from monopolistic competition.

at least one Tit-for-Tat player is involved. However, a detailed analysis of this case would go beyond the intentions of this work. In addition to the punishment strategy, it is important to note that a Tit-for-Tat player never defects first. Thus, with respect to our model, when both airlines use the Tit-for-Tat strategy in a infinitely repeated game, there will be cooperation forever, independently of the length of a detection lag.

To summarize the above analysis we may derive two main theoretical reasons for the existence of cooperation, as it is observed in bilateral agreements for city-pair markets. It was shown that cooperation can persist in an infinitely repeated game if information lags are absent or sufficiently short. If we face a finitely repeated game or an infinitely repeated game with long information lags, a certain number of periods of cooperation may still occur when at least one of the players chooses the Tit-for-Tat strategy. In order to continue the analysis on cartel stability, we now focus on some qualitative arguments that are specific to the airline industry.

5.4.4 Stability of Collusion in the Airline Industry

Reflections on the nature of the supply variables derived in the models lead to the straightforward proposition that changes in flight frequency and connecting destinations in a city-pair market are easily observed, whereas the detection of price changes and the collection of reliable information on inverse load factors deserves additional elaboration. This indicates that supply variables have different information lags, which influence the profitability of defection relative to cooperation. Furthermore, the detection lag for the entire supply equals the lowest detection lag of single variables. Thus, a cheating airline may have strong incentives to hold the number of flights and connecting destinations constant and only change the ticket prices and the inverse load factor at best.

The detection of price changes is usually more difficult in industries where a seller faces a small number of large buyers than in industries with a large number of small buyers. For a small number of large buyers, the seller can make deals that are specific to each buyer and are not public. In this case, the competitors of the seller may only observe price cuts with a lag or indirectly by the change in their market shares.[12] In the case of a large number of small buyers, secret price deals with individual consumers would be very costly and, therefore, prices are quoted publicly. This makes it easier for competitors to observe price changes, which lowers the detection lag and reduces incentives for defection. For the airline industry, this theoretical distinction may explain differences in institutional arrangements for scheduled and non-scheduled air services in Europe. Non-scheduled air services (charter services) are usually not covered by pool arrangements.[13] In order to be exempted from bilateral agreements for scheduled air services, charter airlines are not allowed to sell tickets to consumers directly. They have to sell the seats to ‹charterers› (travel agencies, tour operators etc.) that resell complete holiday packages. While airlines offering scheduled services face a large number of individual buyers, charter airlines face a relatively small number of large buyers. Thus the stability of price fixing ought to be higher for scheduled services than for charter services. This may explain the absence of pool arrangements in the non-scheduled market.

The detection of inverse load factors is more difficult than the observation of price changes. Although the availability of seats influences demand, it is not necessary to quote inverse load factors publicly in order to sell tickets. Thus, inverse load factor variations can be held secret for a while, because the partner is not able to detect this defection directly. One possible solution to the problem may be a contract that fixes total capacity, as is done in some European pool arrangements. A change in total capacity is easily detected, because it either has to be carried out by a change of flight frequency or the employment of new aircraft with a different size. However, since cheating involves a reduction in fares and a decrease in inverse load factors, capacity may not have to be increased, and defection stays secret until the competitors detect fare changes.

If direct observation of supply variables is impossible or too costly, any defection from the cartel agreement can still be detected through changes of one's own output. However, such attempts are constrained by the fact that

12 See, for example, *Stigler (1964)*.

13 According to the COMPAS-Report, virtually all European pools cover scheduled services only. Cf. *OECD (1988)*, p. 34.

demand may change due to business cycles. Assuming unobservability of the competitors' prices and inverse load factors but perfect observability of all the other supply variables, a single airline does not know whether a decrease in its demand was triggered by the business cycle or defecting behavior by the competitor. Therefore, the question arises whether the cause of a demand change can be determined by a single airline. The models of *Green and Porter (1984)* and *Rotemberg and Saloner (1986)* examine secret price cuts under the assumption of demand fluctuations. As a starting point, both models assume that price changes are not observed directly. *Green and Porter (1984)* show that for imperfect observability of demand, price wars can be triggered by an unexpectedly low demand because oligopolists may confuse low demand resulting from business cycles with cheating by the partner. Therefore collusion may be less stable during recessions. *Rotemberg and Saloner's* theory of price wars during booms shows the opposite. Their model implies that in high demand states, the temptation to cheat may outweigh the punishment, which leads the colluding firms to set a price below the fully collusive level in order to reduce this temptation. But, depending on the demand function, this price can still be above the collusive level of a low demand state.[14]

Although the observability of supply variables favors the stability of coordination once it is established, the *development* of tacit collusion may be limited by several market conditions in the first place. *Scherer and Ross (1990)* for example identify a significant number of sellers, heterogeneity of products and differences in cost structures as factors complicating coordination of oligopolistic supply.

The number of sellers basically influences the development of collusion for three reasons. First, as the number of competitors increases and the market share of one representative firm decreases, the effect of supply variable changes of an individual firm on competitors' actions and on total supply decreases. This means that it is more difficult for the cartel members to detect a cheater as the number of firms increases. In addition, monopoly supply increasingly becomes a ‹public› good rather than a private good, which lowers incentives to take actions in order to form a cartel. Second, the probability that one member of the cartel is a cheater increases with the number of firms. Finally, because

14 See *Tirole (1988)*, p. 250.

different firms are likely to have different notions with respect to the most favorable supply variables, communication in order to reach an agreement becomes more costly. This coordination problem especially arises when there is no central agency like a cartel bureau, which presumably is the case in countries where collusion is prohibited by law. Therefore each firm must tacitly communicate with every other firm, which leads to an almost exponential rise in coordination cost for an increasing number of firms.[15]

The monopolistic competition model for airline markets assumes that firms offer diversified products by offering flights via hubs and to connecting destinations in different regions. The heterogeneity of services imputed thereby may limit the development of collusion. Spatial differentiation can lead to variable conditions on the demand side as well as on the cost side. First, when access and time costs of passengers differ between regions, a complex structure rather than a unique set of supply variables is required for profit maximization. The same is true if market distances differ considerably. As with the number of firms, a complex structure of supply variables raises difficulties with respect to tacit communication. The cost of coordination additionally increases if the regions are in different countries with distinct politics, law systems and economic performances. Second, spatial differentiation may lead to interfirm differences in factor prices and qualities. When these differences are sufficiently large, they require distinct profit maximizing supply variables across firms again, which aggravates difficulties with respect to tacit communication. The same applies when frequent changes of factor prices and qualities at different locations call for frequent renegotiations.

The difficulty of agreeing on supply variables may also increase when firms are characterized by different cost structures, e.g. differences in marginal and average costs across firms. As with the problem of heterogeneity, distinct cost structures require distinct profit maximizing supply variables. Two different sources of inequality in the cost structure are discussed: technological innovation and large overhead costs. The more rapidly airlines' cost functions are changed by new technologies and the more unevenly those changes affect the firms in the industry, the more likely it is that cost differences and, therefore, difficulties regarding the choice of supply variables will occur. The

15 Cf. *Williamson (1965)*, p. 600.

problem of overhead cost arises when there is a substantial downward change in demand. *Scherer and Ross (1990)* show that the probability of price cutting due to a decline in demand is higher in industries with high fixed costs relative to marginal cost than in industries with low fixed costs. Negative demand shocks lead to a decrease in the firms' output and profit. Especially when fixed costs are high, the decrease in profit is particularly high compared to an industry with low fixed costs. Therefore, incentives to increase output in order to spread fixed costs over as many units as possible and to increase profit thereby are higher for high fixed costs.

Summarizing the conditions facilitating and limiting collusion, it can be concluded that collusion in airline markets may be stable once difficulties with respect to the coordination of supply variables have been overcome and if the cooperating airlines operate in an economically and politically integrated area. The stability is due to the fact that frequencies, networks, capacities and publicly quoted fares are observed without or with only short information lags, and that demand and supply shocks are similar in integrated economies. However, note that the long term stability of the IATA based pool arrangements for international air transport is due to other reasons. Because the system of bilateral agreements explicitly tolerates cartels and hardly allows more than two firms to operate in markets between two countries, communication costs are minimal. The negotiation of supply variables within the scope of IATA and required approvement by respective governments increase the protection of the cartel's goals against opportunistic behavior by single member firms. In addition, one has to take into account the fact that the regulation set by bilateral agreements has led to relatively homogeneous products in the sense of the model, because the two national carriers designated by their governments usually operate in the same city-pair markets, integrate their schedules and have interlining agreements. In the US, where cartels are illegal under the anti-trust law, there is less evidence of collusion. The relatively quick adjustment of fares, load factors, frequencies and networks shortly after deregulation and the mergers in the mid 80s point to competitive behavior. This indicates that the coordination of supply variables between the numerous firms operating in the US, where the industry is characterized by large diversified networks, has been too costly up to now.

For European and international markets, the theoretical results above predict that deregulation of the EU airline industry may be accompanied by relatively small changes in supply variables in the short run. The presumed stability of collusion indicates that national carriers will probably be able to keep up collusive supply variables in markets between countries for a certain length of time. In the long run, the entry of new carriers and the development of global networks between the EU and the US may lead to the breakdown of the remaining collusion between national carriers. The development of global networks presumably involves mergers and strategic alliances with foreign carriers, which may change the interests and goals of firms. Networks and other supply variables have to be adjusted, and product differentiation may increase. Therefore, communication problems between the former European partners will arise and eventually lead to the dissolution of cooperation. If the changed industry structure is characterized by a sufficiently large number of firms, collusion presumably will not arise again for a certain period of time. But it is important to note that this development may only occur if there is sufficient deregulation in the US-EU market, e.g. an open-sky agreement is signed between the two, which will lead to a large liberalized area. Otherwise, collusive supply variables may persist for connections within Europe and eventually arise for services between single EU member states and the US.

5.5 Summary and Conclusions

In this chapter, propositions from the results developed in previous chapters were first presented. Second, possible implications of the deregulation process in the EU and in intercontinental markets on the structure of the airline industry were derived. It has been demonstrated that free markets in Europe may lead to different results compared to the deregulation in the US because the EU is smaller in geographical size, air transport faces tougher competition from ground transport (e.g. the railway system), and major cities are located in the center of the continent while they are mainly located at the edge in the US. A major part of the chapter then was devoted to competition policy, where the issues of integration and collusion were discussed. The respective results and the propositions derived from the models imply the following two main policy recommendations:

a) Deregulation of airline markets

The model developed in Chapter 4 showed that the number of firms increases with the geographic extent of a liberalized area. As a basic implication, this means that passengers can choose from a larger variety of products as the size of a deregulated area increases. Further implications are derived from the welfare effects of the development of global networks and the possibility of collusion. First, as the size of the area in terms of regions increases, the development of global networks more likely will lead to an increase in consumer surplus. Second, as the number of firms increases, communication between carriers and, therefore, the joint determination of supply variables become more difficult. Therefore, the current developments in the airline industry, for example mergers and strategic alliances, are likely to be beneficial to consumers, if market entry is free in a sufficiently large geographic area. Thus, open-sky agreements are strongly advocated.

b) Approval of mergers and strategic alliances, prevention of collusive behavior

Like any organization, courts and enforcement agencies in charge of the application of competition law should allocate their resources efficiently. Therefore, a detailed investigation of every attempt by airlines to integrate operations is not feasible. Instead, courts and enforcement agencies should concentrate their investigations on developments that presumably increase market power. In this view, mergers and strategic alliances between carriers that are predominantly operating in different areas are not of primary interest. They usually lead to an increase in online connections and do not reduce competition in the regions concerned. On the other hand, competition authorities should pay attention to mergers and strategic alliances between carriers operating mainly in the same areas. In doing so, they should focus on demand elasticities and the size of the areas as well as on market shares and the number of competitors. In addition, note that that a high time sensitivity of passengers leads to externalities with respect to flight frequency and network size, but it is also one reason for local monopoly situations due to product differentiation. Thus, welfare effects of mergers, takeovers and strategic alliances cannot be judged on the basis of single city-pair markets alone. The relevant market, therefore, is at least composed of the demand and supply between two regions.

With respect to collusion, it has to be remembered that a large liberalized area reduces the probability of coordination because of a high number of competitors. Therefore, the best policy against collusion is the deregulation of a large area. However, airlines that have previously operated under bilateral agreements involving pool arrangements may be able to continue collusion for a certain period of time even in a deregulated environment. These firms have to be watched closely by competition law authorities if industry structures and supply variables do not seem to change after deregulation.

To conclude the analysis, we propose two additional policy recommendations regarding the future development of the international airline industry, although they cannot directly be derived from the theoretical results. First, because deregulation has a large impact on competition, the industry structure and the efficient design of networks, the privatization of national carriers is advocated. In a liberalized environment, only firms that are able to adjust production and services to changed conditions will survive as independent firms or in strategic alliances in the long run. Public enterprises that usually do not follow the goal of profit maximization, may not take the necessary decisions in order to provide efficient transport services in the future, as they were not able to operate profitably in the past despite the absence of competitive pressure. Furthermore, subsidies by their governments may distort competition and harm privately owned competitors as well as consumers and taxpayers. Second, as the networks of large carriers increasingly take on an international dimension, deregulation and competition policy will have to be coordinated internationally. Although a multinational framework for large deregulated areas could eventually be established through bilateral agreements, we advocate a multilateral open-sky agreement. Not only would it be more efficient because of presumably lower administrative costs, it would also provide uniform rules all over the world. Moreover, since mergers, takeovers and strategic alliances increasingly cover air transport between many countries located on different continents, the investigations of competition law authorities should also be coordinated at an international level.

Concluding Remarks

In this work we have developed models that should enhance the understanding of market structures in a deregulated international airline industry. As major assumptions, we have proposed that passengers are time sensitive with respect to the frequency of service, the availability of seats, and access to the closest airport, that airlines develop hub-and-spoke networks for cost reasons, and that airlines differentiate products with respect to connecting destinations. Extending the results of earlier studies that take time sensitivity of passengers and respective costs into account, we have demonstrated that the provision of air transport services between two regions may lead to a natural monopoly situation, especially when passengers are very time sensitive with respect to flight frequency. In addition, it was shown that in a deregulated environment, airlines are tempted to develop multiple-hub networks in order to increase the number of online connections and, thereby, further reduce passengers' opportunity costs from time. On the one hand, the development of multiple-hub networks increases the concentration of firms. On the other hand, if it is assumed that airlines are tempted to differentiate their products geographically, the free-entry equilibrium number of firms increases with the size of a deregulated geographic area. These results suggest that an increase in market concentration is likely to be beneficial for consumers if it leads to an increase in quality with respect to the saving of time costs and if the behavior of single firms is still constrained by a sufficiently large number of competitors. For international aviation policy, this implies that countries should either increase the number of open-sky agreements or agree on a multilateral liberalization policy.

The development of multiple-hub networks can already be observed in today's airline industry. In the US, for example, the deregulation of air transport markets led to a large number of mergers and acquisitions, which was followed by a large increase in the number of online connections via hubs but also by an increase in concentration. A similar development is now on the way in the increasingly liberalized air transport markets between the US and Europe. Large carriers are signing strategic alliances in order to provide intercontinental online connections. Product differentiation with respect to the location of hubs can be observed in the US as well as in Europe. In both economic areas, there are regions that are predominantly served by the carrier that operates a hub in that region. This may lead to regional monopoly situations, especially for services to local destinations and direct flights between the hubs. But a large number of passengers will benefit from the increase in online connections and from the competition between large networks in numerous indirect city-pair markets. The models developed in this work seem to explain these developments quite well. However, they still leave open several questions that may provide the basis for future research in this field.

First, it was assumed that firms differentiate products with respect to connecting destinations. Although it has been demonstrated that this assumption is quite realistic, especially when taking into account the fact that the majority of city-pair markets are monopolies even in a deregulated environment, it is very rigorous. Large non-hub cities often enjoy air transport services by several carriers via different hubs, which indicates that airlines do not always differentiate products in that respect. Therefore, it would be interesting to investigate the criteria according to which airlines make location choices for connecting destinations. This may also lead to additional insights with respect to the other supply variables price, inverse load factor and frequency. In the models, it was implicitly assumed that the single firm offers the same price for all connections, regardless of the detailed market structure in the single spokes. It can be presumed that if there are competitors for air transport services between two particular connecting destinations, fare policies of the single firms would be different compared to the case where one airline has local monopoly power for such a connection.

Second, for simplicity, it was assumed that firms basically offer indirect connections over one or two hubs and that there only is demand for air transport between the connecting destinations. These assumptions are also very restrictive. Large non-hub cities often are served by a certain number of direct connections despite the growing importance of hub-and-spoke systems. Again, it seems that market density influences the structure of supply. Therefore, the models could be extended by analyzing destinations of different size and by taking the time sensitivity of passengers with respect to actual trip time into account.

Third, the models provide additional opportunities for empirical studies of the effects of deregulation and market concentration, especially with respect to the deregulation of air transport between Europe and North America. Finally, the results obtained in this work may similarly apply to other transport sectors. For example, for public transport in urban and suburban areas, time sensitivity of passengers plays an important role. As public transport usually is confronted with competition from private cars, variables like frequency of service and access to the transport system are central determinants of supply. Similar market structures may be found in scheduled bus and train services.

Although many features and details of air transport markets have not been discussed in this work, and although it was necessary to underlay some strong assumptions that may not pass empirical tests, I believe that the simple structure of the models provides a valuable framework for the analysis of market structures and recent developments in the international airline industry.

References

Aschinger, G. (1984): «Contestable Markets. Ein neuer Weg zur Charakterisierung des Wettbewerbs und der Industriestruktur», WiSt, vol. 13, pp. 217-223.

Aschinger, G. (1986): «Contestable Markets – der Mehrprodukte Fall», Jahrbuch für Sozialwissenschaft, vol. 37, pp. 298-320.

Aschinger, G. (1991): «Benchmarks for Competition – Determination of Contestable Equilibria in the Multiproduct Case», ISES-Working Paper no. 186, University of Fribourg, Switzerland.

Bailey, E. and Panzar, J. (1981): «The Contestability of Airline Markets During the Transition to Deregulation», Law and Contemporary Problems, vol. 44, Winter, pp. 125-145.

Bailey, E., Graham, D. and Kaplan, D. (1985): «Deregulating the Airlines», Cambridge (Mass.).

Bain, J. (1959): «Industrial Organization», New York.

Baumol, W. and Bradford, D. (1970): «Optimal Departures From Marginal Cost Pricing», American Economic Review, vol. 60, pp. 265-272.

Baumol, W., Panzar, J. and Willig, R. (1982): «Contestable Markets and the Theory of Industry Structure», New York.

Baumol, W. and Willig, R. (1986): «Contestability: Developments Since the Book», Oxford Economic Papers, vol. 38, pp. 8-36.

Borenstein, S. (1990): «Airline Mergers, Airport Dominance, and Market Power», AEA Papers and Proceedings, vol. 80, no. 2, May, pp. 400-404.

Borenstein, S. (1989): «Hubs and High Fares: Dominance and Market Power in the U.S. Airline Industry», Rand Journal of Economics, vol. 20, Autumn, pp. 344-365.

Brown, J. (1991): «An Economic Model of Airline Hubbing-and-Spoking», Logistics and Transportation Review, vol. 27, no. 3, pp. 225-239.

Brueckner, K. and Spiller, P. (1991): «Competition and Mergers in Airline Networks», International Journal of Industrial Organization, vol. 9, pp. 323-342.

Brueckner, K., Dyer, N. and Spiller, P. (1992): «Fare Determination in Airline Hub-and-Spoke Networks» , Rand Journal of Economics, vol. 23, no. 3, pp. 309-333.

Button, K. and Swann, D. (1989): «European Community Airlines - Deregulation and its Problems», Journal of Common Market Studies, vol. 27, no. 4, pp. 259-282.

Carlton, D., Landes, W. and Posner, R. (1980): «Benefits and Costs of Airline Mergers: A Case Study», Bell Journal of Economics, vol. 11, Spring, pp. 65-83.

Caves, D., Christensen, L. and Tretheway, M. (1984): «Economies of Density versus Economies of Scale: Why Trunk and Local Airline Costs Differ», Rand Journal of Economics, vol. 15, no. 4, Winter, pp. 471-489.

Chamberlin, E. (1933): «The Theory of Monopolistic Competition», Cambridge (Mass.).

D'Aspremont, C., Gabszewicz, J., and Thisse, J.-F. (1979): «On Hotelling's Stability in Competition», Econometrica, vol. 47, no. 5, September, pp. 1145-1150.

De Vany, A. (1974): «The Revealed Value of Time in Air Travel», Review of Economics and Statistics, vol. 54, February, pp. 77-82.

De Vany, A. (1975): «The Effect of Price and Entry Regulation on Airline Output, Capacity and Efficiency», Bell Journal of Economics, vol. 6, Spring, pp. 327-345.

Dempsey, P. and Goetz, A. (1992): «Airline Deregulation and Laissez-Faire Mythology», Westport (Conn.).

Doganis, R. (1985): «Flying Off Course: The Economics of International Airlines», London.

Douglas, G. and Miller, J. (1974): «Economic Regulation of Air Transport», Washington D.C..

Dwivedi, T. and Srivastava, V. (1978): «Optimality of Least Squares in the Seemingly Unrelated Regression Equation Model», Journal of Econometrics, vol. 7, pp. 391-395.

Eaton, B. and Lipsey, R. (1989): «Product Differentiation», in R. Schmalensee and R. Willig (ed.), Handbook of Industrial Economics, vol. 1, pp.723-770.

Evans, W. and Kessides, I. (1993): «Localized Market Power in the U.S. Airline Industry», Review of Economics and Statistics, vol. 75, pp. 66-75.

Fisher, F. (1987): «Pan American to United: The Pacific Devision Transfer Case», Rand Journal of Economics, vol. 18, Winter, pp. 492-508.

Gaynor, M. and Trapani III, J. (1994): «Quantity, Quality and the Welfare Effects of US airline deregulation», Applied Economics, vol. 26, pp. 543-550.

Good, D., Röller, L. and Sickles, R. (1993): «U.S. Deregulation: Implications for European Air Transport», Economic Journal, vol. 103, July, pp. 1028-1041.

Göpfert, I. (1994): «Interlining, Code-Sharing und Trucking», WiSt, vol. 23, pp. 460-462.

*Graham, D., Kaplan, D. and Sibley, D. (1983): «*Efficiency and Competition in the Airline Industry", Bell Journal of Economics, Spring, vol. 14, no. 1, S. 118-138.

*Greene, W. (1993): «*Econometric Analysis», Englewood Cliffs, NJ.

Green, E. and Porter, R. (1984): «Noncooperative Collusion under Imperfect Price Information», Econometrica, vol. 52, no. 1, pp. 87-100.

Hendricks, K., Piccione, M., and Tan, G. (1995): «The Economics of Hubs: The Case of Monopoly», Review of Economic Studies, vol. 62, pp. 83-93.

Hirshleifer, J. (1984): «Price Theory and Applications», Englewood Cliffs, NY.

Hotelling, H. (1929): «Stability in Competition», Economic Journal, vol. 39, March, pp. 41-57.

Jordan, W. (1970): «Airline Regulation in America: Effects and Imperfections, Baltimore.

Keeler, T. (1972): «Airline Regulation and Market Performance», Bell Journal of Economics and Management Science, vol. 3, Autumn, pp. 399-424.

Kreps, D., Milgrom, P., Roberts, J. and Wilson, R. (1982): «Rational Cooperation in the Finitely Repeated Prisoners' Dilemma», Journal of Economic Theory, vol. 2, pp. 245-252.

Krugman, P. (1987): «Is Free Trade Passé?», Economic Perspectives, vol. 1, no. 2, Fall, pp. 131-144.

Landes, W. and Posner, R. (1981): «Market Power in Antitrust Cases», Harvard Law Review, vol. 94, no. 5, March, pp. 937-995.

Leibenstein, H. (1981): «Microeconomics and X-efficiency Theory: If there is no Crisis, there ought to be», in: Bell, D. and Kristol, I. (ed.), The Crisis in Economic Theory, New York.

Marín, P. (1995): «Competition in European Aviation: Pricing Policy and Market Structure», Journal of Industrial Economics, vol. 43, no. 2, pp. 141-159.

Moore, T. (1986): «U.S. Airline Deregulation: Its Effects on Passengers, Capital and Labor», Journal of Law and Economics, vol. 29, April, pp 1-28.

Morrison, S. and Winston, C. (1986): «The Economic Effects of Airline Deregulation», Waschington D.C..

Morrison, S. and Winston, C. (1987): «Empirical Implications and Tests of the Contestability Hypothesis», Journal of Law and Economics, vol. 30, April, pp. 53-66.

Morrison, S. and Winston, C. (1989): «Enhancing the Performance of the Deregulated Air Transportation System», Brooking Papers on Economic Activity: Microeconomics, pp. 61-112.

Organization for Economic Co-Operation and Development OECD (1988): «Deregulation and Airline Competition», Paris.

Panzar, J. (1979): «Equilibrium and Welfare in Unregulated Airline Markets», American Economic Review, vol. 69, no. 2, pp. 92-95.

Rotemberg, J. and Saloner, G. (1986): «A Supergame-Theoretical Model of Price Wars during Booms», American Economic Review, vol. 76, no. 3, pp. 390-407.

Salop, S. (1979): «Monopolistic Competition with Outside Goods», Bell Journal of Economics, vol. 10, Spring, pp. 141-156.

Scheffman, D. and Spiller, P. (1987): «Geographic Market Definition under the U.S. Department of Justice Merger Guidelines», Journal of Law and Economics, vol. 15, April, pp. 123-147.

Scherer, F. and Ross, D. (1990): «Industrial Market Structure and Economic Performance», 3rd edition, Boston.

Schmalensee, R. (1977): «Comparative Static Properties of Regulated Airline Oligopolies», Bell Journal of Economics, vol. 8, Autumn, pp. 565-576.

Steiner, P. (1957): «Peak Loads and Efficient Pricing», Quarterly Journal of Economics, vol. 71, pp. 585-610.

Stigler, G. (1964): «A Theory of Oligopoly», Journal of Political Economy, vol. 72, pp. 44-61.

Stigler, G. (1971): «The Theory of Economic Regulation», Bell Journal of Economics and Management Science, vol. 2, Spring, pp. 3-21.

Strotz, H. (1956): «Myopia and Inconsistency in Dynamic Utility Maximization», Review of Economic Studies, vol. 23, pp. 165-180.

Tirole, J. (1988): «The Theory of Industrial Organization», Cambridge (Mass.).

Varian, H. (1992): «Microeconomic Analysis», New York.

Williamson, O. (1965): «A Dynamic Theory of Interfirm Behavior», Quarterly Journal of Economics, vol. 79, pp. 579-607.